© Wilfried Fest 1978

Published in the United Kingdom by
George Prior Publishers
37–41 Bedford Row, London WC1R 4JH

Reprinted 1980

British Library Cataloguing in Publication Data

Fest, Wilfried
  Dictionary of German History 1806–1945.
  1. Germany – History – 1789–1900 – Dictionaries
  2. Germany – History – 20th century – Dictionaries
  I. Title
  943′.07′03   DD203

  ISBN 0–86043–108–8

Typeset by
Computacomp (UK) Limited, Fort William, Scotland
Printed in the United Kingdom by
Biddles Limited, Guildford, Surrey

CONTENTS

PREFACE

This dictionary lists the salient facts and dates of Germany's political, social and economic history in alphabetical sequence from the dissolution of the Holy Roman Empire of the German Nation in 1806 to the collapse of the German Reich in 1945. Though 1806 has been chosen as the starting point, the author is well aware of the importance of the transitional period from 1789 to 1806 for the beginning of a 'modern' Germany and references to this period can be found under captions dealing with the national awakening of Germany. It was far easier to draw the line at the end of the chronological ladder, for 1945 still means a clear break in the development of Germany as the end of 75 years of national unity. All movements and events after 1945 are still related to contemporary politics, even more so with the separate development of two German states since then.

The subject-matter of the dictionary is the heritage of present-day Germany; or, rather, Germans: the movement for and the realization of national unity; the quest for imperial glory and the fall of the monarchy; the attempt at the destruction of democracy; the rise of total dictatorship and the calamities of total war. Some 700 topics are included in the book in an attempt to do equal justice to all these aspects, although 20th-century affairs slightly predominate because of their more imminent impact on the events of the day. Considering the dynamism of history the presentation of historical data in dictionary form will always remain problematic. Due to the limitations of space, the omission of some interesting and important topics was unavoidable. Nevertheless I have tried to include the men, moments and events that determined the course of German history: personalities of rank and influence; institutions and offices; bills and laws; parties and associations; negotiations and agreements; discords and revolts; wars and peace treaties. There are some entries on political writers and their works, but no paragraphs on literary and cultural history as such. Likewise purely economic, technological and scientific history is not included except for innovations and their creators that had a direct bearing on political or social change.

Although affairs covering the whole of Germany predominate, I reserved some space for regional matters. Individual territories, however, are only summarized where there are few or no topics or biographies about that territory listed elsewhere (eg Rhineland and Westphalia are in – Bavaria and Prussia are out). Knowledge of the general context of European and world history is taken for granted and familiar expressions and names are not explained where mentioned.

This dictionary has been written by a German national who might be forgiven the occasional Germanism. Many things in his country are 'typically German' indeed and therefore difficult to explain in another tongue. The author tried to convey the 'spirit' of each topic or expression by clinging as closely as possible to the original, if sometimes at the cost of linguistic elegance rather than that of inaccuracy. It is in the precision that the reader will find his compensation.

Apart from giving accurate information on historical data, I felt entitled to add brief evaluations wherever it seemed suitable or necessary. My interpretations are based on the findings of historical research as published and widely accepted in the year 1977. I have tapped many valuable sources and tried to summarize their content. It is impossible to acknowledge them all individually and no reference is given except for the bibliographical notes at the end of many entries. These are restricted to the topic under consideration and only include works published after 1950. Together with my personal comments, they should be taken as a stimulant to the reader's own research, for this book is meant as an aid to study, not as a substitute for it.

Free University of Berlin
September 1977   *Wilfried B Fest*

ACKNOWLEDGMENTS

In the compilation of a work of this size I was advised and assisted by a number of colleagues and friends. I have to thank in particular my two pupils U Gräfe and H Schätzel, who helped me in the planning and researching of large sections of the book.

My greatest debt is to Mr Lalit Adolphus, who completely revised and edited the final manuscript. Without his patience and devotion to this work it could not have been published.

Of course, I alone am responsible for any misinterpretation and inaccuracy that it may contain.

My mother has helped me re-type part of the manuscript and my wife has provided the homely atmosphere that enabled me to concentrate on the preparation of this dictionary, which therefore is dedicated to them.

Free University of Berlin
September 1977   *Wilfried B Fest*

ABBREVIATIONS

ADAV	Allgemeiner Deutscher Arbeiterverein
ADGB	Allgemeiner Deutscher Gewerkschaftsbund
DAF	Deutsche Arbeitsfront
DDP	Deutsche Demokratische Partei
DNVP	Deutschnationale Volkspartei
DVP	Deutsche Volkspartei
KPD	Kommunistische Partei Deutschlands
OHL	Oberste Heeresleitung
OKW	Oberkommando der Wehrmacht
SA	Sturmabteilung
SD	Sicherheitsdienst
SPD	Sozialdemokratische Partei Deutschlands
SS	Schutzstaffel
USPD	Unabhängige Sozialdemokratische Partei Deutschlands

NOTE

Agreements, pacts and treaties are generally listed under the name of the place where they were concluded, except when better known under another term, eg London Naval Agreement, but Ribbentrop-Molotov Pact. Invasions, campaigns and battles are frequently listed under the code-word for their German operations (eg Barbarossa, but Battle of Britain). Cross-references to other articles in the book have been indicated by the use of italics in the text.

Aachen, Congress of. Meeting of the four Great Powers – Russia, Prussia, Austria and Britain – in Sept–Oct 1818. The most important agenda was the memorandum of the Russian state councillor Count Stourdza 'On Germany's Present Condition'. It regarded the universities as the seed-bed of a revolution aiming at a democratic nation state and demanded the limitation of academic freedom and press censorship as well as reprisals against demagogic groups. The discussion at Aachen formed the basis for the *Carlsbad Decrees* of 1819. In Aachen the policy of European solidarity ('Congress System') reached its climax.

Abgeordnetenhaus. Second chamber of the Prussian *Landtag* according to the constitution of 5 Dec 1848. By the decree of 30 May 1849 it was elected on the basis of the *three-class-suffrage*. It had budgetary and taxation powers (ratification by the *Herrenhaus*). The principle of ministerial responsibility as envisaged by the constitution was never really put into practice. The Abgeordnetenhaus was the instrument of the Liberals for influencing state legislation (*Constitutional Conflict*).

ADAV (Allgemeiner Deutscher Arbeiterverein). Socialist party founded on 23 May 1863 by *Lasselle*. The *ADAV* had split from the 'Educational Tradesmen's Union' in Leipzig. After one year it commanded a membership of 46,000. The *ADAV* fought for universal suffrage and workers' associations. In 1875 it merged with the 'Sozialdemokratische Arbeiterpartei' (founded in 1869) to form the 'Sozialistische Arbeiterpartei Deutschlands', a forerunner of the *SPD*.

ADGB (Allgemeiner Deutscher Gewerkschaftsbund). Central organization of the *Freie Gewerkschaften* founded in 1919 to replace the loose union of the 'general commission'. After the death of C Legien (1920), Th Leipart (1867–1947) became its president. Attached to the *ADGB* were the 'Afa-Bund' for employees and the 'ADB' for civil servants. In its aims and activities the *ADGB* was closely connected with the *SPD*. It displayed an increasing tendency towards bureaucratization and alienation of members from union officials. Contrary to the pre-war period, the *ADGB* later succeeded in impressing reformist union views on the Social Democratic party. In 1924 the *ADGB* comprised 41 unions with 4.6 million members, a number that remained stable until 1933, when it was suppressed.

Adlerangriff. German code-word for *Battle of Britain*.

Adolf-Hitler-Schulen. See *National Socialist Schools*.

Afrika Korps. Troops sent in 1941 to aid the Italians fighting in Libya. They comprised two tank divisions and a motorized infantry division under the command of *Rommel*. Within 14 days the Afrika Korps conquered the whole of Cyrenaica except Tobruk, which fell in the offensive started on 27 May 1942, pushing the British back to the Egyptian frontier. The Afrika Korps advanced

1

up to El Alamein, where it was forced into the defensive by the British, who cut the German supplies. The Afrika Korps had to withdraw behind Bengazi and after the Allied landings in Morocco (8 Nov 1942), was soon reduced to bridgeheads in Tunisia, the last of which surrendered on 12 May 1943. The defeat of the Korps led to the imprisonment of 252,000, secured final hegemony in the Mediterranean for the Allies and paved the way for Germany's subsequent collapse.

R Lewin: The Life and Death of the Afrika Korps (1977).

Algeciras. South Spanish town, where an international conference of the Great Powers was summoned on 16 Jan 1906 to settle the dispute between Germany and France over Morocco (*Tangier, landing in*). Germany's hope for Anglo-American support at the conference table proved illusory. The official settlement reached on 7 April 1906 formally respected the Sultan's authority and Germany's prestige by providing for an international police control of Morocco. But the original German aim of demonstrating to France the weakness of the entente cordiale failed due to the misjudgment of the diplomatic constellation, for which *Holstein* had to take responsibility by resigning one day before the signing of the Act of Algeciras.

A J P Taylor: 'La Conference d'Algésiras', in Revue Historique 208 (1952).

Alldeutscher Verband. Patriotic union founded in 1891 as 'Allgemeiner Deutscher Verband', from 1894 known as Alldeutscher Verband. It was initiated by *Hugenberg* in reaction to the *Heligoland-Zanzibar Treaty*. As the mouthpiece of Pan-Germanism, it agitated for German national aims abroad. With the call for an active *Kolonial-* and *Flottenpolitik* it became a vociferous pressure group for annexionist demands supported by leading industrialists (*Kirdorf, Kardorff*). The majority of its members belonged to the intellectual middle class (teachers, professors etc.) and numbered 20,000 in 1900. During World War I, under the leadership of H Class, it exercised an influence on the shaping of German war aims (*September Programme*). After 1918 it became part of the 'national opposition' whose anti-Semitic propaganda prepared the ground for the rise of National Socialism. When colonial claims were dropped by the Nazi rulers, the Alldeutscher Verband was dissolved in 1939.

A Kruck: Geschichte des Alldeutschen Verbandes 1890–1939 (1954).

Allgemeine Zeitung. Daily newspaper founded in 1798 by Cotta, published in southern Germany. The bourgeois Allgemeine Zeitung was the most important political paper up to 1850.

Alsace-Lorraine. Territory west of the Upper Rhine ceded by France to Germany at the Peace of Frankfurt in 1871. It was constituted as a 'Reichsland' (condominion) which was directly subordinate to the Reich. It was neither accorded the status of a federal state nor was it attached to another German state. In 1874 the Reich constitution was promulgated, allotting Alsace-Lorraine 15 seats in the *Reichstag*. In 1879 a 'Statthalter' (governor) with powers to declare martial law (withdrawn in 1902) was appointed. In 1911 Alsace-Lorraine was granted a constitution of its own with three votes in the *Bundesrat* (which were not counted if they overruled Prussia). The population of Alsace-Lorraine was 87 per cent German speaking; but on the whole it rejected German administration. In the elections up to 1890 they returned Francophile candidates who protested against the German regime in Berlin, although Alsace-Lorraine profited from the economic prosperity of the Reich. The strained relations between the German army and the indigenous population was exemplified at *Zabern* in 1913. In Nov 1918 Alsace-Lorraine was occupied by French troops and the Treaty of *Versailles* returned it to France. Between the wars the 'Home League' led by E Ricklin called for the cultural autonomy of Alsace-Lorraine within France, while German *Revisionspolitik* aimed at its reannexation. On 25 Aug 1939 *Hitler* informed the French government that Germany had renounced all claim to Alsace-Lorraine but in May–June 1940 it was occupied in the western *Blitzkrieg*. Part of the territory was incorporated in Baden, part in the 'Westmark'. The National Socialist administration attempted to germanize it by expelling 70,000 French-speaking people from Lorraine. Nationalistic politics and the fact that about 18,000 Alsatians were killed on the eastern front renewed the anti-German sentiments. In Feb 1945 French administration was restored.

D P Silverman: Reluctant Union. Alsace-Lorraine and Imperial Germany, 1871–1918 (1972); L Kettenacker: Nationalsozialistische Volkstumspolitik im Elsass (1973).

Alvensleben Convention. Agreement concluded in St Petersburg on 8 Feb 1863 between the Prussian envoy Gen v Alvensleben (1803–81) and the Russian Vice-Chancellor Gorchakov. The convention entitled Prussian and Russian military commanders to mutual assistance in the repression of the Polish uprising, even to crossing the border if necessary. It was indicative of a rapprochement between Prussia and Russia foreshadowing the latter's benevolent neutrality during the Austro-Prussian *Seven Weeks' War* of 1866.

Anglo-German Alliance Negotiations. See *Eckardstein*.

Angola-Treaty. Anglo-German treaty signed on 30 Aug 1898 in London. It provided for German economic preponderance in Angola in exchange for the recognition of British influence in Mozambique. In the event of Portugal abandoning her colonies they were to be split between the signatories, but prospects for this were greatly diminished by the Windsor treaty of 1899, in which Britain reiterated her respect for Portuguese sovereignty over her colonies. In 1913–14 Anglo-German negotiations were resumed with a view to confirming German aspirations to Angola, but the outbreak of World War I prevented the signing of a supplementary treaty. The Angola Treaty expressed the desire of *Weltpolitik* to achieve a *Mittelafrika* empire.

Anschluss. Annexation of Austria by Germany. The Anschluss was facilitated by the common historical heritage of the two countries, resulting in a pro-German

3

feeling among the majority of the Austrian population. The Nazis regarded Anschluss as an essential stage on the way to the *Grossdeutsches Reich* and recognized Austria's importance for their aspirations for hegemony in South East Europe. (*Mitteleuropa, Hossbach-Minutes*). Anschluss was also promoted by close economic ties between Austria and Germany (*Customs Union*). The first attempt to bring about Anschluss was represented by the National Socialist putsch in Austria in July 1934 with the assassination of the Austrian Chancellor Dollfuss. It failed because of German isolation and Italian resistance, which ended in 1936 when the *Rome-Berlin Axis* came into being. In 1937 plans for a military intervention were worked out. On 12 Feb 1938, at his meeting with Chancellor Schuschnigg, *Hitler* secured recognition of the Austrian *NSDAP* and the appointment of its leader *Seyss-Inquart* to the cabinet. On 9 March Hitler forced the renunciation of the plebiscite and on 11 March Schuschnigg's resignation. When President Miklas refused to name Seyss-Inquart chancellor, Austria was occupied by German troops within a few hours on 12 March 1938. At a plebiscite held on 10 April 99.7 per cent of the votes cast favoured the *Anschluss*.

J Gehl: Germany and the Anschluss, 1931–1938 (1963).

Ansiedlungskommission. State commission founded in 1886 (after the expulsion of Poles in 1885) to finance German settlements in the eastern provinces of Posen and West Prussia. Until 1914 the *Ansiedlungskommission*, whose competence was extended to the entire Reich in 1890, spent almost 1,000 million Goldmark and created more than 20,000 settlements with an average size of 35.5 acres. But most of the land was purchased from German Junkers rather than the Polish landed nobility and the *Ansiedlungskommission* alone did not achieve the aim of strengthening the German element by a 'germanization of the soil' (*Lebensraum*). From 1904 new settlements in the districts with a Polish population required the permission of the president in office and in 1908 the Prussian *Landtag* passed a bill of expropriation against the Poles (once enforced in 1912) to support the *Ansiedlungskommission*, which was indicative of the anti-Polish nationality policy in Prussia.

H U Wehler: 'Polenpolitik im Deutschen Kaiserreich, 1871–1918', in id: Krisenherde des Kaiserreiches (1970).

Anti-Comintern Pact. Treaty concluded between Germany and Japan on 25 Nov 1936. It obliged both parties to provide information to each other on the activities of the Comintern and to take counsel on defence measures. A secret supplementary clause bound both partners to neutrality in the event of any of them coming into conflict with Russia. Although the pact was a purely defensive alliance, it fore-shadowed the formation of the *Three Powers' Pact*, as became apparent with the entry of Italy and Germany's other allies to the Anti-Comintern Pact in 1937.

Th Sommer: Deutschland und Japan. Vom Antikominternpakt zum Dreimächtepakt (1962).

Anti-Fascists. Term used in Marxist historiography for socialist resistance groups against the Nazi regime. The Anti-Fascists were rooted in the illegal cells of the *KPD* and were supported by the international Communist movement. Their main task was to enlighten the working class about *National Socialism*. After the German attack upon Soviet Russia (*Barbarossa*), they intensified the sabotage of the armament production. The main Anti-Fascist group was headed by H Schulze-Boysen and A Harnack, who disposed of their own espionage ring, the 'Rote Kapelle'. Cooperation with Social Democrats (*Leber, Leuschner*) largely failed because of mutual ideological prejudices, but partly materialized in the *Nationalkomitee Freies Deutschland*. The Anti-Fascists, who were numerically the largest resistance group, paid for their activities with the highest toll, but they failed to mobilize the working class masses against the Nazi dictatorship.

G Perrault: Auf den Spuren der Roten Kapelle (1969); D Gerhard: Antifaschisten Lehren und Beispiele aus dem proletarischen Widerstand 1933–1945 (1975).

Anti-Semitism. Expression coined in 1879 by W Marr, based on the pseudo-anthropological division between 'Aryans' and 'Semites'. In spite of the emancipation of Jews (1812), anti-Semitism re-emerged after the *Wars of Liberation* (1813–15) with popular outbreaks in 1819. Anti-Semitism declined in the mid-19th century but reappeared more vigorously in the wake of the *Gründerzeit* (1873), when the Jews were made a scapegoat for the depression. In the 1880s numerous movements and political parties with anti-Semitic programmes were founded: 'Antisemitenliga' (1879), 'Soziale Reichspartei' (1880), 'Deutscher Volksverein' (1881). Chief agitator was A *Stoecker* of the 'Christlich-soziale Arbeiterpartei'. Bayreuth in North Franconia became the cultural centre of anti-Semitism (*Wagner, Chamberlain*). In Berlin *Treitschke* was the intellectual leader of the movement and influenced student corporations (*Burschenschaften*). On 13 Apr 1881 a mass petition to exclude Jews from public appointments was presented to the Prussian *Abgeordnetenhaus*. From 10–12 Sept 1882 the first international anti-Jewish congress took place in Dresden; on 10–11 June 1889 the most important anti-Semitic groups convened at Bochum to formulate a common programme that demanded the annulment of the emancipation and various sanctions against the Jews. The conservative participants united in the 'Deutschsoziale Partei', rivalled from 1890 by the 'Antisemitische Volkspartei' (from 1893 'Reformpartei', which then held 11 of the 15 seats won by the anti-Semitic parties in the *Reichstag* election. These splinter groups never influenced legislation, but anti-Semitism was included in the programme of the *Deutschkonservative Partei* at the 'Tivoli' conference of 1892. Their demands for the exclusion of Jews from army and civil service posts were met in practice by the administration, because the allies were gradually influenced by anti-Semitism, although the courts kept aloof from it. Anti-Semitism was propagated with economic arguments (over-representation in the textile industry, defects in the credit system) by the *Deutschnationaler Handlungsgehilfenverband* and the *Bund der Landwirte*. After World War I anti-Semitism became a mass movement which protested against the Jewish

5

plutocracy and cultural 'overalienation'. Anti-Semitism was included in the programme of the *DVNP*, whose radical wing, the 'Deutschvölkische' ('Freiheitspartei') united with the *NSDAP* in 1922. Its party programme of 1925 declared that no Jew could be a *Volksgenosse* and brandmarked the *Weimar Republic* and parliamentary democracy as 'Jewish'. After the world slump of 1929–32 the latent anti-Semitism of wide middle class groups switched to pogroms (*Crystal Night, Jews, boycott of*) and anti-Semitic legislation (*Aryan Clause, Nuremberg Laws*) and ended in persecution and extermination (*Concentration Camps, Final Solution*) of c. 500,000 German Jews (1933) and millions of others in occupied territories.

P Pulzer: The Rise of Political Anti-Semitism in Germany and Austria (1964).

Arbeitgeberverbände. See *Employers' Federations.*

Ardennen Offensive. German counter-attack launched on 16 Dec 1944 on the western front with the aim of reaching the coast and driving a wedge between the Allied troops in order to destroy them separately. Favoured by poor visibility, three German army units succeeded in breaking into the American lines; but the improvement of weather enabled the superior Allied air forces to intervene. By mid-January 1945 the Germans were pushed back to their starting-point. Simultaneously, urged by the western powers, the Red Army began its offensive on the Vistula. Thus the Ardennen Offensive marked the beginning of the last phase of World War II.

P J Elstob: Hitler's Last Offensive (1971); H Jung: Die Ardennen-Offensive 1944–45 (1971).

Arndt, Ernst Moritz (26 Dec 1769–29 Jan 1860). Political writer and poet. After calling on his countrymen to shake off the French yoke he was forced to emigrate to Sweden in 1806, but he continued to communicate his patriotic ideals in pamphlets and poems, eg 'What is the German's fatherland?' His work included the call for German unity, renewal of the empire and a new national consciousness. In 1812 he became *Stein*'s private secretary; in 1818 he was appointed professor of history at the University of Bonn. When he criticized the reactionary policy of the German states after the Congress of *Vienna*, he was suspended from his university post until 1840. After the outbreak of the *Revolution of 1848* he became a member of the *Frankfurt National Assembly* and was associated with H v *Gagern*'s group. He joined the deputation to the *Kaiser* in Berlin. His disappointment at its failure led to his withdrawal from public life.

J Paul: Ernst Moritz Arndt. Das ganze Deutschland soll es sein (1971); K H Schäfer: Ernst Moritz Arndt als politischer Publizist (1974).

Arnim Clause. §353a of the Code of Criminal Law (*Strafgesetzbuch*). It was inserted in 1876 to penalize disobedience and misleading reporting to the *Auswärtiges Amt* by its diplomats. The clause derived its popular name from the ambitious ambassador Harry Count Arnim (1824–1881), who acted

6

arbitrarily against *Bismarck*'s orders. He was dismissed in 1874 and sentenced in 1876 to five years' penal servitude for repeated violations of official secrets.
G O Kent: Arnim and Bismarck (1968).

Aryan Clause (Arierparagraph). Decree of 7 April 1933 legalizing the exclusion of non-'Aryans' (*Aryan racial doctrine*) from public offices. Until 1935 the Aryan Clause did not apply to civil servants in office before 1 Aug 1914 and those who fought on Germany's side in World War I. The clause was gradually extended to all professions which then required the 'proof of Aryan descent'. The Aryan Clause, together with the boycott of *Jews*, paved the way for the exclusion of the Jews from Germany's legal and economic system.

Aryan racial doctrine. Ideology directed against the ethics of Christianity. It linked up the 19th century anti-Semitism of Gobineau, de Lagarde, Dühring, and H St *Chamberlain* with the neo-romanticist ideas of *Nietzsche* and had a close connection with neo-paganism as expressed by R *Wagner*. The doctrine proclaimed the 'Aryans' as the creative race in world history and the Jew as their eternal enemy. The purest form of the Aryan was to be found in the German people and it was the task of the National Socialist state to safeguard its racial purity, because inter-breeding would lead to corruption. After the *Nazi seizure of power* the aims of this doctrine first found expression in the *Aryan Clause* and the boycott of *Jews*. During World War II it found expression in the enslavement of the slave population of the occupied territories and the *final solution* of the Jewish question.
L Poliakov: The Aryan Myth (1974).

Atlantic, Battle of. See *U-Boat Warfare*.

Auswärtiges Amt. Office for foreign affairs which came into being on 1 Jan 1870 as a federal office of the *North German Confederation* by taking over the Prussian ministry for foreign affairs. In 1871 it became a *Reichsamt* under the direction of a secretary of state (for foreign affairs). In 1919 it was replaced by a ministry for foreign affairs (*Reichsminister*).
L Cecil: The German Diplomatic Service, 1871–1914 (1977).

Autobahnen. Arterial highways constructed from 1934 under the direction of the *Organisation Todt*. Based on an idea conceived in the late *Weimar Republic*, they provided employment to a large labour force and were a crucial point of Nazi propaganda. Their construction was carried out mainly from the point of view of strategical considerations.

Axis. Code word for German military intervention in Italy to cope with the situation created by the fall of Mussolini on 25 July 1943 and the Italian surrender of 8 Sept. Germany was then faced with the task of stopping the Allied advance in Italy single-handed and suppressing indigenous resistance. Rome was occupied by German troops, the Italian army was disarmed, and a

German commando liberated Mussolini, who ineffectively set up a Fascist Republic in Northern Italy and remained a German puppet. Allied landings on the Italian mainland stiffened German resistance centred at Monte Cassino, which only fell in mid-May 1944. Only in the final phase of the war did the German forces in Italy collapse. They ceased fire on 2 May 1945. The name Axis was derived from the *Rome-Berlin Axis*.

J Schroder: Italiens Kriegsaustritt 1943 (1969).

Baden, uprisings in. Uprisings in the south-western *Land* of Baden in 1848–49, when the *Revolution of 1848* reached its climax in Baden with its traditionally liberal-democratic movement. The first uprising in Baden in Apr 1848, also called *Hecker* putsch after its leader, aimed at the separatist republican solution for South Germany but failed on account of lack of popular support and the superior military strength of the dynasties. Later, in May 1849, appalled by the agony of the *Frankfurt National Assembly*, an 'Offenburger Landesversammlung' of Palatinate Liberals resolved to enforce the new constitution in the other states by means of arms. The revolutionaries were joined by the regular Baden army, which fraternized with the people. In June Prussian operations were launched with a view to liquidating the uprisings in Baden. Under the leadership of the Polish general Mieroslavski the Baden people's army succeeded in resisting superior forces until 23 July, when it had to surrender in front of Rastatt fortress. The defeat of the Baden uprisings signalled the final failure of the German revolutions of 1848–49.

W Dressen (ed): 1848–49: Bürgerkrieg in Baden (1975).

Ballin, Albert (15 Aug 1857–19 Nov 1918); shipowner. From 1899 he was general director of the *Hapag*, which he developed into the greatest shipping company in the world. A friend of *Wilhelm II*, Ballin tried to reduce the naval rivalry (*Flottenpolitik*) between Germany and Britain. His contacts with the British banker E Cassel led to the abortive Haldane mission of 1912. During World War I Ballin warned of the ill effects of an unlimited *U-Boat Warfare*. After the armistice the *Zentrum* and the *SPD* expected him to conduct the peace negotiations, but he committed suicide under the impact of the November Revolution.

L Cecil: Albert Ballin (1967).

Bamberger, Ludwig (22 July 1823–14 Mar 1899); Liberal politician. In 1849 he took part in the Republican uprising in the Palatinate and was sentenced to death in absentia. After the amnesty he returned to Germany as a financial expert and became an advisor to *Bismarck*, who invited him to take part in the negotiations which led to the Peace of *Frankfurt*. From 1871 Bamberger sat in the *Reichstag* as a National Liberal. He was responsible for the monetary law of 1873 and the establishment of the *Reichsbank*. As a free trader he led the secessionists of 1880 ('Liberale Vereinigung'). He attacked the *Kolonialpolitik* and the *social insurance policy* as a member of the Freisinnige Partei, after whose split he joined the Freisinnige Vereinigung. In the 1880s he belonged to

Friedrich III's circle, but he retired in 1893 when his hopes for a liberal government were dashed.

St Zucker: Ludwig Bamberger, German Liberal Politician and Social Critic, 1823–1899 (1975).

Barbarossa. Code word for the operation against Soviet Russia, ordered by *Hitler's* 'B'-directive No 21 of 18 Dec 1940 and originally scheduled for 15 May 1941. In his conversation with the *Wehrmacht* commanders on 30 March 1941 Hitler had stressed that the Russian campaign differed from that in the West inasmuch as it was a life-and-death struggle between two ideologies and was above international law (as exemplified by the 'commissar order' of 6 June 1941 exempting political officers from the Geneva Convention). Barbarossa was to serve Nazi Germany's primary war aim of reshaping Eastern Europe to create *Lebensraum*. Germany attacked Russia on 22 June 1941 in violation of the *Ribbentrop-Molotov Pact*, succeeded in frontier battles and slowly advanced towards Moscow with the central army group. Contrary to the Supreme Army Command's intention of waging the decisive battle before Moscow (*Halder*), Hitler had ordered operations in the Ukraine and north of Leningrad. Only at the end of Nov did the German Panzer spearheads under General Guderian come as near as 30 km from Moscow. Then the offensive came to a halt, the German forces being exhausted and short of supplies. On 5 Dec the Russian counter-offensive pushed the Germans back. On 19 Dec 1941 *Brauchitsch* was removed as a scapegoat and Hitler put himself in command of the army, whose first defeat was due to an underrating of the Red Army, bad weather conditions, and the united resistance of the Russian people.

A Clark: Barbarossa (1966); A Seaton: The Russo-German War 1941–1945 (1971); B A Leach: German Strategy against Russia 1939–1941 (1973); B Whaley: Codeword 'Barbarossa' (1973); R Cecil: Hitler's Decision to Invade Russia 1941 (1975).

Bartenstein. Site of the Russo-Prussian headquarters in East Prussia, where on 26 Apr 1807 the two allies concluded a treaty against France. It was a reaction to Napoleon's pressure on Prussia to desert Russia. According to a memorandum by *Hardenberg*, Bartenstein envisaged the co-operation of Russia, Prussia, Britain and Austria against France, but after the Russian defeat at Friedland in July 1807 Czar Alexander accepted Napoleon's offer for collaboration, which was a violation of the short-lived Bartenstein alliance.

Basserman, Ernst (26 July 1854–24 July 1917); National-Liberal politician. From 1893 deputy in the *Reichstag*, he became leader of the parliamentary party after *Bennigsen's* resignation in 1898 and party leader in 1904. He tried to strengthen the position of Parliament and strove for an all-embracing Liberalism. As a Western German economist (member of the board of directors of several firms) Basserman was cool towards the East Elbian Junkers. He opposed the *Umsturzvorlage* (Subversion Bill), but approved all army and naval bills. He was the strongest supporter of *Bülow*'s 'block policy'.

Basserman, Friedrich D (24 Feb 1811–29 July 1855); Liberal political publicist.

In 1841 he founded the *Deutsche Zeitung* in collaboration with *Mathy*. From 1844 he openly demanded an all-German parliament. As a member of the Baden chamber Basserman urged the promulgation of liberal principles (eg freedom of the press, juries). During the *Revolution of 1848* he was a member of the *Frankfurt National Assembly* belonging to the *Erbkaiserliche*. He became secretary of state in the federal government and travelled to Berlin, where he tried in vain to persuade *Friedrich Wilhelm IV* to accept leadership in a federal German state.

Battle of Britain (Adlerangriff). German air offensive against England, initiated by the *Luftwaffe* on 15 Sept 1940 with the aim of wiping out the Royal Air Force to make possible the invasion of Britain (*Sea Lion*). During the first phase (23 Sept to 6 Oct) there were daily attacks of c.1000 aircraft on airports and naval bases, involving heavy losses without achieving the aim of the battle. On 7 Oct the Luftwaffe switched to night raids, particularly on London. The climax was reached on 15 Oct (Battle of Britain Day), when the Germans suffered record losses. The battle phased out with bombardments of industrial targets (raids on Coventry on 14 Nov 1940) which could not decisively weaken the British war economy. The Battle of Britain ended with a final raid on London on 11 May 1941.

B Collier: The Battle of Britain 1940 (1962).

Bauer, Gustav Adolf (6 Jan 1870–16 Sept 1944); trade unionist and statesman. From 1903 he was engaged in the *Freie Gewerkschaften* and became chairman of the 'general commission' in 1908. In 1918 he entered *Max von Baden*'s government as secretary of state. In 1919 he was a member of the first government of the *Weimar Republic* as *Reichsminister* for labour. In June he succeeded *Scheidemann* as *Reichskanzler*, but the events of the *Kapp-Putsch* led to his resignation on 26 Mar 1920. Thereafter he was minister of transport in H *Müller*'s cabinet; then minister of the treasury and vice-chancellor in *Wirth*'s government. He was subsequently involved in a case of corruption and withdrew from politics in 1925.

Bauernbefreiung. See *Peasants' Liberation*.

Bayrische Volkspartei. Bavarian party which emerged in 1918 from the Bavarian section of the *Zentrum*. Its supporters came from rural, later also from industrial, bourgeois circles. It stood for an anti-Socialist, federalist policy. It had strong parliamentary representation in the Bavarian *Landtag*, and formed the government in Bavaria from 1920. In national politics it participated in the cabinets of 1922–23 and 1925–32. It demanded constitutional revision in favour of state autonomy and promoted fascist-nationalist forces. After consenting to the *Enabling Act* it was dissolved on 4 July 1933.

K Schönhoven: Die Bayrische Volkspartei 1924–1932 (1972).

Bayrischer Bauernbund. Bavarian farmers' league founded in 1893 by rural *Zentrum* voters who opposed *Caprivi*'s trade policy. After 1919 it participated in Bavarian governments.

Bebel, August (22 Feb 1840–13 Aug 1913); leader of the labour movement. From 1865 he was chairman of a Workers' Educational Association in Leipzig, where he contacted W *Liebknecht*, who became his mentor and helped him to found the 'Sächsische Volkspartei' (1867), which they represented in the *Reichstag*. In 1869 there followed the foundation of the 'Sozialdemokratische Arbeiterpartei', of which Bebel soon became the uncontested leader. He was largely responsible for its amalgamation with *Lasalle*'s *ADAV* to form the *SPD* in 1875. A parliamentary expert on financial and military affairs, Bebel protested against *Bismarck*'s *kleindeutsch* solution. For his speech against the war loan of 1871 Bebel was sentenced to two years for high treason, which he utilized for the study of *Marx* and *Engels*. During the time of the *Sozialistengesetz* (1878–90) Bebel prevented his party from disintegration by opposing all tendencies towards terrorism. In the struggle with the party opposition of the Radicals he insisted on the principle of universal suffrage, but condemned all reformist deviations (*Bernstein*). Bebel shaped the history of Social Democracy for half a century and lived to see the day when the *SPD* became the strongest party in the Reichstag (1912: 110 seats). He combined a utopian socialist belief with promotion of the immediate needs of the working class, while lacking a political theory for the systematic integration of the working class into the state.
E Schraepler: Bebel-Bibliographie (1961).

Beck, Ludwig (29 June 1880–20 July 1944); general. From 1935 chief of the general staff of the army, he was opposed to *Hitler*'s two-front war plans and resigned during the *Sudeten* crisis of 1938. He then joined the resistance movement and the conspirators of the *July Plot* looked upon him as provisional head of state. After the failure of the plot he committed suicide.
N Reynolds: Treason Was No Crime (1976).

Bekennende Kirche. See *Kirchenkampf.*

Bennigsen, Rudolph v (10 July 1824–7 Aug 1902); Hanoverian politician. In 1859, together with *Miquel*, he founded the *Nationalverein*, whose president he was until 1867. In 1866 he failed to prevent an alliance between Hanover and Austria. After the annexation of the former by Prussia he and his political friends entered the *Nationalliberale Partei*. As its leader the gifted orator and eminent parliamentarian played a leading role in the foundation of the new German empire in 1871, when he participated in the negotiations at Versailles (*Kaiserproklamation*). As president of the Prussian *Abgeordnetenhaus* (1873–79) he supported *Bismarck* but failed to become a minister in 1877 because of the disapproval of *Wilhelm I* and Bennigsen's demand that the *Reichskanzler* should be closely bound to the *Reichstag* majority. After

Bismarck turned away from the National Liberals Bennigsen temporarily laid down his mandate (1883), but remained the leader of the party. He was responsible for the acceptance of the *Bürgerliches Gesetzbuch* in 1896. He retired in 1898.

Berlepsch. Hans Herrmann Baron v (1843–1926); politician. He was first confronted with industrial and social problems in the *Rhineland*. He was convinced that the labour movement could not be suppressed by force and conducted the negotiations with the workers during the miners' strike in May 1889 (*Ruhr Strike*). As Prussian minister of commerce (from 1890) he attempted an integration of the working class into the state as opposed to the mere welfare tendency of *Bismarck's Sozialpolitik*. His plans for a real partnership between state and workers on the local level were deprived of any chances of success with the advent of the '*Stumm*' era (1894–95) and he resigned in June 1896.

Berlin-Baghdad Railway. Project for a railway in Asia Minor to meet the Turkish strategic needs to shift troops from Asia to Europe. In Oct 1888 the *Deutsche Bank* had obtained a concession for an Anatolian railway, which was completed as far as Ankara in less than five years. In 1889 a preliminary concession for the Berlin-Baghdad Railway was obtained by the Anatolian railway company. But the Germans, lacking the capital to build the section to Baghdad and Basra alone, offered a share to the French and British, who declined under the pressure of public opinion, though the Germans had disclaimed any colonial ambitions. But soon the German railway construction was accompanied by the presence of military advisers (Linman von Sanders mission) and coincided with the Kaiser's visits to the Middle East, while the *Alldeutscher Verband* propagated the catchword 'Berlin Baghdad'. Thus the project provoked the suspicions of Russia and Britain, which were only removed after Germany recognized Britain's exclusive rights in Iran and Mesopotamia by promising to terminate the railway at Basra. In 1914 850 km (200 km beyond Aleppo) of the railway were ready except for some passes which were completed during World War I, which, however, led to the termination of the project. The projects manifested the limits of *Weltpolitik* and facilitated the Anglo-Russian entente.

Berlin, Battle of. The last phase of World War II in the European theatre began on 12 Jan 1945 with the offensive of the Red Army. The *Ardennen Offensive* enabled the Russians to cross the Oder line in Mar–Apr and start their assault on Berlin which was encircled on 25 Apr. The last fightings took place around the *Reichskanzlei* in which Hitler is believed to have committed suicide on 30 Apr. The surrender of Berlin on 2 May 1945 was soon followed by Germany's *unconditional surrender*.

Berlin (Congo) Conference. Meeting of representatives of 15 nations in Berlin from 15 Nov 1884 to 26 Feb 1885, convened by Germany and France to discuss the status of the Congo basin, which was claimed by King Leopold II of Belgium as the president of the International Congo Association. The conference was presided over by Bismarck, who for tactical reasons participated only in its opening and closing session, but achieved a breakthrough for German *Kolonialpolitik* by demonstrating to Britain her isolation and secured a market for German overseas trade, for the conference created a free trade zone in Central Africa (*Mittelafrika*). The Berlin agreement of 1885 not only prevented a British trade monopoly, but proved an obstacle to the Cape to Cairo railway project, against which Germany successfully protested in 1894.

Berlin, Congress of. Diplomatic convention of the leading European statesmen (Disraeli, Salisbury, Andrássy, Gorchakov, Shuvalov) which took place under *Bismarck*'s chairmanship from 13 June to 13 July 1878. The Congress of Berlin revised the Russo-Turkish peace of San Stefano, which had given Russia a preponderance in the Balkans unacceptable to Austria-Hungary and Britain. It renounced the Russian protectorate over 'Greater Bulgaria', restored Turkish sovereignty over Eastern Rumelia and Macedonia, placed Bosnia-Herzegovina under Austrian military administration and recognized the independence of Rumania and Serbia. But it failed to solve the Eastern Question. The Balkan population remained discontented. Only the Habsburg Monarchy made real gains. Russia was embittered at her reduced influence, for which she held Germany responsible. Russia's alienation from Germany led to the conclusion of the *Dual Alliance* in 1879.

Berlin National Assembly (Berliner Nationalversammlung). Prussian Constituent Assembly elected on 8–10 May 1848 by an indirect system of voting. It was constituted on 22 May in Berlin. The majority of the representatives were moderate Liberals, mainly civil servants and teachers. The assembly was chiefly concerned with the preparation of a constitution for Prussia. The *Camphausen* government presented a draft that provided for a bicameral system, the first chamber consisting of elected representatives, the second of those appointed by the King. On 17 Sept *Friedrich Wilhelm IV* commissioned General v Pfuel to form a new cabinet which was close to the *Camarilla* but also sought an understanding with the Liberals. The King appointed *Brandenburg* prime minister on 8 Nov, although the assembly had expressed itself against such a cabinet. Simultaneously the removal of the assembly to the provincial town of Brandenburg was ordered. The refusal of part of the assembly was answered by the Crown with an open coup d'état, the entry of troops in Berlin under *Wrangel* on 10 Nov. On 5 Dec the assembly was dissolved by royal decree; a constitution was imposed, which, however, contained concessions to the Liberals. A bicameral system was introduced, in which suffrage to the second chamber was dependent on landed property. The chambers were given the right to confirm and revise the constitution. On 30 May 1849 the constitution was amended by a royal decree which introduced the *three-class suffrage*. The Prussian constitution included the human and civil rights (except free assembly); the second chamber (*Abgeordnetenhaus*) possessed the right to sanction and control taxation and expenses. Although ministers were not responsible to parliament and the army remained under the control of the monarch, this was an improvement on the conditions prior to the *Revolution of 1848*.

Berlin Treaty. German-Russian treaty of friendship and neutrality, 24 Apr 1926. It was concluded by *Stresemann* on behalf of Germany and confirmed the Treaty of *Rapallo*. By the Berlin Treaty Germany achieved an understanding in the East and left the anti-Soviet front of *Locarno*. Both partners promised mutual neutrality except in the event of aggression by one of the partners. This clause was in harmony with Germany's obligations to the League of Nations, but the western powers did not react to the treaty favourably. It was renewed by *Brüning* in 1931 and again in 1933 (for 5 years), but lost its importance in the thirties because of the changes in the European political scene.

Berlin University, founded on 16 Aug 1809 by royal charter and opened in 1810. It was structured on *Humboldt*'s principles and became the model for other new universities in Prussia. Prominent academics (Scheiermacher, Niebuhr) were appointed as professors. The first rector was Fichte, who was succeeded by Savigny. The number of students was small in the beginning (256) and diminished further during the *wars of liberation* (1813–15). In 1815 the university recovered but the *Wartburg Festival* (1817) and *Sand*'s murder of Kotzebue introduced a political struggle in it which developed into a fight for academic freedom and the autonomy of universities in Germany.

Berliner Tageblatt. Berlin daily newspaper which was developed into an influential Liberal organ by Th Wolff (1861–1943). It opposed *Weltpolitik* and advocated an understanding with Britain. In World War I it renounced annexations and called for a true parliamentary system. In 1918 Wolff helped to found the *DDP*, whose policy the newspaper supported in the *Weimar Republic*.

G Schwarz: Th Wolff und das Berliner Tageblatt (1968).

Bernstein, Eduard (6 Jan 1850–18 Dec 1932); Social-Democratic theorist. After the *Sozialistengesetz* was passed in 1878 he emigrated to Switzerland, where he was the chief editor of the party organ 'Sozialdemokrat' in the 1880s. From 1888 to 1901 he lived in England and came into contact with the Fabians. He was a close friend of *Engels*, after whose death he evolved his theory of revisionism, and wrote about it in the "Neue Zeit". According to him, the expectation of the imminent collapse of the bourgeois society was wishful thinking; hence he advocated a peaceful policy of reform ('Evolutionary Socialism', 1902). In 1901 he returned to Germany and was a deputy in the Reichstag, representing the *SPD* during the years 1902–06, 1912–18 and 1920–28. In 1919 he joined the *USPD* and, because of his pro-British attitude, he could no longer win much support after his return to the Social Democrats.

P Gay: The Dilemma of Democratic Socialism (1952).

Bethmann Hollweg, Theobald v (29 Nov 1856–2 Jan 1921); statesman. Son of a Frankfurt banker, he joined the civil service and was appointed Prussian minister of the interior in 1905 and state secretary of the *Reichsamt* of the interior in 1907. On 14 July 1909 he became *Reichskanzler* and Prussian minister-president. He was the first to attain to this office from administrative ranks. His moderate conservatism seemed suitable to a cautious approach to reform, but his bills to revise the *three-class suffrage* were twice rejected (1906–1910) by the Conservatives and the Radicals. He shrank from social legislation designed to confer equal rights on the working class. In 1911 he granted universal suffrage to *Alsace and Lorraine* but damaged his reputation by his involvement in the *Zabern* affair. In 1913 his army bills strengthened Germany's military position on land, after his failure to reduce the naval programme of *Tirpitz* and *Wilhelm II (Flottenpolitik)* to a level acceptable to Britain. Bethmann Hollweg himself initiated the July crisis of 1914 with his *blank cheque* to Austria. His belated negotiations with Vienna and London could not reverse his former subordination to the army command, an attitude which was continued during the war. His *September Programme* of 1914 summarized the annexionist aims of the war party, to which he succumbed. Consequently he could not succeed in his diplomatic attempts to split the Allies by a peace based on compromise. In mid-1916 he approved of the appointment of *Hindenburg* and *Ludendorff* as leaders of the military high command and in Jan 1917 he yielded to their demand for an unrestricted *U-Boat-Warfare*. In home policy Bethmann Hollweg had secured the public peace of 1914 by a 'new orientation' towards the right of the *SPD*. When the radical Socialist opposition became vociferous in 1918 (*Spartakus*), Bethmann Hollweg realized that drastic internal changes were necessary and initiated plans for a franchise reform. But his position vis-à-vis the military party and the *Reichstag* had become too precarious and on 13 July 1917 he resigned over the debate on the *peace resolution*. His 'policy of the diagonal' did not satisfy any of the rival sections of the ruling classes. Though personally opposed to the war and content with a return to the status quo, his loyalty to the monarchy and its traditional pillars made him yield to the forces of militarism against his own convictions.

K Hildebrandt: Bethmann Hollweg. Der Kanzler ohne Eigenschaften? (1970); H G Zmarzlik: Bethmann Hollweg als Reichskanzler 1909–1914 (1957); F Stern: Bethmann Hollweg und der Krieg (1968); K H Jarausch: The Enigmatic Chancellor (1973).

Betriebsrätegesetz. See *Work Councils Act.*

Beust, Friedrich, Count (13 Jan 1809–24 Oct 1886); diplomat. In 1848 he became Saxon ambassador in Berlin. In Feb 1849 he entered the cabinet of civil servants that succeeded the previous Liberal government. In Apr 1849 he encouraged the King to reject the constitution drawn up by the *Frankfurt National Assembly* and to call for Prussian aid against the Dresden uprising. A Conservative particularist with pro-Austrian inclinations, he was responsible for Saxony's entry in the *Seven Weeks' War* of 1886. Bismarck was instrumental in causing his dismissal from the service of the Saxon government. Thereupon Breust moved to Austria, where he served as chancellor of the Habsburg Monarchy.

H. Potthof: Die deutsche Politik Beusts von 1866 ... bis ... 1870–71 (1968).

Bierkeller Putsch. See *Munich (Bierkeller) Putsch.*

Bismarck, Otto v, from 1871 Prince (1 Apr 1815–30 July 1898); statesman. Influenced by East Elbian Conservatism Bismarck became its spokesman in the *Vereinigter Landtag* (1847), the *Abgeordnetenhaus* and the *Erfurt Parliament* (1849–50). From 1851 to 1859 he was Prussian ambassador to the Frankfurter Bundestag. As ambassador in St Petersburg (1859) and Paris (1862) Bismarck became acquainted with centres of European diplomacy and was converted to *Realpolitik.* At the climax of the *constitutional conflict* he was appointed Prussian minister-president and foreign minister (1862). He was convinced that the political union of Germany was necessary to preserve Prussia's position as a great power, but unification had to be obtained by Austria's exclusion from the *Deutscher Bund* and against the other European nations, notably France. He openly declared that the German question could only be solved with 'iron and blood' – paving the way for the wars of 1864 (*Schleswig-Holstein*) and 1866 (*Seven Weeks' War* against Austria). The resulting preponderance of Prussia in Germany led to the foundation of the *North German Confederation* (1867) under Bismarck's leadership (*Bundeskanzler*). He answered France's opposition to German unity with the *Ems Telegram* and after the ensuing *Franco-Prussian War* (1870–71) achieved the foundation of the new German empire in 1871 (*Kaiserproklamation*). As *Reichskanzler* he dominated German politics for 19 years. He then aimed at securing the position of the empire, which he regarded as territorially satiated (*Kissinger Diktat*). He strove to isolate France by a complex system of pacts (*Dual Alliance, Triple Alliance, Reinsurance Treaty*). His international reputation was enhanced by his role of an 'honest broker' at the Congress of *Berlin*. It was only with hesitation that he agreed to the acquisition of the *Schutzgebiete*, because he feared that German *Kolonialpolitik* would estrange Britain, an alliance with whom he regarded as the ultimate aim of his foreign policy. In home affairs he was frequently confronted with an opposition in the *Reichstag*, which was elected by universal suffrage (Reich *constitution* of 1871). At first he collaborated with the Liberals, and to break the power of the *Zentrum* and the *SPD* he initiated the *Kulturkampf* and the *Sozialistengesetz*. When he did not succeed in his fight against the workers' party, he tried to win them over for the state by *Sozialpolitik*, particularly the *social insurance*. In economic policy he paved the way for the transition from free trade to protection (1878–79), which gave him the united support of the Junker party and the representatives of the iron and ore industry (*Sammlungspolitik*) after the break with the Liberals. After 1888 he came into conflict with the young *Wilhelm II* and was forced to resign on 18 Mar 1890. In retirement he attacked the *Neuer Kurs* of his successors from his private estate of Friedrichsruh, where he wrote memoirs of literary value.

16

Bismarck's foreign policy, which was determined by his *cauchemar des coalitions*, was moderate in its aims and genial in his understanding of the 'art of the possible'. In domestic affairs he fought passionately against Liberalism and the labour movement. Here the 'iron chancellor' unscrupulously sacrificed the development of German democracy to the preservation of the old Prussian order.

E Eyck: Bismarck and the German Empire (1950); A J P Taylor: Bismarck, the Man and the Statesman (1955); O Pflanze: Bismarck and the Development of Germany (1963); L Gall (ed): Das Bismarck-Problem in der deutschen Geschichtsschreibung nach 1945 (1971); A Palmer: Bismarck (1977).

Björkö. Meeting-place in Finland, where on 24 July 1905, *Wilhelm II* cajoled the Czar into signing the text of a Russian-German defensive alliance. The Kaiser's jubilation over 'the turning-point in the history of Europe' was premature because the alliance was incompatible with existing Russo-French ties. After this was explained by the Russian government the chimera of a *continental league* on the basis of personal monarchic diplomacy vanished for ever.

Blank Cheque. German assurance of full support given to an Austrian envoy on 5–6 July 1914 under the impact of the assassination at Sarajevo. When the Austrians asked in Berlin to what extent they could count on *Nibelungentreue* in their reprisals against Serbia, *Wilhelm II* assured them of unqualified support and told them that he regarded the moment as favourable for speeding up action even if Russia intervened. He was later seconded by *Bethmann Hollweg*, whose consent made the blank cheque constitutionally valid. German political leadership wilfully accepted the risk of a great war and was mainly responsible for initiating the July crisis, during which the *Wilhelmstrasse* continued the course prescribed in the blank cheque, ie wishfully hoping to divide the entente partners by an unqualified support of Austrian policy.

Bleichröder, Gerson (22 Dec 1822–19 Feb 1893); Jewish banker. The Berlin representative of the Rothschilds, he was summoned to Versailles in 1871 by *Bismarck* to take part in the negotiations for a French war contribution (Peace of *Frankfurt*). As British Consul General, Bleichröder became an informant of the *Auswärtiges Amt*. Germany would not have acquired any possessions in the South Sea (*German New Guinea*) without his assistance. As an owner of steel trusts he was among the initiators of a protective tariff policy. His close relationship with Bismarck, for whom he administered the *Reptilienfonds*, gave rise to anti-Semitic propaganda. At his death Bleichröder was the richest citizen of Berlin.

F Stern: Gold and Iron: Bismarck, Bleichröder and the Building of the German Empire (1977).

Blitzkrieg. Strategic concept employed by the Germans in the early phase of World War II to avoid wars of attrition on several fronts. Motorized and armoured formations launched quick, concentrated attacks on the enemy territory, forming circles within which the enemy was destroyed. Success was secured by *Luftwaffe* attacks on the enemy's concentrations. The economic basis of the attacks was a flexible allocation of resources to produce selected munitions. The blitz attacks were successful against Poland, in the West, and in the Balkans, but failed in Operation *Barbarossa*.

H A Jacobsen: Fall Gelb (1957); M L Creveld: Hitler's Strategy 1940–41, The Balkan Clue (1973); J Lukacs: The Last European War, September 1939–December 1941 (1976).

Blomberg, Werner v (2 Sept 1878–14 Mar 1946); general and minister. From 1919, Blomberg, who had belonged to the general staff of the imperial army, served in the *Reichswehr* ministry. In 1931 he led an army delegation to the disarmament conference at Geneva, demanding military equality for Germany. On 30 Jan 1933 he became Reichswehr minister in *Hitler*'s first cabinet and was appointed supreme commander of all three branches of the services by *Hindenburg*, after whose death he caused the *Wehrmacht* to take an oath of allegiance to *Hitler*. But on 5 Nov 1937 he objected to *Hitler*'s war plans (*Hossbach Minutes*). He was dismissed on 4 Feb 1938, when Hitler himself took over his post, thus completing his total dictatorship.

Blücher, Gebhardt v (16 Dec 1742–12 Sept 1819); Prussian general. He fought the war of 1806–07 against France (*Jena-Auerstedt*) after which he was removed at Napoleon's behest for his attempt to organize resistance after the fall of Berlin. After the outbreak of the *wars of liberation* (1813), Blücher was put in charge of the Silesian army on *Scharnhorst*'s initiative. Assisted by *Gneisenau*, Blücher won decisive victories at Katzbach (Silesia) and *Leipzig*. He was created field marshal in 1814 and led the Prussian troops that conquered Paris in 1815. He was recalled upon Napoleon's return from Elba, and thereafter quickly advanced to Waterloo, where he decisively supported Wellington in the battle. He was very popular in Prussia but his plans for a citizen's army diminished his influence with the reactionary governing circles. Blücher's outstanding achievement was the successful transfer of *Gneisenau*'s theory into practice. The King rewarded him for this by creating him Prince of Wahlstatt in 1814.

R Parkinson: Blücher (1976).

Blum, Robert (10 Nov 1807–9 Nov 1848); revolutionary. Originally an outspoken Liberal, Blum fought for a democratic republic in the *Revolution of 1848*. He became vice-president of the provisional parliament and deputy in the *Frankfurt National Assembly*, where he was leader of the parliamentary party of the moderate Left ('Deutscher Hof'). In Oct 1848 he moved to Vienna as a delegate and took part in the armed struggle during which he was shot by the Austrian authorities.

Bohemia-Moravia. German protectorate established on 15–16 Mar 1939 effecting the destruction of the Czechoslovak state. After the separation of the *Sudeten Germans* by the *Munich Agreement* (1938) Germany favoured the segregation of Slovakia, which became a German vassal state. On 15 Mar the Czech

President Hacha, on his visit to Berlin, was forced to appeal for a German protectorate which *Hitler* proclaimed the next day in Prague. Officially the autonomy and self-government of the Czechs was acknowledged, but *de facto* all power passed into German hands. *Neurath* became the 'protector' of Bohemia-Moravia and *Henlein* the head of its civil administration. During World War II *Heydrich* wielded the executive power and terror against the population increased. The 'Generalplan Ost' envisaged the germanization of Bohemia-Moravia by assimilation and immigration.

Bormann, Martin (17 June 1900–2/3 May 1945); leading National Socialist. A member of the Deutschvölkische Freiheitspartei (see *Anti-Semitism*) in his youth, he entered the *NSDAP* via the 'Frontbann' (*SA*). He rose rapidly in the party. In 1933 he was appointed 'Reichsleiter' of the NSDAP and chief of the staff of the *Führer's* deputy. This office enabled him to become an eminence grise in the party, because of his close relationship with *Hitler*, who appointed him to his personal staff in 1928. In May 1941 Bormann became chief of the party chancery with the rank of minister and in 1943 was named Hitler's private secretary. Bormann had a share in such National Socialist crimes as the organization of *euthanasia*. As leader of the *Volkssturm* he was responsible for the partial realization of the *Nero Order*. On 2 May 1945 Bormann, who had been named as Hitler's executor, disappeared from the *Reichkanzlei*. In 1946 he was sentenced to death in his absence by the *Nuremberg Tribunal*. In Nov 1972 previous speculations about his alleged escape to South America were proved false by the identification of his remains, indicating that he fell in the battle for *Berlin*. During the last years of World War II Bormann, who hardly appeared in public, was the most influential figure in the National Socialist hierachy under Hitler.

L Besymenski: Die letzten Notizen von Martin Bormann (1974); J v Lang: Der Sekretär. Martin Bormann: Der Mann, der Hitler beherrschte (1977).

Boyen, Herrmann v (23 July 1771–15 Feb 1848); Prussian military officer. After the *wars of liberation* (1813–15) he succeeded *Scharnhorst* as Prussian minister of war. Boyen drafted the military law of 3 Sept 1814 which stipulated conscription in times of peace and decreed the *Landwehr* regulations. The conflict over the union of army and Landwehr led to his resignation in 1819. Boyen was again minister of war from 1841 to 1847 and played an important role in the reform of the Prussian army.

Brandenburg, Friedrich Wilhelm, Graf v (24 Jan 1792–6 Nov 1850); Prussian statesman. Son of a morganatic marriage of the Prussian King Friedrich Wilhelm II. On 2 Nov 1848 he was appointed Prussian minister-president of a reactionary ministry under the influence of O v *Manteuffel*. Brandenburg dissolved the *Berlin National Assembly* and decreed a new constitution on 5 Dec 1848, thereby confirming the monarchic principle against democratic aspirations. His *kleindeutsch* policy failed at the time because of Austrian and Russian resistance.

Brauchitsch, Walter v (4 Oct 1881–18 Oct 1948); general. After serving in World War I as a member of the general staff of the imperial army he joined the *Reichswehr* and subsequently became supreme commander of the army with increased competence after the dissolution of the ministry of war (*Blomberg, Fritsch Plot*) on 4 Feb 1938. Brauchitsch was opposed to a military coup d'état to prevent the war, and after its outbreak he, together with *Halder*, led the military campaigns against Poland, France, Yugoslavia and Greece and the attack on Soviet Russia (*Barbarossa*). Brauchitsch became field marshal on 19 July 1940 but resigned on 7 Dec 1941. Thereupon *Hitler* personally took over his position.

Braun, Otto (28 Jan 1872–15 Dec 1955); Social-Democratic politician. From 1911 to 1922 he was a member of the executive committee of the *SPD*, from 1913 to 1933 a member of the *Abgeordnetenhaus*, from Nov 1918 to 1920 Prussian minister for agriculture and from 1920 to 1933 (with two interruptions in 1921 and 1925) Prussian minister-president. He championed the *Weimar Coalition* and split from the extremists. In 1925 he unsuccessfully stood for the office of *Reichspräsident*. In 1930 he used his influence in favour of the toleration of *Brüning*'s *Notverordnungen* by the *SPD*'s parliamentary party in the *Reichstag*, of which Braun was also a member. After the elections of 1932, when no new government could be formed in Prussia, Braun was removed from office by *Papen*'s coup d'état of 20 July. Braun appealed to the *Staatsgerichtshof*, which gave a ruling in favour of the restoration to him of the rights (25 Oct) of which he was deprived by Hindenburg's intervention on 6 Feb 1933. In Mar 1933 Braun emigrated to Switzerland.

Bremen Socialist Soviet Republic. It was established after the *November Revolution* of 1918 and liquidated in Feb 1919. In 1920 the city parliament passed a democratic constitution.

P Kuckuck: Revolution und Räterepublik in Bremen (1969).

Brest-Litovsk, Treaty of. On 15 Dec 1917 a Russo-German armistice was concluded at Brest-Litovsk where peace negotiations began on 22 Dec. They continued for several months without concrete results. On 9 Feb 1918 the Central Powers concluded a separate peace with the Ukraine and on 18 Feb they resumed their military advance. On 3 Mar the Russians were forced to accept a dictated peace, by which the Baltic countries, Finland, the Caucasus and the Ukraine were separated from the former Russian Empire. But the economic exploitation of the Ukraine did not fulfill the hopes for a 'bread peace'. The negotiations of Brest-Litovsk were continued at Bucharest. The Rumanians were likewise humiliated. Besides the cession of the southern Dobrudja, the Central Powers claimed the Rumanian petrol and grain resources. The Treaty of Bucharest was signed on 7 May 1918. The two treaties were formally invalidated by the German armistice in the West (*Compiègne*).

Brockdorff-Rantzau, Ulrich Graf v (29 May 1869-8 Sept 1928); diplomat. Held

20

several diplomatic posts until 1918, when he took over the *Auswärtiges Amt*. In 1919 he led the German delegation to the Paris Peace Conference. As an opponent of the Treaty of *Versailles* he resigned from *Scheidemann*'s cabinet on 20 June 1919. From 1922 ambassador in Moscow, Brockdorff-Rantzau did not approve of *Rapallo*, because he viewed it as a threat to détente with the West. But he was equally opposed to a unilateral orientation towards the Western powers and criticized the policy of *Locarno*. He contributed much to German-Soviet agreements such as the *Berlin Treaty*.

U Wengst: Graf Brockdorff-Rantzau und die aussenpolitischen Anfänge der Weimarer Republik (1973).

Brüning, Heinrich (26 Nov 1885–30 Mar 1970); Catholic politician. He started his career as managing director of the 'Christliche *Gewerkschaften*'. From 1924 he represented the *Zentrum* in the *Reichstag*, where he was its parliamentary leader from 1922 to 1929. In Mar 1930, in a Germany shaken by the world economic crisis, he became *Reichskanzler*. He governed without a parliamentary majority with the help of *Notverordnungen* and was greatly dependant on *Hindenburg*. Brüning hoped to overcome the crisis with a deflationist policy, including an increase in taxes and cuts in unemployment insurance, and also with reduction of wages, salaries and public expenditure. These measures had little effect and fostered extremism in the elections of Sept 1930, when the *NSDAP* increased its share and put pressure on Brüning, who tried in vain to win their co-operation. Abroad he gained the confidence of the Allies in the negotiations over *reparations*. He was responsible for their partial remission (*Young Plan*). On 30 May 1932 Hindenburg withdrew his support after Brüning had become the victim of an intrigue by *Schleicher*. In 1934 Brüning emigrated to the USA. His appointment marked the end of parliamentary democracy; his dismissal was the beginning of dictatorship.

R Morsey: Brüning und Adenauer. Zwei deutsche Staatsmänner (1972); E Lohe: Heinrich Brüning (1969).

Bülow, Prince Bernhard (3 May 1849–28 Oct 1929); diplomat and statesman. Ambassador in Rome from 1894, Secretary of the *Auswärtiges Amt* from 1897, *Reichskanzler* in 1900: (also Prussian minister-president). Bülow's career was enhanced by court protection, for his charm and cleverness flattered *Wilhelm II*. Bülow had no original ideas and in foreign policy he repeated the slogans of his time, demanding a 'place in the sun' overseas and 'a free hand' in the choice of Germany's partners. He earned his country the reputation of a blackmailer for the sake of small colonial advantages and together with *Tirpitz* supported the building of a navy (*Flottenpolitik*). He publicly denounced Chamberlain's call for an Anglo-German alliance. After the *Reichstag* elections of 1907 he formed the 'Bülow bloc' of Conservatives and Liberals against *SPD* and *Zentrum*. This combination split over the question of franchise (*three-class suffrage*) and the financial reform of the Reich. Bülow was the first chancellor to face defeat in parliament. Realizing after the *Daily Telegraph Affair* that he could not free himself from dependence on the Kaiser, Bülow resigned in 1909. He liked to be

21

regarded as *Bismarck*'s heir, but his policy ignored social and political changes, leaving Germany weaker at home and isolated abroad. In 1914–15 Bülow was again ambassador in Rome, where he tried in vain to prevent Italy's entry into World War I (*Triple Alliance*). His 'Memoirs' are extremely subjective.

L Namier: 'Men Who Floundered into the War. Prince von Bülow', in Vanished Supremacies (1958); P Winzen: Bülows Weltpolitik (1977).

Bund der Geächteten (League of the Outlaws). League of Socialist emigrés founded secretly in Paris in 1834, under the influence of French republicanism. Its political pamphlets also spread to Germany, where it tried to win over the working class to socialist ideas. The league propagated civil rights in a resurgent Germany. Its main support in France came from travelling artisans, who were under the influence of Utopian Socialism and came into conflict with the league's intellectual leadership. This led to the foundation of the *Bund der Gerechten* in 1836.

Bund der Gerechten (League of the Just). Secret league of German travelling artisans in Paris after their split from the *Bund der Geächteten* in 1836. Influenced by French Utopian Socialism and British Chartism, the league soon spread to Germany, where it took part in the social struggle which resulted in strikes in the 1830s. In 1839–40 the most important 'communities' of the league were established in Brussels and London. In 1840 the founding of the German Workers' Educational Association by Weitling helped to spread the revolutionary theses of the league within the working class. In 1847 the league was incorporated into the *Bund der Kommunisten*.

Bund der Industriellen (League of Industrialists). League of leading industrialists of the light and ready-made goods industries (textiles, chemicals), founded in 1895 as a rival organization to the *Centralverband deutscher Industrieller*. The league was more moderate than the *CVDI* on *Sozialpolitik*: it approved of wage agreements and recognized the trade unions as partners in negotiation. Its interests were represented in parliament by the left wing of the National Liberals (eg *Stresemann*). In 1919 the league was merged in the *Reichsverband der Deutschen Industrie*.

HP Ullmann: Der Bund der Industriellen (1976).

Bund der Kommunisten (League of Communists). Communist league which came into being at the London Congress of the *Bund der Gerechten* in 1847. It aimed at the overthrow of bourgeois domination with a view to establishing a new classless society without private property. In the beginning it was under the influence of *Marx* and *Engels*. In Germany it was assisted by the Workers' Educational Associations, which tried to propagate ideas among the working class. In 1847 it ordered the drawing up of the *Communist Manifesto*. During the *Revolution of 1848* its members left their Western European exiles to entice the German workers to lead the uprising. The failure of the revolution and differences within its leadership led to the dissolution of the league in 1852.

Bund der Landwirte. Farmers' League founded in 1893 in reaction to the reduction of import tariffs on corn. The programme of the league declared agriculture to be the first and most important trade and demanded protection and representation by agricultural chambers. Its claims were only partly met by the renewal of the trade treaties in 1902. Its membership rose to 300,000 before World War I, of which 1.5 per cent were big landowners. These Junkers determined the league's policy under its chairman C v Wangenheim (1899–1920) in co-operation with the *Deutschkonservative Partei.* The league was continued by the *Reichslandbund.*

S R Tirell: German Agrarian Politics after Bismarck's Fall. The Formation of the Farmers' League (1951); H J Puhle: Agrarische Interessenpolitik und preussischer Konservatismus im wilhelminischen Reich (1966).

Bundeskanzler. (1) Chancellor of the *North German Confederation* (1867–70). He was appointed by the 'Bundespräsidium', ie the King of Prussia, and presided over the *Bundesrat.* Besides the *Auswärtiges Amt* the Bundeskanzler was the only federal office; in practice both were filled in personal union by Bismarck. (2) In current usage, the term refers to the chancellor (ie prime minister) of the Federal Republic of Germany, founded in 1949. See also *Reichskanzler.*

Bundesrat. Supreme federal organ of the *North German Confederation* (1867–70) and the German Empire (1871–1918), representing the Princes and Free Cities that had joined the Confederation. In the Bundesrat Prussia had 17 out of 43 (from 1911: 61) votes and could always count on a majority. The Bundesrat was presided over by the *Bundeskanzler* (from 1871: *Reichskanzler*). In the Federal Republic of Germany founded in 1949, the term designates the upper house, representing the Länder, of the two-chamber parliament.

Bundestag. The only federal organ of the *Deutscher Bund* from 1815 to 1886 at Frankfurt. Members of the Bundestag (also called 'Bundesversammlung') were the representatives of the member states. In the Federal Republic of Germany, founded in 1949, the term designates the lower house of the two-chamber parliament.

Bürgerliches Gesetzbuch. Civil code for the entire Reich. It was passed on 18 Aug 1896 and came into force on 1 Jan 1900. It was prepared by a commission of the *Bundesrat.* Its draft was amended by the *Bundesrat* and the *Reichstag.*

Bürgerräte. Self-help organizations of the citizens originating in the *November Revolution* (1918). In the free cities of Hamburg and Lübeck the Bürgerräte were committees responsible for the observance of the constitution.

Burgfriede. Civil truce at the outbreak of World War I by which all political parties agreed not to criticize either each other or the government. The truce had a special bearing on the *SPD*, whose 110-member parliamentary party in the *Reichstag* gave its consent to the war credits on 3 Aug 1914. The Social

Democrats were convinced that Germany was unjustly threatened by the other imperialist powers and especially resented the Russian declaration of war. The truce was declared when the Kaiser said: 'There are no more parties; I see only Germans!'

Burschenschaften. National student corporations founded in 1813–14 under the stimulation of the *Wars of Liberation*. They derived inspiration from the tradition of the 18th century 'Landsmannschaften' and the ideas of *Jahn*, who advocated the unity of students for the strengthening of the patriotic forces. They expressed their allegiance visibly by wearing the colours of the *Lützow Korps* and spread quickly, mainly in central and southern Germany. Their first national congregation was the *Wartburg Festival* of 1817. The radical sections within the corporation (Follen, *Sand*) sparked off reactionary countermeasures (persecution of *demagogues*), which caused the collapse of the enthusiasm of the corporations. After 1848 many *Burschenschaften* imitated the non-political, neo-aristocratic 'Corps', who concentrated on social/student traditions with much drinking and singing. The scar ('Mensur') which resulted from their duelling became the symbol of the membership of the academic upper class.

P Wentzke: Geschichte der deutschen Burschenschaften (1965); E Wiskemann: 'The German Student Corporations', in History Today IV (1954).

Cabinet of Barons. Cabinet formed in 1932 by *Papen*. It consisted mainly of aristocrats and industrialists; 8 of them were members of the *DNVP*, 5 without party membership. The Cabinet of Barons was succeeded by *Schleicher*, who had previously influenced its formation.

Camarilla. Term used to denote an influential lobby at the court of King *Friedrich Wilhelm IV* of Prussia. It was a royalist body and it intrigued against Liberals and Democrats. In the *Revolution of 1848* it worked against constitutional change (*Berlin National Assembly*) by making use of its influence with the King, the *Kreuzzeitung* and conservative clubs. The leaders of the Camarilla were the *Gerlach* brothers, and its supporters included *Wrangel* and *Manteuffel*. The Camarilla rejected the *Union Plan*, which it regarded as a limitation of the rights of other monarchs. The Camarilla exercised a strong influence on the conservatives in the Prussian *Landtag* and in the *Herrenhaus* until the coming of the *New Era*. Later the term Camarilla was also applied to the favourites of Emperor *Wilhelm II* (*Bülow, Eulenburg*).

Cameroons, the. German protectorate (*Schutzgebiete*) from 14 July 1884, after *Nachtigal* had made a 'treaty' with the native King Bell. German sovereignty over the Cameroons was recognized by Britian in return for the renunciation of German claims in Nigeria, and by the French by the agreement of 4 Dec 1885, reached at the *Berlin* (*Congo*) *Conference*. After expeditions into the interior the borders were defined in 1893–95, when the Cameroons comprised 519,000 sq km. On 4 Nov 1911 further territory was added by the *Moroccan Agreements*, which provided access to the Congo-Ubangi. In 1913 the Cameroons had

2,650,000 inhabitants. In World War I they were invaded by British and French troops and the *Schutztruppe* retreated to Spanish-Guinea on 9 Feb 1916. In 1919 the Cameroons were divided between the mandatary powers, Britain and France.

H Stöcker et al: Kamerun unter deutscher Kolonialherrschaft (1960); K Hausen: Deutsche Kolonialherrschaft in Afrika. Wirtschaftsinteressen und Kolonialverwaltung in Kamerun vor 1914 (1970).

Camphausen, Gottfried L (10 Jan 1803–3 Dec 1890); Rhenish entrepreneur. He was the leader of the moderate Liberals in the Rhineland seeking an understanding with the Prussian government. On 29 Mar 1848, during the *Revolution of 1848*, he and D *Hansemann* formed the Prussian ministry. After the fall of his cabinet Camphausen was Prussian plenipotentiary at the federal ministry in Frankfurt. After the triumph of the reaction he sat in the *Herrenhaus* but abstained from political activity.

Canaris, Wilhelm (1 Jan 1887–9 Apr 1945); admiral. He was appointed chief of the 'Abwehr' office in the war ministry on 1 Jan 1935. He developed his department into the espionage centre of the *Wehrmacht*, and was responsible for the organization of the 'fifth columns' abroad. When he realized that German defeat in World War II could not be averted, he began to support resistance movements and took part in the *July Plot* to assassinate *Hitler*. He was arrested and executed shortly before the end of the war.

I Colvin: Canaris (1973).

Caprivi, Count Leo (24 Feb 1831–6 Feb 1899); general and statesman. He held key naval and military positions before succeeding *Bismarck* as *Reichskanzler* and Prussian minister-president on 20 Mar 1890. He initiated the policy of the *Neuer Kurs*. To counteract the danger of a two-front war, he sought an understanding with Britian, dropping colonial claims in the *Heligoland-Zanzibar Treaty*. While his trade policy was 'liberal', his scheme for the confessional *Volksschule* made him appear reactionary in the eyes of the Liberals and led to his resignation as minister-president (1892). Because of his bad relationship with *Wilhelm II* and the intrigues of the *Camarilla*, he resigned the chancellorship in 1894. His failure was due not to his personality but to Germany's social structure, which then had no future for Liberalism.

J A Nicholls: Germany after Bismarck. The Caprivi Era 1890–1894 (1958).

Carlsbad Decrees. Decrees agreed upon by the representatives of the German states on 20 Sept 1819 in Carlsbad (Bohemia) on the basis of the *Teplitz Punktation*. The decrees sanctioned the persecution of *demagogues* and were a reaction against the rise of the liberal movement. They were unanimously passed by the *Bundestag*. They envisaged the elimination of university professors who undermined public institutions, preventive censorship of publications exceeding 20 sheets and the installation of a central commission of investigation in Mainz. An executive regulation of 3 July 1820 completed the decrees by providing for federal courts. Initiated by Metternich, the decrees were the climax of Austrian influence in the *Deutscher Bund*, which from then on became an instrument of the suppression of liberal and national forces. The decrees had a paralysing effect on Prussian plans for a *Nationalrepräsentation*.

Cartel. See *Kartell*.

Catholicism, Political. Catholic ideology favouring the defence of ecclesiastical interests by political means. It aspired to see its creed placed above the self-interest of citizens, estates and the state. Its main representative was *Ketteler*. Political Catholicism was closely connected with the Christian democratic and the Christian social movement. It aimed at solving the social question on the basis of Christian ethics. It inspired the foundation of the *Zentrum* as a counterweight to the Prussian state authority dominated by the Protestants (*Kulturkampf*).

R J Ross: Beleaguered Tower. The Dilemma of Political Catholicism in Wilhelmine Germany (1976).

Central Powers. Collective expression for Germany and her allies (Austria, Bulgaria, Turkey) in World War I. The Central Powers, which were united by the monarchical principle, were linked by bilateral treaties. Though Germany played the predominant part among them, she did not succeed in pressing her war aims upon the other partners. Thus the Central Powers could never agree upon a common concept of foreign policy. Their only co-ordinated appearance in public diplomacy was the peace offer of 12 Dec 1916 (which was rebuffed by the Allies as being insincere) and the negotiations for the treaty of *Brest-Litovsk*. The Central Powers as a bloc were dissolved with the conclusion of separate armistices in late 1918.

W Steglich: Bündnissicherung oder Verständigungsfrieden. Untersuchungen zum Friedensangebot der Mittelmächte vom 12. Dezember 1916 (1958).

Centralverband Deutscher Industrieller. League of German entrepreneurs, founded in 1876. It aimed at a greater influence on economic policy, in particular the introduction of protective tariffs. In the 1890s, the Rhenish-Westphalian heavy industry assumed its leadership, which co-operated with the *Freikonservative Partei* in parliament (W v *Kardorff*) and after 1897 co-ordinated its interests with that of the agrarians in the *Sammlungspolitik*. The league was the most eminent industrial pressure group in the Wilhelmine era. In 1919 it merged with the *Bund der Industriellen* to form the *Reichsverband der Deutschen Industrie*.

H Kaelble: Industrielle Interessenpolitik in der Wilhelminischen Gesellschaft. Centralverband Deutscher Industrieller, 1895–1914 (1967).

Chamberlain, Houston Stewart (9 Sept 1855–9 Jan 1927); philosophical writer. British-born but educated on the continent, he was impressed by the music and the *Pan-Germanism* of *Wagner*, whose daughter Eva he married in 1908, when he settled in Bayreuth. Chamberlain enunciated a national-mystic ideology, his 'philosophy of life' – a mixture of scientific and philosophical ideas. In his work 'The Foundations of the 19th Century' (1899) he became the champion of Social Darwinism and the *Aryan Racial Doctrine*, which greatly influenced *National Socialism*. Chamberlain did not live to see the rise of *Hitler*, whom he met on 30 Sept 1923.

Chancellor. See *Bundeskanzler* and *Reichskanzler*.

Christlich-sozialer Volksdienst. Right-wing party which split from the *DNVP* in 1929 as a reaction to the election of *Hugenberg* as chairman of the DNVP. The party stood under strong Protestant influence. It was loyal to the *Constitution* of the *Weimar Republic*. In the elections for the *Reichstag* it won 14 seats in 1930 and in 1933. Its supporters came from petty bourgeois circles in Protestant areas. It was disbanded in 1933.

G Opitz: Der christlich-sozialer Volksdienst (1969).

Clausewitz, Karl v (1 June 1780–16 Nov 1831); Prussian general and military theorist. A disciple of *Scharnhorst*, he fought in the Napoleonic Wars. In 1818 he became director of the War Academy in Prussia. His posthumously published work *On War* made him the father of the modern theory of war. His critical approach to strategic problems emphasized the preferability of a defensive war against the triple target of the enemy's forces, his resources and his will to fight. He maintained that war is but the continuation of politics with different means. Whereas this had little impact on 20th-century German military policy, Communist theory on war since Lenin is largely derived from him.

J L Wallach: Das Dogma der Vernichtungsschlacht. Die Lehren von Clausewitz und Schlieffen und ihre Wirkungen in zwei Weltkriegen (1967); P Paret: Clausewitz and the State (1976).

Cologne disorders (Kölner Wirren). Struggle between the Roman Catholic Church and the Prussian state, 1836–1841, caused by the curial denunciation of doctrine on mixed marriages held by the theologian G Hermes. A Prussian decree of 1803 provided that children were to be brought up in the denomination of the father. When this regulation was applied in the Rhineland in 1825, Archbishop C A v Droste Vischering (1773–1845) indicated that he would only accept it on certain conditions. He was therefore taken into custody and held in the fortress of Minden. The Cologne disorders created a common political consciousness among German Catholics, as expressed in J v Görres's pamphlet 'Athanasius' (1838).

R Lill: Die Beilegung der Kölner Wirren 1840–42 (1962).

Colonial ... See *Kolonial–*.

Colonies. See *Schutzgebiete*.

Commercial and trade associations (Handels- und Gewerbevereine). Commercial and trade societies, which were founded in the early 19th century to represent the interests of the traditional merchants as well as the rising class of industrialists. They also propagated the new technological civilization with its consequences for the educational system, eg 'The Association for the Promotion of Technical Knowledge' founded in Prussia in 1821 by P Beuth (1818–1845). The 'Society of German Merchants and Manufacturers' was founded in 1819 by F *List* to propagate a *Customs Union*. The commercial and trade associations developed into important political forces and subsequently became the basis of political parties.

Commissar Order. See *Barbarossa*.

Communist Manifesto. Programme of the Communist movement drawn up in 1847–48 by K *Marx* and F *Engels* on behalf of the *League of Communists*. The Communist Manifesto analysed the capitalist order from the point of view of scientific socialism. It demanded the participation of the Communists in the democratic bougeois revolution in Germany without concealing the hostility between bourgeoisie and proletariat. The Communist Manifesto was the starting-point for the programmes of the Socialist and, later, the Communist parties.

Compiègne. Place where the armistice between Germany and the Allies was signed (8–11 Nov 1918) in a railway carriage. It was the first action of the new German government after the *November Revolution*. The German delegation was led by *Erzberger*, who procured only minor concessions. According to the conditions imposed, the Germans had to evacuate France, Belgium, *Alsace and Lorraine* within 15 days and the left bank of the Rhine within 25 days, to accept an occupied zone in the *Rhineland*, to surrender a fixed amount of war material, to withdraw all troops from the East, and cancel the treaty of *Brest-Litovsk*. These conditions did not comply with the German request for an armistice on the basis of W Wilson's Fourteen Points. Hence the seeds of a *Revisionspolitik* were sown at Compiègne. On 22 June 1940 *Hitler* chose Compiègne as the site for the armistice with France after the western campaign to symbolize the successful revenge for the disgrace of 1918.

Concentration camps (Konzentrationslager). Camps for internment in National Socialist Germany and occupied territories. The first concentration camps were erected on the basis of the *Schutzhaftbefehle* in 1933. Besides political opponents, other groups imprisoned in these camps were Jews, gypsies, criminals and homosexuals. The inmates were victims of forced labour, malnutrition and insufficient medical treatment. From 1934 under the direction of the *SS*, they became labour camps for the armament industry in 1942. During World War II the number of these camps increased from 30 (best known: Dachau, Buchenwald) to 85. Terror reached its climax in the extermination camps of the occupied territories in the East (Auschwitz, Treblinka), where Jews (*final solution*) and Russian prisoners were brutally killed and *euthanasia* was practised.

E Kogon: Der SS-Staat. Das System der deutschen Konzentrationslager (1947).

Confessing Church. See *Kirchenkampf.*

Constitutional Campaign (*Reichsverfassungskampagne*). Attempt of the Democrats to enforce the constitution passed by the *Frankfurt National Assembly* in the German states. The assembly's resolution of 11 Apr 1849 demanding the recognition of the constitution was complied with by 29 smaller states, but the middle states of Hanover, Bavaria and Saxony refused, encouraged by the resistance of Austria and Prussia (*Kaiserdeputation*). After putting pressure on the government the Prussian *Abgeordnetenhaus* was dissolved on 27 Apr. On 4 May the Frankfurt National Assembly, in the absence of many moderates, appealed to all public corporate bodies and to the German people to compel the observance of the constitution. This led to revolutionary unrest in Saxony, in the Rhineland, and in southwest Germany, mainly supported by wage labourers in alliance with bourgeois Democrats (eg R *Wagner*). Everywhere Prussian troops intervened to suppress the campaign: in Dresden, in Düsseldorf and Elberfeld, and at Rastatt (uprisings in *Baden*), while the rump parliament in Stuttgart was dispersed on 18 June 1849. The failure of the campaign, which united national, radical-democratic and social-revolutionary elements, marked the end of the German *revolutions of 1848–49.*

Constitutional Conflict. Constitutional conflict in Prussia culminating in a crisis of the monarchy in 1862–64. The conflict was caused by the military reorganization undertaken from 1860 by War Minister *Roon*. Originally approved by the *Abgeordnetenhaus* (1860–61), the increasing hostility of the progressive Liberals (Deutsche *Fortschrittspartei*) led to the cancellation of all means for the army reform in the budget in 1862. Thereupon the *Herrenhaus* rejected the budget and no budget law for 1862 was passed. Then King Wilhelm I, who was strongly in favour of army reform, appointed *Bismarck* minister-president on 24 Sept 1862. Bismarck believed in the possibility of governing without a budget, because the constitution did not provide for the eventuality of both houses failing to agree upon a budget. This 'gap theory' transformed the army conflict into a constitutional conflict. Bismarck's attempt to solve it by new elections to the Abgeordnetenhaus failed in autumn 1863, when the Liberal opposition obtained a huge majority. Only in the aftermath of victory in the *Seven Weeks' War* (1866) did he succeed in solving the conflict with the help of the *Indemnity Bill.*

E N Anderson: The Social and Political Conflict in Prussia, 1858–1864 (1954).

Constitutions (Reichsverfassungen). (1) Constitution of the German Empire (1871–1918); adopted on 16 Apr 1871 on the basis of the *November Treaties* as a scarcely revised version of the constitution of the *North German*

Confederation. Accordingly the *Deutsches Reich* was a federal state of 22 single states governed by monarchs, 3 Free Cities and the 'Reichsland' *Alsace-Lorraine.* The empire consisted of partial states with equal rights; its power was borne by the unity of the 'Länder' as embodied in the *Bundesrat.* Prussia had a preponderant position of power over the other federal states: the King of Prussia was at the same time *Deutscher Kaiser*, the *Reichskanzler* in most cases was the Prussian prime minister: its influence in the Bundesrat was considerable (17 out of 61 votes). The South German states possessed a number of *reserved rights.* The presidency of the empire lay with the Emperor. He was the international representative, commander-in-chief of the army, proclaimed the laws, appointed and dismissed the chancellor and the imperial civil servants, but did not participate in the legislation; he could declare war (with the consent of the Bundesrat) and conclude peace; treaties with foreign states needed the approval of the Bundesrat and the *Reichstag*; if the public security was threatened he could declare martial law. The Reichskanzler was the leader of the administration, and the Reichstag was the body which represented the German people. The most important constitutional change (introduction of the parliamentary system by the law of 28 Oct 1918) did not become effective in practice because of the collapse of the empire. (2) The constitution of the *Weimar Republic* was enforced on 14 Aug 1919 by the *Weimar National Assembly.* It determined the structure of the new republic. The *Reichspräsident* was head of state, the *Reichskanzler* head of government responsible to parliament (*Reichstag*). The federal nature of the Reich was preserved, although the *Reichsrat* had little influence. The Länder (federal states) exercised judicial and administrative power in their territories, but the law of the Reich superseded that of the Länder (*Reichsexekution*). The constitution of 1919 guaranteed human rights for the individual and contained plebiscitary elements (*Volksbegehren Volksentscheid*).

Continental League. Idea of a continental alliance to be formed against Britain between 1895 and 1905. Hopes for such an alliance were always fostered when Anglo-German relations were at a low ebb. Such a league was meant to serve a double purpose: either to draw Britain out of her reserve toward Germany, or (in case of its realization) to exclude the dangers of a war on two fronts. Moves towards a league were made by *Wilhelm II* in his correspondence with the Czar. The Kaiser and *Bülow* wanted to achieve a mutual guarantee of the *status quo* in Europe including *Alsace-Lorraine*, which made French consent to a league illusory. Schemes for a league were thwarted by the formation of the entente cordiale, although the Kaiser made a final personal offer in 1905 at *Björkö.* Interest in a continental league in Berlin showed that policy-makers there were conscious of Germany's forthcoming encirclement. The project was doomed to failure, since Germany's aims were irreconcilable with those of the other continental powers.

Crystal Night (Kristallnacht, Night of the Broken Glass). Term used to denote the anti-Jewish pogrom of 9–10 Nov 1938. It was initiated by *Goebbels* (assisted by the *SA*) after the assassination of the German diplomat v Rath in Paris by a 17-

year old Jew. The pogrom, which was expected to entail a spontaneous popular outburst, did not produce the anticipated results. There was little participation of the German population, other Nazi leaders (*Göring*, *Himmler*) refused to co-operate, and public opinion abroad was shocked. The Jews suffered terribly: 91 were killed, several hundreds driven to their death, 35,000 arrested, 191 synagogues burnt down, and 7,000 shops destroyed. The decrees of 12–13 Nov 1938 sealed their complete exclusion from economic life by confiscating the major part of Jewish wealth and imposing a huge punitive fine of 1 billion marks upon the Jewish community.

L Kochan: Pogrom, November 10, 1938 (1957); R Thalman and E Feinermann: Crystal Night, 9–10 November, 1938 (1974).

Cuno, Wilhelm (2 July 1876–3 Jan 1933); shipowner and statesman. One of the most prominent economic experts of his time, he was the general director of *Hapag* and took part in the armistice and peace negotiations of 1918–19. In Nov 1922 Cuno, who was not a member of any political party, succeeded *Wirth* as *Reichskanzler*. Cuno formed a minority government which was supported by the *DVP* and the *Zentrum* and tolerated by the *SPD*. His cabinet was welcomed by the public but his attempts to solve the *reparations* problem and to stabilize the currency failed. His call for passive resistance after French intervention in the *Rhineland* (*Ruhrkampf*) in Jan 1923 was a contributory cause of inflation. His cabinet resigned on 12 Aug 1923. In 1926 he became president of Hapag and in 1930 he merged the company with *Norddeutscher Lloyd*.

Customs Union (Zollverein). Customs Union creating a free trade area in Germany. Economic progress in the industrial age was hampered by the division of the country into many independent states with their own fiscal policy, particularly by transit tariffs. This situation gave rise to an agitation for a customs union, which was favoured by the commercial bourgeoisie and the manufacturers (Handels-und Gewerbevereine). In Prussia the idea was taken up under the minister of finance, F v Motz (1775–1830) in 1825. Internal customs duties in Prussia had been abolished in 1818. By 1820 the various enclaves on Prussian territory had agreed to enter the new customs area. In 1828 Prussia formed a customs union with Hesse-Darmstadt, providing a link between the Rhineland and Bavaria, which in the same year concluded a union with Württemberg. In defence against Prussian domination the North and Central German states, led by Hanover and Saxony, formed a 'Middle German Commercial Union'. When the South German union united with Prussia, the customs union was born on 1 Jan 1834. The states which had hitherto opposed it gradually joined the union: in 1851–54 the 'Duty Association' of 1834 (ie Hanover-Oldenburg), in 1868 Mecklenburg and Lübeck, in 1888 the Hanse cities of Hamburg and Bremen. The customs union removed anachronistic tariff barriers but soon erected new ones to protect the rising industry of Prussia, thereby indirectly preparing the ground for a *kleindeutsch* solution of German unification.

W O Henderson: The Zollverein (2nd ed., 1968).

31

DAF (Deutsche Arbeitsfront). National Socialist organization uniting employers and employees and claiming to represent all working Germans. It was founded by *Ley* in Nov 1933 after the dissolution of the trade unions. The *DAF* as part of the *NSDAP* enabled the party to exercise influence in social-political and economic affairs. The *DAF* rejected class warfare and only approved of wage rises after rises in productivity. Only 10 per cent of the workers succeeded in avoiding *DAF* membership which stood at 30 million in 1939. Their contributions (1.5 per cent of their income) plus confiscated trade union funds enabled the *DAF* to develop its own economic enterprises (*Volkswagen*) and to finance the holidays of members (*Kraft durch Freude*). Besides such welfare activities the *DAF* did nothing to represent the workers' interests and was a mere propaganda institution to integrate the working class into the totalitarian state.

Dahlmann, Friedrich Ch (13 May 1785–5 Dec 1860); historian. He became professor at Göttingen in 1829, when he began to urge political reforms by constitutional means. During the *Revolution of 1848* he was deputy of the Prussian government in the *Bundesrat* and the *Frankfurt National Assembly*. He resigned after the failure of the deputation to the *Kaiser* and worked for the *Union Plan*.

H Heimpel: Zwei Historiker. F C Dahlmann, J Burckhardt (1962).

Daily Telegraph Affair. Public stir after the publication on 28 Oct 1908 in the *Daily Telegraph* of an interview with *Wilhelm II*, in which the Kaiser declared himself to be a friend of Britain but, as such, in a minority in Germany. He claimed to have prevented a *continental league* against Britain during the Boer War, for which he had sent a strategic plan to Queen Victoria, as a result of which the British defeated the Boers. The interview, which offended Britain and her allies, had been approved by the negligence of an official in the *Auswärtiges Amt* and hence *Bülow* offered his resignation, which was not accepted by the Kaiser. In the ensuing public debate over the affair, *Bülow* did not take responsibility for the incident and in common with all parties admonished *Wilhelm II* to restrain himself in future. The Kaiser's self-confidence was shaken and the forces favouring parliamentary democracy were strengthened.

W Schussler: Die Daily-Telegraph-Affaire (1952).

DANAT Bank. Abbreviation for 'Darmstädter und Nationalbank', founded in 1922 as a merger of the Darmstadt Bank for Commerce and Industry (founded in 1853) and the Berlin 'Nationalbank für Deutschland' (founded in 1881). The DANAT Bank ran into difficulties after the collapse of the Viennese 'Creditanstalt' and on 13 July 1931 it had to suspend payments. All banks closed down temporarily. This marked the climax of the great banking and financial crisis of the *Weimar Republic*. It was a belated repercussion of the world economic crisis after the Wall Street crash in Oct 1929 and as a result of the failure of the *Young Plan*. Together with record unemployment figures (over 6 million in the winter of 1931–32), the DANAT crash largely contributed to the undermining of confidence in the *Brüning* government.

Danzig. Free City established by articles 100–108 of the Treaty of *Versailles*, despite its 95 per cent German population, to give Poland an outlet to the Baltic. From 1920 to 1939 it was under the protection of the League of Nations, which appointed a high commissioner to administer it. The senate was the supreme governing authority, responsible to parliament, according to the constitutions of 11 Aug 1920 and 14 June 1922. In 1922 its economic life was integrated with that of Poland. In 1933 the *NSDAP* gained the majority in Danzig, which became a source of continuous tension between Nazi Germany and Poland. In 1939 Danzig was conquered in the *Blitzkrieg* and was incorporated in the new *Gau* Danzig-West Prussia.

Ch M Kimmich: The Free City. Danzig and German Foreign Policy 1919–34 (1968).

David, Eduard (11 June 1863–24 Dec 1930); Social-Democratic politician. He joined the *SPD* in 1893 and was its *Reichstag* deputy from 1903–1918. He was an extreme exponent of *Bernstein's* revisionism and pleaded for the *Burgfriede* in 1914. He approved of moderate war aims. In Oct 1918 he became under-secretary in the *Auswärtiges Amt* under *Max v Baden.* At the Weimar party congress in 1919 he opposed all attempts at nationalization. He was the first president of the *Weimar National Assembly.* From 1920 again a deputy, he was minister without portfolio in the cabinets of Scheidemann, Bauer, and Müller (briefly *Reichsminister* of the interior in 1923). His activities contributed much to the shaping of the *Weimar Republic.*

S Miller and E Matthias (eds); Das Kriegstagebuch des Reichstagsabgeordneten E David (1965).

Dawes Plan. Scheme for the payment of German *reparations* worked out by the American Charles Dawes. The Plan, which was accepted by the Treaty of London of 16 Aug 1924, envisaged the payment of an annual quota of 2.4 billion Goldmark. This sum had to be paid to the *Reichsbank.* A transfer committee provided the transfer to the creditors. In the first years German payments were made possible by foreign loans, but by 1928 the untransferable amount increased to such an extent that the Dawes Plan was replaced by the *Young Plan.* The Dawes Plan made provision for a supervision of the *Reichsmark,* thereby interfering with German sovereignty. The implementation of Germany's obligations was controlled by a commission chaired by the USA, preventing the sanctions by a single power (France, *Ruhrkampf*).

DDP (Deutsche Demokratische Partei). Progressive Liberal party founded on 20 Nov 1918 by the journalist T Wolff by uniting parts of the *Fortschrittliche Volkspartei* and the left-wing of the *Nationalliberale Partei.* The DDP won 74 seats in the elections for the parliament in 1919, but the defection of the National Liberals (as *DVP*) led to a loss of members and votes in 1920. The DDP obtained 45 *Reichstag* seats, which were reduced to 25 in 1928. It aimed at building up a social democracy within the parliamentary set-up of the *Weimar Republic* and participated in most state and federal governments. In 1930 the DDP was renamed 'Deutsche Staatspartei', but this transformation could not prevent its further decline. It only commanded 5 seats in 1933, when it was dissolved.

L Albertin: Liberalismus und Demokratie am Anfang der Weimarer Republik. Eine vergleichende Analyse der DDP und der DVP (1972); R A Pois: The Bourgeois Democrats of Weimer Germany (1976).

Delbrück, Hans (11 Nov 1848–14 July 1929); historian and publicist. Editor of the 'Preussische Jahrbücher', in which he propagated a programme of 'power and culture' for which he tried to win the educated bourgeoisie. His approval of a '*Weltpolitik* without war' and his intervention for a 'moderate and rational' compromise peace in World War I proved illusory. After 1918 he was a severe critic of the *stab-in-the-back legend* and the *war guilt* theory.

A Thimme: H Delbrück als Kritiker der Wilhelminischen Epoche (1955).

Demagogues, persecution of. Reactionary measures of the *Deutscher Bund* against liberal tendencies, launched after the murder of the poet Kotzebue by *Sand* on 23 Mar 1819. This incident served as a pretext for intervention against what was regarded as demagogic agitation. On the basis of the *Carlsbad Decrees* the *Bundestag* conducted the persecutions by instituting a central commission of investigation. The persecutions hit the *Burschenschaften,* the gymnasts (*Turnen*) and the patriotic societies (*Tugenbund, Deutsche Gesellschaften*). University professors (*Arndt, Jahn,* Welcker) were dismissed as demagogues. The persecutions were revived in the 1930s (after the *Hambach Festival*), when reactionary forces tried to nip revolutionary elements in the bud by the repressive *Six Articles* of 28 June 1932.

Dernburg, Bernhard (17 July 1865–14 Oct 1937); banker and politician. He was appointed director of the colonial department of the *Auswärtiges Amt* in 1906 and became secretary of state of the newly created 'Reichskolonialamt' in 1907. He started his office with the suppression of the native risings in the *Schutzgebiete*, but as a skilled financial expert he soon improved the colonial economy by promoting the construction of railways. After the disintegration of *Bülow*'s bloc he had to resign in 1910. In 1914–15 he directed German propaganda in the USA. In 1919 he represented the *DDP* in the *Weimar National Assembly* and from April to June 1919 he was minister of finance and 'vice-chancellor' in *Scheidemann*'s cabinet.

W Schiefel: Bernhard Dernburg 1865–1937, Kolonialpolitiker und Bankier im wilhelminischen Deutschland (1975).

Deutsche Bank. Big bank founded in 1870 by G v Siemens (1839–1901) in Berlin. In addition to being a domestic credit institute it became active abroad. Like its competitors (the Dresdener Bank, Disconto Bank, Darmstädter Bank) the Deutsche Bank had a large share in German industry. The Deutsche Bank was also indispensable to the plan of nationalization of the railways (*Reichsbahn*). Internationally its most controversial project was the *Berlin-Baghdad Railway*, in the financing of which it played a leading role.

F Seidenzahl: 100 Jahre Deutsche Bank, 1870–1970 (1970).

Deutsche Bauernpartei. Agrarian democratic party founded in 1927 in Bavaria. Its nucleus was the *Bayrischer Bauernbund*. It first featured in the *Reichstag* elections of 1928 and was represented with 8 deputies up to 1933. The party had about 200,000 members in 1928.

Deutsche Christen. See *Kirchenkampf.*

Deutsche Gesellschaften. Patriotic societies founded in 1814 in the Rhineland and in Nassau at the suggestion of E M *Arndt.* Their supporters were partly · involved in the persecution of *demagogues.* In 1815 the reactionary forces began to suppress them.

Deutsche Zeitung. Daily newspaper published from 1847 to 1850. Edited by *Mathy* and *Gervinus*, it was an organ of the Liberals in Baden and played an important part in propagating their views during the *Revolution of 1848* and the *constitutional campaign* of 1849.

Deutscher Bund. Confederation of the German states (1815–1866), founded by the Final Act of the Congress of *Vienna.* At first 34 sovereign states and four Free Cities belonged to it, but in 1866 the number of states was reduced to 28. Foreign members included Denmark (for Holstein and Lauenburg), Britain (for Hanover) and the Netherlands (for Luxembourg and Limburg); Austria and Prussia were only members with those territories which had belonged to the Holy Roman Empire before 1806. The only federal organ was the *Bundestag.* As each member-state had its sovereignty guaranteed, it was impossible to develop the Deutscher Bund into a nation-state (ie from a confederation to a federal state). This aroused the opposition of the national-democratic movement, which was continuously suppressed by the resolutions of the Deutscher Bund (*Carlsbad Decrees*). During the *Revolution of 1848* attempts were made to transform the Deutscher Bund and the Bundestag ceded part of its responsibility to the *Reichsverweser.* In 1850 Austria restored the full power of the Bundestag against Prussian opposition. After the *Olmütz Punktation* Prussia returned to the Bundestag, a reform of which failed in 1863 because of Austro-Prussian rivalry. The Deutscher Bund finally broke up in 1866 after Austria mobilized the federal troops against Prussia. Prussia seceded from the Bundestag and Austria acknowledged the dissolution of the Deutscher Bund in the Peace of Prague on 23 Aug 1866.

Deutscher Kaiser (German Emperor). Official title of the German Emperor (1871–1918). Originally *Wilhelm I* insisted on the version 'Kaiser von

35

Deutschland' (Emperor of Germany), while the Crown Prince (Friedrich III), supported by his Liberal friends preferred the title 'Kaiser der Deutschen' (Emperor of the Germans). *Bismarck* wanted to avoid any constitutional implications and did not go beyond the formula Deutscher Kaiser, which had been suggested by *Ludwig II* of Bavaria. At the *Kaiserproklamation*, Grand Duke *Friedrich* of Baden evaded the problem by toasting 'Kaiser Wilhelm'.

Fehrenbach, E: Wandlungen des deutschen Kaisergedankens 1871–1918 (1969).

Deutsches Reich. Official name given to the German national state at the foundation of the German Empire in 1871. After the *Anschluss* and the inclusion of the *Sudeten Germans* within Germany in 1938 the Nazis proclaimed the 'Grossdeutsches Reich'.

Deutschkonservative Partei. Conservative party which emerged from the old Conservatives after the split over *Bismarck*'s policy in 1876. Its supporters came from the aristocracy, the big landowners (Junkers), the army, the clergy and the higher civil service. It was the strongest party in Prussia until 1918. Its uncontested leader from 1911 to 1918 was *Heydebrand*; its organ was the *Kreuzzeitung*. The maximum number of seats won by it in the *Reichstag* was 80 in 1887. The party emphasized Crown and Christianity as the foundation of the nation. In 1909 it renounced the co-operation with the liberal parties in the *Bülow* block. In 1912 the party sank to 40 seats. In World War I it favoured an annexationist peace and opposed parliamentary reform (eg the abolition of the *three-class suffrage*). After 1919 it was merged in the *DNVP*.

Deutschland, Deutschland über alles. German national anthem by the decree of the *Reichspräsident* of 11 Aug 1922. It was written by Hoffmann v Fallersleben (1798–1879) in Aug 1891 on the island of Heligoland. The initial words 'Deutschland, Deutschland über alles ...' were sung to the tune of the old Austrian imperial anthem composed by Haydn in 1797.

Deutschnationaler Handlungsgehilfenverband. National union of commercial employees founded in 1893. It took an anti-Socialist and anti-Semitic stand and was associated with the Deutschsoziale Partei (1900–14). After 1918 it co-operated with the *Christian Gewerkschaften* and supported the *DNVP*. In 1932 it reached a membership of 400,000, which increasingly voted for the *NSDAP* after 1930. It was dissolved by the Nazis in 1934.

I Hamel: Völkischer Verband und nationale Gewerkschaft. Der Deutschnationale Handlungs-gehilfenverband, 1893–1933 (1967).

DNVP (Deutschnationale Volkspartei). Right-wing party founded in Nov 1918. It was instilled with a monarchic spirit and stood for national unity, private property and enterprise. The party opposed the Treaty of *Versailles* and the policy of *fulfilment*. Under the leadership of *Helfferich* and *Westarp* the DNVP had supporters in all sections of society, particularly in the rural areas in the East. The DNVP was the strongest bourgeois party of the *Weimar Republic*, but

36

it opposed its parliamentary system. The party joined *Luther*'s cabinet, only to leave it after *Locarno*; in 1927–28 it re-entered the government under W *Marx*. After losses in the elections of 1928 (78 seats) the DNVP resumed its anti-Republicanism under the new chairman *Hugenberg*. In 1929–30 half of the parliamentary party split away, some of them forming the *Volkskonservative Vereinigung*. In 1930 the strength of the DNVP was reduced to 41 seats. A seizure of power by the *Harzburg Front* failed. In 1933 the DNVP supported the appointment of *Hitler*, in whose cabinet Hugenberg became minister of economics. But the influence of DNVP rapidly decreased. On 26 June 1933 the party was dissolved.

Dönitz, Karl (16 Sept 1881–); admiral. Having served in the *U-Boat warfare* of World War I (1916–18), he joined the Reichswehr. In 1936 he was put in charge of the submarines. He recognized the submarines as the most effective weapon in commercial warfare and organized their construction and employment. In 1943 he succeeded *Raeder* as supreme commander of the navy. His close relationship with *Hitler* became apparent when the latter appointed Dönitz leader of the executive government, which he formed on 21 May 1945. Dönitz failed to come to a settlement with the Western powers and had to accept *unconditional surrender*. On 23 May he was arrested. The *Nuremberg Tribunal* held him responsible for the conduct of war and sentenced him to ten years' imprisonment.

M G Steinert: Die Tage der Regierung Dönitz (1967); W Görlitz: Karl Dönitz, der Grossadmiral (1972).

Dresden Conference. Meeting of representatives of the states in the *Deutscher Bund* at Dresden from Dec 1850 to Mar 1851. They were initiated by Austria to secure her position in Germany. At the conferences Prussia won support from the smaller states against the Austrian idea of a strong executive in Austrian hands which would have restored the *Bundestag* of the pre-1848 period. As a compromise result of the conferences it was decided to retain the old federal constitution of 1815 unchanged, notwithstanding the *Revolution of 1848*. By 1853 Austria's attempts at entering the *customs union* and the establishment of a huge *Mitteleuropa* were disappointed.

Drittes Reich. See *Third Reich.*

Droysen, Johann Gustav (6 July 1808–19 June 1884); historian and politician. Droysen took part in the German movement in *Schleswig-Holstein*. In 1848–49 he became a member of the *Frankfurt National Assembly* as a leader of the *Erbkaiserliche Partei*. He gave historical legitimation to the *kleindeutsch* solution. His theory of history ('Historik') aimed at a symbiosis between history and politics.

J Rüsen: Begriffene Geschichte. Genesis und Begründung der Geschichtstheorie J G Droysens (1969); K H Spieler: Untersuchungen zu J G Droysens 'Historik' (1970).

Dual Alliance (Zweibund). Defensive alliance between Germany and Austria-Hungary, concluded on 7–15 Oct 1879, promising mutual assistance in case of an attack by Russia or another power supported by her. The alliance which gave security against the two-front war, was accomplished by *Bismarck* despite the Russophile inclinations of *Wilhelm I*. After Germany's mediating role at the Congress of *Berlin* (1878) a 'limited option' for Austria seemed inevitable to Bismarck, but that involved no break with Russia and the *Three Emperors' Alliance* was prolonged (1881). The Dual Alliance secured German influence in the Danube region (*Mitteleuropa*) and determined the foreign policy of the later Bismarckian era, but was not necessarily the starting-point of the block formation leading to the pre-World War I situation. In 1882 the alliance was extended to form the *Triple Alliance* (Dreibund).

Duisberg, Carl (29 Sept 1861–19 Mar 1935); chemist and industrialist. His entrepreneurial activity in the aniline dyes stuffs industry culminated in the foundation of the *IG Farben* cartel in 1925. As president of the *Reichsverband der deutschen Industrie* he tried to implement the *Dawes Plan* and demanded the economic integration of Europe.

Dunkirk, one of the famous battles of World War II. It was fought in May and June 1940 by Germany against British and French forces which had been encircled near Dunkirk. German troops reached the Channel on 20 May 1940 but the onward march was stopped on 24 May in order to enable the exhausted soldiers to have a rest. The Germans planned a *Luftwaffe* offensive to destroy Allied forces which had been pushed back to Dunkirk, but the Luftwaffe failed to prevent the rescue of about 340,000 men by Britain in vessels of all descriptions by 4 June 1940.

DVP (Deutsche Volkspartei). Political party founded in Dec 1918 as a union of the right wing of the *Nationalliberale Partei* and parts of the *Fortschrittliche Volkspartei*. The DVP was a bourgeois party with support from big industry (*Stinnes*), intellectuals and the middle rank. In 1920 it achieved its best result in *Reichstag* elections, polling 13.9 per cent of the votes (62 seats). From 1920 to 1928 its strength fluctuated between 8 and 10 per cent. The DVP gradually accepted the new republic, taking part in the coalition of 1923 and the right wing governments of 1925, 1927–28, 1928–30, which it supported for reasons of economic policy. In foreign policy it tended towards the *SPD*, guided by its chairman *Stresemann*. During the world economic crisis the *DVP* was reduced to a splinter party. In 1933 it was forced to disband.

W Hartenstein: Die Anfänge der DVP 1918–1920 (1962); W Liebe: Die DVP 1918–1924 (1956).

Dolchstosslegende. See *Stab-in-the-back legend*.

Ebert, Friedrich (4 Feb 1871–28 Feb 1925); Social-Democratic statesman. He was chairman of the *SPD* from 1913 and co-leader (with *Scheidemann*) of its parliamentary party from 1916. He was offered the office of *Reichskanzler* by

Max von Baden on 9 Nov 1918 and he accepted, although he had been in favour of the retention of the monarchy. On 11 Nov he became chairman of the *Rat der Volksbeauftragten*; on 11 Feb 1919 he was elected *Reichspräsident* (in 1922 his term was extended by the *Reichstag* to 1925). In this office Ebert acted in a neutral and impartial manner, also appointing Conservative chancellors (*Cuno,Luther*). He used the *Notverordnungen* to protect the young democracy of the *Weimar Republic* against attacks from the Left and the Right (*Spartakus, Kapp-Putsch*). He earned the reputation of an able mediator between the factions.

G Kotowski: Friedrich Ebert, vol. 1 (1963).

Eckardstein, Hermann Freiherr v (5 July 1864–21 Nov 1933); diplomat. As official in the German embassy in London from 1891 to 1898 and as councillor in 1899, he initiated negotiations between his chief, Ambassador Hatzfeldt (1831–1901), and Joseph Chamberlain on 18 Mar 1901, with a view to bringing about an Anglo-German alliance. Eckardstein had proposed such an alliance himself, but sent a misleading report to Berlin to the effect that Chamberlain had made the offer. His conduct confused both governments, but the failure of the Anglo-German talks lay in deeper causes: British reluctance to enter into a binding agreement and the German conception of *Weltpolitik*.

H W Koch: 'The Anglo-German Alliance Negotiations: Missed Opportunity or Myth', in History (1969).

Eichmann, Adolf (19 Mar 1906–31 May 1962); National Socialist civil servant. Expert on Jewish questions in the head office of the *SD*. He was responsible for carrying out the *final solution* and the extermination of 2 million European Jews. In 1945 he fled to South America. In May 1960 he was discovered in Argentina by the Israeli secret service and kidnapped to Israel, where he was tried and sentenced to death in 1961 and executed in 1962.

Eiderdänen. Danish party claiming the River Eider to be the national boundary. The party was the mouth piece of Danish nationalism, aspiring to incorporate *Schleswig* within Denmark, thereby detaching it from Holstein.

Eight-Hour Day (Achtstundentag). Standard of 8 working hours per day, introduced by the *Rat der Volksbeauftragten* in 1918–19. The eight-hour day was an important success of the Socialists in the *November Revolution*. The attempts of heavy industry to revoke it caused a government crisis in 1923, when the forces of order demanded a greater labour effort to reduce the mortgages of the *reparations*. In Oct 1923 the eight-hour day was abolished by *Stresemann*'s enabling act, which the *SPD* approved with reservations. The new working hours decree of 21 Dec 1923 extended the working day to a maximum of 12 hours.

Einjährige. Short for Einjährige-Freiwillige, ie one-year volunteers for national service. From 1815 they were required to serve for one year in Prussia (later in imperial Germany) because they had passed the final examination at a secondary school (*Gymnasium* or 'Realschule').

Einsatzgruppen. Operational units of about 3,000 men of the special Nazi police forces (Security Police, *SD*). After the invasion of Soviet Russia (*Barbarossa*) they began the systematic shooting of the Jewish population on conquered territory in western Russia and the Ukraine. Up to the end of 1941 they had killed about 1.4 million people.

Eisner, Kurt (14 May 1867–21 Feb 1919); Socialist politician. He belonged to the consistent anti-war opposition and took part in the foundation of the *USPD* (Independent Social Democratic Party), becoming its chairman in 1917. On the night between 7 and 8 Nov 1918 he proclaimed the *Munich Soviet Republic*. He then headed a Bavarian government of independent Socialists. Eisner's belief in the success of the revolution was shattered by the Bavarian *Landtag* elections in 1919, when his party won only 3 out of 180 seats. He is believed to have decided to resign at the opening session of parliament on 21 Feb 1919, but on his way to the session he was assassinated by Count Arco-Valley, a counter-revolutionary officer.

F Schade: Kurt Eisner und die bayrische Sozialdemokratie (1961).

Employers' Federations (*Arbeitgeberverbände*). Employers' associations directed against socialist trade unions. The first of them was founded in 1869 in the printing trade. After the May celebrations in 1890 another 29 were formed. The employers united to assist each other with strike funds and to co-ordinate lock-outs. From 1907 they sponsored the *Gelbe Gewerkschaften*. The employers' federations refrained from expressing political views and concentrated on the promotion of a business relationship between employers and workers. After 1919 the central federation of the employers' federations subordinated its activities to the *Reichsverband der Deutschen Industrie*.

G Erdmann: Die deutschen Arbeitgeberverbände im sozialgeschichtlichen Wandel der Zeit (1966).

Ems Telegram. Telegram to all Prussian embassies edited and published by *Bismarck* on 13 July 1870, reporting the shortened version of *Wilhelm I*'s refusal to assure the French ambassador that he would never tolerate the *Hohenzollern candidacy*. The telegram phrased this statement in such a way as to make it impossible for France to save face without declaring war upon Prussia (which she did on 20 July). Thus the telegram achieved the calculated effect of providing an immediate cause for the *Franco-Prussian War*.

E Kolb: Kriegsausbruch 1870 (1970).

Enabling Act (Ermächtigungsgesetz). Term used to denote the act for the 'elimination of need from the people and the nation', passed by the *Reichstag* on 23 Mar 1933. The act empowered the government to proclaim and enforce laws without the approval of parliament. It required a two-third' parliamentary majority to be passed, which was achieved, because the *KPD* deputies forfeited their seats, several Social Democrats were arrested and thus not present. The *Zentrum* and the small liberal parties of the centre consented to it after *Hitler* gave them guarantees that the constitution would be respected (which did not prove to be the case). By passing the Enabling Act the Reichstag gave up its powers and laid the legal basis for the Nazi dictatorship.

Encirclement (*Einkreisung*). The contention that Germany was systematically encircled by the other great powers by the conclusion of alliances and ententes prior to 1914. The expression was first used by *Bülow* in his *Reichstag* speech of 14 Nov 1906. After 1918 the encirclement theory featured in the historians' debate over the responsibility for World War I (*War Guilt Clause*). H. Kantorowicz ('The Myth of the Encirclement', 1929) was the first German historian to point out that Germany's isolation was largely the result of her *Weltpolitik*.

Engels, Friedrich (28 Nov 1820–5 Aug 1895); social philosopher and businessman. He sympathized with the *Junges Deutschland* movement in his youth and later with the *Neo-Hegelians*. In 1842 he met Karl *Marx* in Cologne. During his employment at the Manchester branch of his father's textile shop he became interested in Chartism and wrote a study on 'The Condition of the Working-Class in England in 1844'. He then closely collaborated with Marx on the *Communist Manifesto* and the 'Neue Rheinische Zeitung'. In 1849 Engels took part in the rising in the Palatinate. In late 1849 he returned to England, where he supported Marx financially and politically and assisted him in his writing. In 1885 and 1894 he was responsible for the posthumous publication of volumes II and III of Marx's 'Das Kapital'. Engels is important both for his theoretical and practical work for the Socialist movement. In his pamphlet 'Anti-Dühring' (1878) he explained dialectical materialism and contributed to its subsequent popularity in the 20th century.

S Bünger: Friedrich Engels und die britischen sozialistischen Bewegungen 1881–95 (1962). W O Henderson: The Life of Friedrich Engels (1976).

Erbkaiserliche. Group in the *Frankfurt National Assembly*, which enforced the election of the Prussian King as hereditary monarch in a *kleindeutsch* empire. It consisted mainly of moderate Liberals of the so-called 'Fraktion Casino'. After the rejection of the imperial crown by *Friedrich Wilhelm III* part of the group supported the Prussian *Union Plan* at the Gotha conference on 28 June 1849 and was represented in the *Erfurt Parliament*.

Erfurt Parliament. Conference which took place in Erfurt on 20 Mar 1850 to discuss a new constitution for Germany on the basis of the *Union Plan*. It was elected with little participation of the population (*three-class suffrage*). It consisted mainly of the Conservative right of those *Erbkaiserliche* who had opted for the formation of the Prussian union at the Gotha conference (28 June 1849). After the *Olmütz Punktation* the question of a future constitution was referred to the *Dresden Conference* of 1850–51.

Ermächtigungsgesetz. See *Enabling Act*.

Ernst August (5 June 1771–18 Nov 1851); King of Hanover. He was the fifth son of King George III of England. His accession ended the 125-year personal union between England and Hanover. Whereas his niece Victoria became Queen of England, the German law of heredity did not make provision for a government by a woman until after the extinction of the entire male line. Ernst August spent most of his life in England, where he was the staunch leader of the High Tories in the House of Lords. He ascended his throne at the age of 66 without much knowledge of German affairs. His first political actions (cancellation of the constitution of 1833, dissolution of the estates) aroused public protest (*Göttingen Seven*). In 1848–49 he was forced to appoint the progressive Stüve as minister of the interior and to sign a liberal constitution, which he observed. He opposed the movement for German unity, remaining neutral in the conflict between Prussia and Austria.

Erzberger, Matthias (20 Sept 1875–26 Aug 1921); parliamentarian and minister. A specialist on budget and colonial questions of the left wing of the parliamentary party of the *Zentrum* in the Reichstag (from 1903), he became prominent for his work for democratization (*Interfraktioneller Ausschuss*) and peace (*Peace resolution*) in 1917, when he played a part in the downfall of *Bethmann-Hollweg*. As a member of the armistice commission and secretary of state without portfolio he signed the terms of *Compiègne*. In Bauer's cabinet he was vice-chancellor and Reichsminister for finance, carrying out financial reforms that strengthened the position of the central government. He was opposed by the parties of the right. *Helfferich*'s pamphlet 'Away with Erzberger' (1920) provoked a libel action, but Erzberger could not disprove the charge of having mixed state affairs and private interests. He was shot by two naval officers (*Feme murders*).

K Epstein: Matthias Erzberger and the Dilemma of German Democracy (1962). T Eschenburg: Matthias Erzberger (1973).

Eulenburg, Philipp, from 1900 Prince (12 Feb 1847–17 Sept 1921); diplomat. For many years he belonged to the entourage of *Wilhelm II*, on whom he exercised immense influence. For example, the decision to appoint *Hohenlohe* chancellor was taken on a visit of the Kaiser to Eulenburg's estate. Gradually recognizing Wilhelm's weakness he tried to moderate the Kaiser's activities and promoted *Bülow*, whom he held able to guide the monarch. From 1894 to 1903 he was ambassador in Vienna. In 1906 he was compromised in the press by *Harden*, who suspected him of homosexuality and perjury. The trial was suspended in 1909 because of Eulenburg's poor health and the accusations remained unproved, but the Kaiser sacrificed his friend to public opinion.

J C Röhl: Philipp Eulenburgs politische Korrespondenz. Vol. I (1976).

Euthanasia. Besides the extermination of the Jews as a parasitic race (*final solution*), *National Socialism* also intended the purification of the German nation from the incurable and insane who were subjected to 'mercy killing'. According to the 'law for the protection of the hereditary health of the German people' (1935) the euthanasia programme was initiated during the war and until 1941 more than 70,000 men were killed. Since euthanasia could not be kept secret – it had been denounced as murder by Bishop Galen – it was officially called off, but continued illegally.

Evangelisch-sozialer Kongress. Christian political union founded in 1890 by A *Stoecker* and other Protestant intellectuals. It advocated social reforms to overcome class differences, but its aims were neither supported by the ruling class nor by the Church, which refused to make compromises with the working class movement. After 1919 the union tended towards the left and was in line with the *Weimar Coalition*. After 1933 it confined itself to purely theological questions.

Expatriation Act. Law of 25 April 1874 during the *Kulturkampf*, enabling the imperial government to impose draconic measures against the clergy, confining them to certain areas or even expatriating them. It also abolished their exemption from military service. In Prussia vacant parishes were to be filled through communal election; vacant bishoprics could be administered by a commissioner appointed by the Prussian minister of culture.

Extermination Camps. See *Concentration camps*.

Falkenhayn, Erich v (11 Nov 1861–8 Apr 1922); general. From July 1913 to Jan 1915 Prussian minister of war, he became chief of the general staff on 14 Sept 1914. He sought a decision in vain in the West by subjecting the French to a crushing defeat at *Verdun* in Aug 1916, when he was replaced by *Hindenburg*, whose demands for a concentration on the Eastern front he had disapproved. In Dec 1916 von Falkenhayn led the victorious German army against Rumania. Thereafter he commanded the Turkish forces in Palestine, where he could not hold out against the British and was replaced by Liam von Sanders.

K H Janssen: Der Kanzler und der General. Die Führungskrise um Bethmann Hollweg und von Falkenhayn, 1914–1916. (1967).

Federal ... See *Bundes—*

Fehrenbach, Konstantin (11 Jan 1852–26 Mar 1926); politician. He was a *Zentrum* deputy in the second Baden chamber (Ständekammer) in the 1880s and again from 1903, when he also sat in the *Reichstag*, where he was chairman of its budget committee in 1917–18. He tried to prevent the revolution by convening parliament in his capacity as president of the Reichstag, an office which he also held in the *Weimar Republic*. In June 1920 he became *Reichskanzler* of a minority government tolerated by the *SPD*. His policy contributed to inflation. He failed in his attempts to obtain concessions on the question of *reparations* and disarmament. He resigned on 3 May 1921, one day before the *London Ultimatum*.

Feme murders. Expression derived from the term Feme for secret medieval trials, mainly in *Westphalia*, where they were finally abolished by the French authorities in 1810. In the *Weimar Republic* the term designated political murders of politicians of the parties of the centre and the left, committed by right-wing extremists. From 1919 to 1923 about 300 murders were committed. The most notable victims were *Eisner, Erzberger, Rathenau*, and *Scheidemann*; others included 'traitors' belonging to self-defence organizations (such as the *Organisation Konsul*), Communist informers, and deserters from the 'black' *Reichswehr*. Sentences given to the culprits were often absurdly light, resulting in loss of faith in the republic.

Final Solution (Endlösung). Final solution of the Jewish question as logical consequence of the *Aryan racial doctrine*. After the legal and economic elimination of the German Jews (*Aryan clause, Nuremberg Laws*) the final solution was included in the 'General-plan Ost' which envisaged the germanisation of Eastern Europe. In early 1942 *Heydrich* (commissioned by *Göring*) explained its details at the *Wansee Conference*. From 1942–43 the Jews of Germany and the occupied territories were deported to the larger concentration camps in the eastern part of the 'fortress Europe'. Extermination was generally executed by gassing, in use from 1941 by means of a gas van. The number of Jews killed is estimated at about 6 million.

G Reitlinger: Die Endlösung (4th ed, 1961); P Hilberg: The Destruction of the European Jews (1967).

Flag decree (Flaggenverordnung). Flag decree of 5 May 1926 according to which the trading flag (black-white-red, national colours prior to 1919) was to be displayed besides the national flag (black-red-gold) at all consular representations overseas. The decree was regarded as an attack upon the republican form of government by the Democrats and Social Democrats, who successfully moved a vote of no-confidence against *Luther* (who had countersigned Hindenburg's decree).

Flottenpolitik. Naval policy inaugurated in the 1890s by *Wilhelm II* and *Tirpitz*, both supporters of the new navalism in a country with no maritime tradition. After 1871 a modest 10–year programme of construction had begun to improve the small coastal force of the *North German Confederation*, but until 1896 Germany possessed only 6 first class battleships. The rise of overseas trade, the scramble for colonies (*Kolonialpolitik*) and *Weltpolitik* in general showed Germany's weakness at sea, particularly in diplomatic conflicts with Britain. Under the impact of anti-British feeling, provoked by the Boer-War (*Krüger Telegram*) the campaign in favour of a strong navy was launched in 1895. The first Navy Law of 1898 provided for 19 battleships, 8 coastal armoured ships, and 12 large and 30 small cruisers within 7 years. Technical necessities and the interest of the iron and steel industry, supported by public opinion (*Flottenverein*), led to the second Navy Law in 1900, which envisaged the doubling of the battleship contingent by 1916. A last vain attempt of the

Flottenpolitik to achieve equality with Britain was the construction of dreadnoughts from 1907, but the hope of rivalling Britain in the naval sphere proved illusory. The pursuit of the Flottenpolitik led Germany astray from the sphere of her vital interests: instead of using her resources for the strengthening of the army and submarines (*U-Boat Warfare*) she engaged in building up a navy that became a strategic and diplomatic liability.

H Schottelius und W Deist (eds): Marine und Marinepolitik im kaiserlichen Deutschland 1871–1914 (1972).

Flottenverein. Society founded in 1898 to "enlighten the German people about German interests at sea and the necessity for a German navy" (*Flottenpolitik*). Along with important members of the ruling class (*Hohenlohe, Miquel, Tirpitz*) the society favoured the *Sammlungspolitik*, but in 1899 during the agitation for the second naval bill it also won the support of university professors, whose appeals attracted middle class members. Between 1906 and 1914 the society developed into a mass organization with 300,000 members. Discredited by the failure of the navy in World War I, it lost mass support after 1918 and was dissolved by the Nazis in 1934 despite its propaganda for naval rearmament.

Fortschrittliche Volkspartei. Progressive liberal party formed by a merger of 'Freisinnige Volkspartei', 'Freisinnige Vereinigung' and the South German People's Party in order to overcome the decline of German Liberalism. In 1912 the party had 120,000 members, mainly from the middle classes. It failed to attract voters from the working class. In World War I it demanded a democratization of the suffrage. In 1919 it merged with the *DDP*.

Fortschrittspartei. Progressive party founded in 1861 by Prussian Old Liberals. It stood for the *kleindeutsch* solution of German unification and formed the majority parliamentary party in the Prussian *Abgeordentenhaus*. The party represented large sections of the bourgeoise. Under E *Richter*'s leadership it opposed *Bismarck*'s policies. In 1866 parts of the party broke away to form the *Nationalliberale Partei*. The Fortschrittspartei then entered a new phase, recruiting its supporters increasingly from petty bourgeois sections. In 1881 it rose to maximum strength with 59 *Reichstag* deputies. In 1884 it merged with the 'Liberale Vereinigung' (secessionists from the National Liberals) to form the Freisinnige Partei. See also *Freisinn*.

H A Winkler: Preussischer Liberalismus und deutscher Nationalstaat. Studien zur Geschichte der Deutschen Fortschrittspartei, 1861–1866 (1964).

Four-Year-Plans. Economic plans of 1933 and 1936. The first plan gave priority to agriculture, since the peasantry was regarded as the main core of the *Aryan race* by *National Socialism*. The second plan aimed at securing the autarky for Germany's economy, putting special emphasis on the development of substitutes for raw materials. The plans provided for a relative restriction of entrepreneurial freedom against the interests of the party and *SS* bureaucracy.

Göring was appointed in charge of the plans and concentrated on the erection of the *Reichswerke*. The war economy with its demand for efficiency prevented excessive state intervention in the organization of production.

D Petzina: Autarkiepolitik im Dritten Reich. Die Vierjahrespläne (1968).

Franckenstein Clause. Amendment to the tax bill of 1879 proposing the increase of indirect taxation (by 300 million marks) on beer, brandy and petrol plus a state monopoly of tobacco and sugar in order to avoid an increase of the *matriculated contributions*. The clause limited the surplus in revenue intended for the Reich to 130 million marks, the receipts beyond that sum being allotted to the individual states, on which the central government remained dependent, because the new revenue was insufficient for the Reich. The Franckenstein Clause had been moved in the *Reichstag* by Franckenstein of the *Zentrum*, which represented federalist interests and united with the Conservatives and some National Liberals against the majority of the *Nationalliberale Partei*, *Fortschrittspartei* and the *SPD*. The political consequence of the clause was the break-up of the National Liberal parliamentary group.

Franco-Prussian War of 1870–71. The war was caused by French opposition to *Bismarck*'s attempts at creating German unity. The immediate cause was the quarrel about the *Hohenzollern Candidacy* (*Ems Telegram*). On 19 July 1870 France declared war on Prussia. While Austria stayed neutral, the South German states allied themselves with Prussia. The German army was far superior in its military leadership (*Moltke*), succeeded in the battles of Weissenburg (4 Aug 1870), Wörth and Spichern (6 Aug), and threw the French Rhine army back to the fortress of Metz. A French relief army was encircled near *Sedan* and capitulated on 2 Aug. A new Republican army under Gambetta continued the war but surrendered on 28 Jan 1871. When a southern army failed to relieve Belfort, a preliminary peace was signed at *Versailles* on 26 Feb 1871, followed by the Peace of *Frankfurt*.

M Howard: The Franco-Prussian War (1961).

Frank, Hans (30 May 1900–16 Oct 1946); National Socialist politician. He entered the *NSDAP* in 1927 and soon rose to an important position as chairman of the National Socialist federation of lawyers. In 1933 he took over the Bavarian ministry of justice and became commissioner of justice to promote the *Gleichschaltung* of the legal institutions. In 1934 he founded the 'Reich's Academy for German Law' as a means to instill the Nazi ideology into the German administration of justice. He was minister without portfolio in 1934 and became head of the *Generalgouvernment* in Poland at the end of 1939. The *Nuremberg Tribunal* sentenced him to death for his atrocities against the Polish people.

Frankfurt Congress of the German Princes. Meeting on 16 Aug 1863 of German princes to consider an Austrian proposal for federal reform, which envisaged a pentagon directory and a parliament out of the delegates of the *Landtage*

46

besides an assembly of princes. The congress failed because Prussia refused participation in order to avoid a defeat in the voting. Bismarck reacted to the congress with a far-reaching reform proposal of his own, which provided for a parliament on the basis of universal suffrage. This Prussian counter-action was designed to estrange public opinion from Austria and to influence the Prussian Liberals to end the *constitutional conflict*.

Frankfurt National Assembly. Constituent assembly of the *Revolution of 1848* which met in Frankfurt am Main. It was initiated by the Heidelberg meeting of prominent Liberals on 5 Mar 1848, when a Committee of Seven was appointed. The committee summoned a provisional parliament at Frankfurt for 30 Mar. Contrary to its recommendations, the state government arranged for indirect elections which were held in May and resulted in a majority for the moderate Liberals, both in the Frankfurt National Assembly and in the constituent assemblies of the states. The deputies who assembled in Frankfurt came mainly from a middle-class background, including about 22 magistrates and lawyers, 100 professors and teachers and only one peasant. They organized themselves in provisional parliamentary parties ('Fraktionen') named after their external meeting-places. The largest of them was the 'Fraktion Casino' of the moderate Liberals (from which the *Erbkaiserliche* evolved); the extreme right met in the 'Café Milani', the left-wing Liberals and the Democrats at the 'Deutscher Hof' and 'Donnersberg'. The national assembly constituted itself on 18 May to draw up a constitution and to determine the territorial extent of its jurisdiction and the modus of an eventual federal executive. H v *Gagern* was elected its speaker (president) and Archduke Johann of Austria *Reichsverweser*. On 28 Mar 1849 it passed a constitution. This provided for a German empire with a unitary monetary and customs system but preserving the internal independence of the German states. The territorial question was solved in a *kleindeutsch* sense, the imperial crown offered to the Prussian King *Friedrich Wilhelm IV (Kaiser, deputation to)*. After his rejection on 13 Apr 1849 the representatives of Prussia, Saxony and Hanover were recalled (thereby following Austria's example). The rump parliament, largely consisting of radicals, changed its meeting-place to Stuttgart on 6 June 1849. On 18 June 1849 it was dissolved by troops of the Württemberg government. While the reaction had been gaining ground in all states, in particular Prussia, the assembly dissipated its energies in constitutional debates and, for lack of an effective executive of its own, remained unable to enforce its resolutions.

F Eyck: The Frankfurt Paliament, 1848–9 (1968).

Frankfurt, Peace of. Peace of 10 May 1871, ending the *Franco-Prussian War* concluded by *Bismarck* and the French Foreign Minister Favre. According to its terms, France agreed to cede *Alsace-Lorraine* except Belfort but including Metz and to pay an indemnity of 5 million francs. North Eastern France remained under occupation until the indemnity was paid in 1873. The Peace of Frankfurt gave rise to revanchist ideas in France and proved a burden to the foreign and economic policy of the new German Empire (*Gründerzeit*).

Freikonservative Partei. Conservative party founded in 1867 in the Prussian *Abgeordnetenhaus*. Its supporters were moderate Conservatives led by *Kardorff*. In contrast to the Old Conservatives the Freikonservative Partei categorically supported *Bismarck* in the *Kulturkampf* and the protective tariff legislation. In the Reichstag it called itself 'Deutsche Reichspartei', reaching its peak in 1878 with 13.6 per cent of the votes. In 1918 it was merged with the *DNVP*.

Freikorps. Volunteer units outside the former imperial army from Nov–Dec 1918, mostly founded by officers and NCOs. They recruited ex-servicemen, students, school-boys and the unemployed. They were generally loyal to the *Weimar Republic* without being convinced republicans. Extremist Freikorps (*Marinebrigade Erhardt*) carried out subversive acts against state authorities too. The units varied in size from company to division strength; some were equipped with aeroplanes and artillery. In all there were about 200 units who believed that their main task lay in fighting the *Spartakusbund*, protecting the frontiers against Russia and Poland (plebiscite districts) and maintaining internal order. They were not regarded favourably by the government, since they were considered a danger to democracy.

R G L Waite: Vanguard of Nazism, The Free Corps Movement (1952); D Venner: Söldner ohne Sold – Die Deutschen Freikorps 1918–1923 (1974).

Freisinn. Liberal and social-reformist political movement organized into the following parties: Deutschfreisinnige Partei (DFSP): Progressive liberal party founded in 1884 by a union of the *Fortschrittspartei* with the 'Liberale Vereinigung' (secessionists from the National Liberals). It stood for a policy of social reform in opposition to that of *Bismarck*. Its chairman was E *Richter* and the most prominent member R *Virchow*. In 1884 it had 67 seats in the *Reichstag*. In 1893 the party split into 'Freisinnige Volkspartei' (FSVP) and 'Freisinnige Vereinigung' (FSV). The latter stood for the principle of free trade. The FSV had 13 deputies in the Reichstag of 1893. They represented the interests of banking and commerce and included intellectuals like F *Naumann* and Th *Mommsen*. The FSVP was virtually the successor to the DFSP. It became one of the most important opposition parties in Wilhelmine Germany with 29 seats in the Reichstag. In 1910 the FSVP merged with the *Fortschrittliche Volkspartei*.

Freisler, Roland (30 Oct 1893–3 Feb 1945); National Socialist judge. From 1925 in the *NSDAP*, he was the party's attorney and rose to become secretary of state in the Prussian (1933) and then in the Reich's ministry of justice (1934). In 1942 he became president of the *Volksgerichtshof*. He was in charge of the trials against the conspirators of the *July Plot* (1944) and used the opportunity to demonstrate his devotion to the National Socialist leadership by a cynical conduct of the cases. He was killed during an air raid shortly before the end of the war.

G Buchheit: Richter in roter Robe (1968).

Fremdarbeiter. Foreign workers from territories under German occupation during World War II. Since volunteers were scarce (about 200,000), the mobilization of labour was organized by a plenipotentiary for labour supply (F Sauckel) in co-operation with the administration in the occupied territories, the *Wehrmacht*, the *SS* and the industries concerned. Altogether 5 to 7 million Fremdarbeiter were deported, mainly from the East. They were hardly treated better than prisoners in *concentration camps*. Prisoners of war were also employed as Fremdarbeiter. The *Nuremberg Tribunal* condemned the treatment of the Fremdarbeiter and sentenced Sauckel to death.

E L Homze: Foreign Labor in Nazi Germany (1967).

Freundeskreise. Groups of financial magnates who promoted *National Socialism*. After its electoral success in Sept 1930 the *NSDAP* was regarded as a mass movement which effectively contested the Socialist parties. In particular the iron and ore industry (*Kirdorff, Thyssen*) and the chemical industry (*Duisberg*) financed the Nazi campaigns. The 'Freundeskreise des Reichsführers *SS*' at Munich financed *Himmler*'s pseudo-research in heredity ('Ahnenerbe'). After the *Nazi seizure of power* groups were joined by businessmen hitherto critical of *Hitler* (*Siemens, Krupp*). Their greatest contribution was the 'Adolf Hitler donation' amounting to RM 700 million, which demonstrated gratitude for the abolition of the trade unions (*DAF*) and an interest in armaments orders. The provision of slave labour from *concentration camps* and the administration of plants in occupied territories proved to be the worst features of Nazi economic policy.

R Vogelsang: Der Freundeskreis Himmler (1972).

Frick, Wilhelm (12 Mar 1877–16 Oct 1946); National Socialist politician. A participant in the *Munich (Bierkeller) Putsch* (1923), for which he was sentenced to 15 months' imprisonment in a fortress which he never served. From 1924 he was a member of the *Reichstag* for the *NSDAP*, from 1928–45 leader of its parliamentary party. As Thüringian minister of the interior (1928–33) he was the first National Socialist member of a government. On 30 Jan 1933 he became *Reichsminister* of the interior. In this capacity he took charge of the *Gleichschaltung*. Most National Socialist laws of terror (*Nuremberg Laws*) were formulated in his ministry. As representative of the central administration he supervised education and the extension of the German laws to the annexed territories. In 1943 he became head of the protectorate of *Bohemia-Moravia*, where he urged germanization. The *Nuremberg Tribunal* sentenced him to death.

Friedrich I (9 Sept 1826–28 Sept 1907); Grand Duke of Baden. He was Prince Regent from 1852, Grand Duke from 1858. He married Princess Luise, a daughter of the Prussian King *Wilhelm I*, a fact which linked him with Prussia and made him the South German protagonist of a *kleindeutsch* solution of German unification. At the *Frankfurt Congress of the German Princes* (1863) he opposed Austrian plans for a reform of the *Deutscher Bund*. Geographical circumstances and public opinion forced him to side with Austria in the *Seven Weeks' War* of 1866, but after the defeat of Baden he allied his duchy with Prussia and took the initiative in the founding of the empire by the German princes (*Kaiserproklamation*). In Baden his reign was characterized by legislative activity, concern for his people's welfare and encouragement of the arts and sciences. As an adviser of *Wilhelm II* he seems to have exercised his influence in favour of *Bismarck*'s dismissal, as Bismarck's *Realpolitik* conflicted with Friedrich's liberalism.

W P Fuchs (ed): Grossherzog Friedrich I von Baden und die Reichspolitik 1871–1907 (2 vols, 1968); L Gall: Der Liberalismus als regierende Partei. Das Grossherzogtum Baden zwischen Restauration und Reichsgründung (1968).

Friedrich III (as Crown Prince known as Friedrich Wilhelm) (18 Oct 1831–15 June 1888); *Deutscher Kaiser* and King of Prussia. He was the son of *Wilhelm I* and married Princess Victoria of England, later called 'the Empress Friedrich', who exercised a great influence on him. Because of his liberal outlook he was opposed to *Bismarck*'s policy. As a commander in war he distinguished himself in the battles of *Königgrätz* (1866) and *Sedan* (1870). When he ascended the throne on 9 Mar 1888 he was already seriously ill with cancer of the throat. During his short reign of 99 days he was unable to change the course of politics, although he dismissed R v *Puttkammer*. It is doubtful whether Friedrich would have ensured the victory of the German liberal movement.

M Freund: Das Drama der 99 Tage (1966).

Friedrich Wilhelm III (3 Aug 1770–7 June 1840); King of Prussia from 16 Nov 1797. Of steady character, he was educated by the famous constitutional lawyer Suarez. Lacking determination to act, his neutral policy towards France only accelerated the collapse of Prussia in 1806 (*Jena-Auerstedt*). At home he preserved traditional 'cabinet' government until 1807, when he sanctioned the reforms of *Stein* and *Hardenberg*. However, the absolutist structure of Prussia remained untouched. In 1813 he finally called upon his people to take up arms against Napoleon (*wars of liberation*), but he did not share the enthusiasm of the army and the population. At the Congress of *Vienna* he was subservient to Czar Alexander I, thereby gaining territories for himself west of the River Elbe. Thereafter Friedrich Wilhelm tried to consolidate his reign by repressive measures (*Demagogues, persecution of*). He dismissed *Boyen* and *Humboldt* in 1819 and the promise of a constitution which had been held out was only partially fulfilled (*Provinzialstände*).

Friedrich Wilhelm IV (15 Oct 1795–2 Jan 1861); King of Prussia. The son of *Friedrich Wilhelm III*, he ascended the throne on 7 June 1840. The great hopes aroused by his accession were soon disappointed, when he expressed unwillingness to fulfil the constitutional aspirations of the Liberals. His generosity and tolerance, together with his unsoldierly and artistic nature, had been mistaken for 'liberal tendencies'. But he was convinced of his divine right and the new ideas of a modern German nation liberated from the rights of the princes, and from their states and institutions, were alien to him. His view of society was hierarchical and only after long delay did he summon the

Vereinigter Landtag in 1847 with the aim of establishing a corporative state. Friedrich Wilhelm was overwhelmed by the *Revolution of 1848*. His order to disperse the crowds from the palace square led to a violent riot, whereupon he made some concessions, appealing 'to my dear Berliners' and paying homage to the fallen soldiers. He then withdrew to Potsdam, where, surrounded by reactionary court advisers (the *Camarilla*), he waited indecisively for events to unfold. Eventually, he cancelled the constitutional arrangements made in March 1848. He appointed Count *Brandenburg* as minister-president, dissolved the *Berlin National Assembly* and imposed a new constitution by royal decree (5 Dec 1848). In Apr 1849 he rejected the Imperial Crown proffered by the *Frankfurt National Assembly* (*Kaiser, deputation to*), thus making it plain that he did not want to become a 'citizen-king'. In the question of German unity he remained disinclined to assert the claims of Prussia against Austria for supremacy in Germany (*Union Plan, Olmütz Punktation*). The final years of his reign were a period of reaction under the bureaucratic regime of O v *Manteuffel*. Friedrich Wilhelm IV was mentally incapacitated by a stroke in 1857, when the future *Wilhelm I* acted as regent for him.

Fritsch Plot. Nazi plot to bring about the removal of the supreme commander of the army, W v Fritsch (1880–1939), because he doubted the capacity of the *Wehrmacht* to achieve Hitler's military aims (*Hossbach Minutes*). Fritsch was unjustly accused of homosexuality in order to force his resignation, which he accepted despite his later rehabilitation by a military court. His replacement by *Brauchitsch* was announced on 4 Feb 1938, but Hitler assumed supreme command of the entire *Wehrmacht*. Fritsch's passive attitude was characteristic of German generals. This helped the National Socialists to gain control of the armed forces.

H C Deutsch: Das Komplott oder die Entmachtung der Generale. Blomberg- und Fritsch-Krise. (1974).

Führer. Title of *Hitler* in imitation of Duce for the leader of Italian Fascism. Hitler as Führer headed the party (*NSDAP*) and the state apparatus, which were both organized according to the Führer principle, ie on authoritarian and hierarchical lines. Hitler also regarded himself as Führer of the entire German nation. He demanded complete obedience and did not tolerate objections to his decisions. After the collapse of internal party opposition (*G Strasser, Röhmputsch*) he succeeded in establishing his total control. His position remained unchallenged to the end.

W Horn: Führerideologie und Parteiorganisation in der NSDAP (1972).

Fulfilment, policy of (Erfüllungspolitik). Term used to denote the policy of implementation of the obligations of the Treaty of *Versailles* as initiated by *Wirth* in 1921, when the government strove to demonstrate to the Allies Germany's capacity for paying *reparations*. The term was applied in a pejorative sense by the right-wing opposition, which denounced the acceptance of the *London Ultimatum* (1921) and the *Locarno* treaties. They also attributed inflation and economic weakness to the policy.

Gagern, Heinrich Freiherr v (20 Aug 1799–22 May 1880): civil servant and politician. He helped to found an all-German *Burschenschaft*. A Hessian Liberal, he rejected a revolutionary unification of Germany. In Mar 1848 he was appointed minister-president of the Grand Duchy. In May 1848 he became president (speaker) of the *Frankfurt National Assembly*. Here Gagern demanded agreements with the princes and the election of Archduke Johann as *Reichsverweser*. He was then chairman of the federal ministry and minister for foreign affairs as well as the interior. He stood for a programme which bore his name. He advocated a Prussian hereditary empire in loose union with Austria. In May 1849 Gagern left the National Assembly and temporarily supported the *Union Plan*, but turned away from it in view of the restoration.

Gas warfare was first employed by the Germans against the Russians in Poland on 31 Jan 1915, but it only became an effective weapon after 22 Apr 1915, when a cylinder attack with chlorine was launched in the Ypres Salient (where French and British lines joined) to break the trench stalemate. Gas warfare came as a complete surprise to unprotected Allied troops and also to the Germans, who did not have enough reserves to exploit the breakthrough for the restoration of open warfare. In the following period the offenders on both sides used new agents independent of wind. In July 1917 mustard gas caused severe burns. The number of deaths from gas warfare increased in the last months of the war. The operation *Michael* was accompanied by a 10-day artillery bombardment with 500,000 mustard gas shells.

Gastein Convention. Agreement concluded on 14 Aug 1865 between *Bismarck* and the Austrian envoy Count Blome, regulating the occupation rights in *Schleswig-Holstein*. According to the convention, Holstein was to be administered by Austria, Schleswig by Prussia; the County of Lauenburg was ceded to Prussia as an indemnity and Prussia was also empowered to erect naval installations in the port of Kiel. Neither the other members of the *Deutscher Bund* nor the people concerned were consulted. The convention temporarily settled an acute bone of contention between the two powers, but it was unable to prevent the *Seven Weeks' War* in 1866.

Gau. Regional division of National Socialist Germany. A Gau comprised a land or province and simultaneously determined the regional sub-division of the *NSDAP*, each headed by a Gauleiter, who was generally also *Reichsstatthalter* of the respective Gau after 1933.

P Hüttenberger: Die Gauleiter (1969).

Geheimer Kabinettsrat (Secret Cabinet Council). According to the decree of 4 Feb 1934 the Geheimer Kabinettsrat was to be an advisory council for *Hitler* in questions of foreign policy. Its chairman was *Neurath*, other members being the chiefs of the branches of the *Wehrmacht* and some cabinet ministers. The council never met. Its membership was merely intended as a compliment to flatter *Hitler*'s ex-allies who had helped him to come to power but who had subsequently been eliminated by him.

Generalgouvernment. After the success of the *Blitzkrieg* against Poland, Germany annexed Poland's western provinces as 'Reichsgaue' (Wartheland and Danzig-West Prussia), in which the Polish population did not obtain German citizenship. The remainder of Poland (except the part occupied by the Russians in consequence of the Ribbentrop-Molotov Pact) was practically made a protectorate as 'Generalgouvernment for the occupied Polish territories' under Governor General H *Frank*. German rule was marked by ruthless economic exploitation and barbaric extermination of the Polish intelligentsia and Jewry, for which the *SS* established huge *concentration camps*. According to the 'Generalplan Ost', germanization, which was at first confined to the annexed territories, was to be extended to the Generalgouvernment at a later stage, when 80 to 85 per cent of the Poles were to be transferred eastwards (*Resettlement*), while the rest were to be assimilated. The German occupation power in the Generalgouvernment was heroically resisted by the Polish people and culminated in the abortive Warsaw rising of 1944.

M Broszart: Nationalsozialistische Polenpolitik (1961).

Geopolitics. Term denoting the theory that national policy is dependent on geography. It was coined shortly before World War I by the Swedish political scientist R Kjellen, who adapted the political-geographical ideas of F Raizel (*Lebensraum*) by declaring that the state is an organism endowed with biological qualities. His treatise was translated into German in 1917 and seized upon by K Haushofer (1869–1946), who contended that the German state was an organism which had been continuously growing for centuries and would spread until it absorbed the whole earth, beginning with *Mitteleuropa* as its 'heartland'. This biological world outlook found an academic platform in the University of Munich and was given wide publicity by the propagandists of *Pan-Germanism*. Geopolitics had an early influence on *National Socialism*, for which it provided an arsenal of catchwords ('blood and soil'). R *Hess* was a disciple of Haushofer; traces of the theory can be found in *Mein Kampf*. The Nazi government officially declared geopolitics to be one of its 'pillars' in 1935 and used the educational system to indoctrinate teachers with it. Haushofer's son Albrecht (who was later involved in the *July Plot*) became a professor in the 'Hochschule für Politik'. Since geopolitics had been of practical assistance to the Nazis in World War II (through maps), it was discredited after 1945. By assuming that political power rested entirely on material wealth which could be statistically computed, geopolitics disregarded the forces generated in a people by nationalism.

A Grabowsky: Raum, Staat und Geschichte. Grundlagen der Geopolitik (1960).

Georg V (27 May 1819–12 June 1878); King of Hanover, 1851–1866. The son and successor of *Ernst August*, blind since the age of 14, his rule was reactionary. On 17 June 1866 *Bismarck* gave him the choice of either allying himself with Prussia (involving the surrender of part of Hanover's sovereignty) or of being treated as an enemy. Georg V chose the latter and sided with Austria in the *Seven Weeks' War*. The defeat of the Hanoverian troops at

Langensalza resulted in the annexation of Hanover by Prussia. When in 1868 Georg established a Welf legion, Bismarck confiscated the royal fortune (*Welfenfonds*).

Gerlach, Ernst L v (7 Mar 1795–16 Feb 1877); Prussian Conservative. Together with his brother Leopold (1790–1861) he directed the *Camarilla*. He was among the founders of the *Kreuzzeitung*, for which he wrote many articles. After 1858, as an alternative to *Bismarck*'s *Realpolitik*, Gerlach developed his illusory concept of a Christian-legitimist policy of principles.

German Christians. See *Kirchenkampf*.

German East Africa. German sphere of influence from 27 Feb 1885, when *Peters* secured an imperial charter after concluding 'contracts' with chiefs in the coastal region opposite Zanzibar. The Sultan of Zanzibar recognized German overlordship of the hinterland, which was confirmed by an Anglo-German agreement in 1886. In 1888 the British navy assisted in quelling an Arab revolt aimed at preventing the transfer of control over the coastal strip to the German East Africa Company. The borders were fixed by the *Heligoland-Zanzibar Treaty* of 1890. On 1 Jan 1891 the Reich took over East Africa as a protectorate (*Schutzgebiete*) under Governor H Schnee. In 1905–1907 the popular uprising of the Maji-Maji led to a more liberal administration and more investment for economic development. The colony became famous for its pioneer coffee-growing on the slopes of the Kilimanjaro. Until 1914, 1645 km of railway were built in a colony of 993,500 sq km with 7,646,000 inhabitants. During World War I it was invaded, but the *Schutztruppe* held out until 14 Nov 1918. The Treaty of *Versailles* ceded most of German East Africa (as Tanganyika) to Britain as a mandatory power: the district of Ruanda-Urundi came under Belgian administration.

K Büttner: Die Anfänge der deutschen Kolonialpolitik in Ostafrika (1959); J Iliffe: Tanganyika under German Rule 1905–1912 (1969); R Tetzlaff: Koloniale Entwicklung und Ausbeutung. Wirtschafts- und Sozialgeschichte Deutsch-Ostafrikas, 1885–1914 (1970).

German New Guinea. North-eastern part of New Guinea acquired by Germany on 16 Nov 1884. By imperial charter of 17 May 1885 sovereignty was transferred to the New Guinea Company, which handed it back to the Reich on 7 Oct 1898. The colony comprised the mainland, the Bismarck Archipelago and the Northern Solomons (from 1899); from 1906 the Micronesian Islands north of the Equator (the Mariana, Caroline and Palau Islands acquired in 1884) as well as Nauru (German in 1888) were also administered by German New Guinea. The area totalled 242,600 sq km with 418,000 inhabitants in 1913. It was peacefully occupied in 1914 by Australia, which acquired the mainland as a mandate in 1919, while the Micronesian Islands were ceded to Japan.

German Southwest Africa. German protectorate (*Schutzgebiete*) from 24 Apr 1884, when *Bismarck* approved *Lüderitz*'s 'treaties' with native chiefs in the no man's land of Angra Pequena, made in 1883. In 1844 *Nachtigal* gained the territory of the Nama and in 1885 that of the Herero. The frontiers with Angola and the Cape colony were fixed in 1886 and 1890, when the *Heligoland-Zanzibar-Treaty* secured access to the Zambesi via the 300 mile-long *Caprivi* strip. German South-West Africa then totalled 836,000 sq km. From 1904 to 1907 the Herero and Hottentots revolted and were fiercely subdued by General v Trotha. The discovery of diamonds (1908) and copper (Otawi mines) attracted many European settlers (15,000 out of 81,000 inhabitants in 1913). In World War I German South-West Africa was invaded by British and Portuguese troops and the *Schutztruppe* surrendered on 9 July 1915. In 1920 it became a mandate of the South African Union.

H Drechsler: Südwest Afrika unter deutscher Kolonialherrschaft (1966); H Bley: Kolonial-herrschaft und Sozialstruktur in Deutsch Südwest Afrika 1894–1914 (1968).

Germanists' Congresses. All-German meetings of philologists in Frankfurt (1846) and Lübeck (1847). The congresses were a reaction to the federal law of 5 Aug 1832, which prohibited all political associations. Led by the *Göttingen Seven*, the congress developed into 'intellectual *Landtage*' (*Treitschke*).

Gervinus, Georg G (20 May 1805–18 Mar 1871); historian. One of the *Göttingen Seven*, he later taught at Heidelberg and temporarily edited the *Deutsche Zeitung*. In the *Revolution of 1848* he was a member of the *Frankfurt National Assembly* from which he resigned because he was appalled by its inactivity. He moved to the left wing of the Liberals and became a pronounced critic of *Bismarck*'s policy (*Union Plan*).

L Gall: 'Georg Gottfried Gervinus' in H U Wehler (ed): Deutsche Historiker, vol V (1972).

Gessler, Otto (6 Feb 1875–24 Mar 1955); Liberal politician. Joint founder of the *DDP*, he became *Reichsminister* for Reconstruction in 1919. In 1920 he succeeded *Noske* in the *Reichswehr* ministry, which he headed for 8 years under 8 different chancellors. Together with *Seeckt* he faced the task of building up the army. In 1926 Gessler left the DDP and in 1928 he resigned over the 'phoebus affair' on clandestine re-armament. His policy strengthened the *Weimar Republic*. For his connection with the *Kreisau Circle* he was sentenced to 7 months' imprisonment in 1944.

Gestapo (Geheime Staatspolizei). Political police in Nazi Germany. Placed under the minister of the interior in 1934, the Gestapo was joined with the criminal investigation department to form the security police, subordinated to the head of the *SD*, *Heydrich*. From 1939 the Gestapo office continued to exist within the *Reichssicherheitshauptamt*, to which all Gestapo men were affiliated automatically. The Gestapo was exempt from the common police law, ie its orders could not be examined by the judiciary. The *Nuremberg Tribunal* declared the Gestapo a criminal organization.

E Crankshaw: Die Gestapo (1959).

Gewerbeordnung (Trade Regulations). Law of 1869 regulating the registration, licence, practice and prohibition of trade. Commercial legislation was influenced by economic liberalism and political reform and first introduced in Prussia with the edicts of 1810–11 promulgating the freedom of trade and abolishing the guilds. The trade regulations of 1869 improved the Prussian regulations of 1845 and 1849, extending the principle of freedom of trade to the *North German Confederation* and soon to the entire German Empire (1871). In 1891 the regulations were amended to include improvements on the lines of *Sozialpolitik* (protection of *labour*). The Gewerbeordnung was the fundamental law of the rising German industrial state.

Gewerkschaften. Trade unions, which developed on the following lines:

I. **Freie Gewerkschaften.** Socialist unions. The first were founded in 1865–66 (cigarette industry workers, book printers). In 1875 there were 30 of them with approximately 50,000 members. The *Sozialistengesetz* interrupted all unionist activities between 1878 and 1890. The new *Freie Gewerkschaften* gained increasing influence on labour conditions by wage agreements. Between 1885 and 1910 they achieved a 100 per cent rise in real incomes, mostly without strikes. In 1919 they were continued by the *ADGB*.

H J Varain: Freie Gewerkschaften, Sozialdemokratie und Staat (1956).

II. **Christliche Gewerkschaften.** Christian unions originating in 1894–95 at Trier and Essen. They were founded in opposition to the *Freie Gewerkschaften* to which they remained inferior in numbers. In 1919 their membership reached 1 million. This had great influence in the Rhineland and in Westphalia from where 50 per cent of the members came in 1929. They were the predominant union in smaller cities. Politically they were connected with the *Zentrum*. Under their leader A *Stegerwald* they rejected class conflict as a means of settling labour questions.

K H Schürmann: Zur Vorgeschichte der Christlichen Gewerkschaften (1958).

III. **Freiheitlich-nationale Gewerkschaften:** see *Hirsch-Dunckersche Gewerkvereine.*

IV. **Gelbe Gewerkschaften.** Peaceful unions based on shop membership. They were conceived as strike beating organizations against the *Freie Gewerkschaften.* The first *Gelbe Gewerkschaften* were founded in 1905. In 1913 there were 287 with 180,000 members. In 1918 an agreement between the other unions and the entrepreneurs (*Employers' Federations*) established a trade union monopoly that encroached on the development of the *Gelbe Gewerkschaften.*

Gleichschaltung. Integration of all political, social and cultural institutions under the control of the *NSDAP* as the only party in Germany from 5 June 1933 in order to create a centralized National Socialist state. The federal structure of the *Weimar Republic* was abolished by the appointment of *Reichsstatthalter* by the law for the reconstruction of the Reich, 30 Jan 1934, which dissolved all provincial parliaments and transferred sovereign rights to the central government. The police was merged with the *SS* (*Gestapo*). Professions were brought into line in National Socialist organizations, and youth organizations in the *Hitler Youth*. For the *Gleichschaltung* of labour, see *DAF*, for that of the cultural scene *Reichskulturkammer*.

Gneisenau, August Count Neidhart v (27 Oct 1760–23 Aug 1831); Prussian general. A mercenary with the British in America in his youth, he first exelled in the defence of the fortress at Kolberg (Pommerania) against Napoleon. His political and military qualifications enabled him to co-operate in *Stein's* reform programme. Gneisenau provided for the foundation of a War Academy, an important step in military reform. He retired in 1808 but served again in the *Wars of Liberation* (1813–15) and after *Scharnhorst's* death he was chief of staff until 1816. Having already been largely responsible for the planning of the Battle of *Leipzig* his career reached its climax at Waterloo, when he became chief of staff to *Blücher* and organized the Prussian countermarch. In 1816 Gneisenau resigned, because his hopes for a reform of the Prussian state on the British model were frustrated.

H Bock: Zwischen Thron und Vaterland. Gneisenau im preussuschen Krieg 1806–07 (1966).

Goebbels, Joseph (29 Oct 1897–1 May 1945); leading National Socialist. He joined the *NSDAP* in 1922 and became the *Gauleiter* of Berlin in 1926. In 1928 he became a member of the *Reichstag*. In 1931 he married the ex-wife of the industrialist Quandt, thereby achieving a powerful financial position, which he utilized to build up the party's propaganda apparatus, which prepared the German people for the *Nazi seizure of power*. On 14 May 1933 he became head of a new Ministry of Propaganda. He organized the suppression of all progressive culture and of intellectuals and directed the dissemination of *National Socialist* ideas (*anti-Semitism, Volksgemeinschaft*) and the propaganda in preparation for World War II. After the failure of the strategy in the East in 1942–43 (*Stalingrad*), he propagated slogans of endurance, as in his speech in the Berlin sports palace on 18 Feb 1943, when he announced total war, for the organization of which he became responsible in the last years of the war. As commissioner for the defence of *Berlin* he mobilized the last resources to delay its fall. Goebbels was envisaged as *Reichskanzler* in Hitler's last will, but he committed suicide on 1 May 1945. His influence within the party was limited, but the effect of his demagogy was disastrous for the German people.

H Fraenkel and R Manvell: Dr Goebbels: His Life and Death (1960); E K Bramstead: Goebbels and National Socialist Propaganda 1925–45 (1965).

Goerdeler, Carl (31 July 1884–2 Feb 1945); Conservative politician. A member of the *DNVP*, he became Mayor of Leipzig in 1930. In 1931 and again in 1934 he was appointed commissioner for prices by *Hindenberg* and *Hitler* respectively. Goerdeler was not opposed to *National Socialism* on principle, but he realized that Germany had hardly any chance of success in a war. He favoured a settlement with the Western Powers. He belonged to the extreme Conservative wing of the resistance movement, though he had also contacts with the *Kreisau Circle* without sharing its ideas of democratic reconstruction. He was envisaged as *Reichskanzler* by the conspirators of the *July Plot* (1944), but was executed soon after the failure of the putsch.

G Ritter: Carl Goerdeler und die deutsche Widerstandsbewegung (1954).

Göring, Hermann (12 Jan 1893–19 Oct 1946); leading National Socialist. Member of the *NSDAP* from 1922 and first leader of the *SA*, Göring fled abroad after the failure of the *Munich (Bierkeller)Putsch* (1923). In 1928 he became a deputy in the *Reichstag* and its president in 1932. As minister-president of Prussia (from 1933) he was responsible for the terror at home. He initiated mass arrests of political opponents, helped to create the *Gestapo* and to organize the *Röhm Putsch*. On 24 Jan 1939 he handed the execution of the *final solution* over to *Heydrich*. In 1936, as commissioner for the *Four-Year Plan*, Göring organized the direction of German industry. In 1940 he became director of the war economy and organized the confiscation of plants in the occupied territories (*Reichswerke*). As supreme commander of the *Luftwaffe* he was responsible for air raids on cities. German defeat in the *Battle of Britain* and the failure to protect the German cities against Allied bombings weakened Göring's position. In 1939 he was still considered the first candidate to succeed the *Führer*, but subsequently lost influence in the National Socialist hierarchy. In 1945 he failed in his unauthorized attempt to negotiate a separate peace in the West and lost all his titles ('Reichsmarschall'). The *Nuremberg Tribunal* sentenced him to death, but he committed suicide before he could be executed.

Ch Bewley: Hermann Göring (1962); L Mosley: Göring (1975).

Göttingen Seven. Seven professors of the University of Göttingen: W Albrecht, F C Dahlmann, H Ewald, G *Gervinus*, J and W Grimm, and W Weber. On 14 Dec 1837 they were dismissed from their chairs, because they had accused the Hanoverian King *Ernst August* of violating the constitution. The dismissal evoked a wave of sympathy from broad sections of the population. Most of the Göttingen Seven later became members of the *Frankfurt National Assembly*.

Green Front. Federation of the farmers' organizations, the *Reichslandbund* and the German agricultural council, formed in 1929. It aimed at overcoming the crisis of German agriculture after the inflation. The Green Front mainly served the interests of the landed proprietors. In 1933 it was merged in the *Reichsnährstand*.

Groener, Wilhelm (22 Nov 1867–3 May 1939); general and minister. He was head of the War Office in 1912 and organized the *Hindenburg Programme*. Dismissed after disagreeing over war aims with *Ludendorff*, he succeeded the latter as general quarter-master in Oct 1918. He was in charge of the retreat and demobilization of the army. After the *November Revolution* he allied himself with *Ebert* against the Bolshevik forces. In 1919 he advocated the signing of the

Treaty of *Versailles* and began a career as a politician. From 1920 to 1923 he was *Reichsminister* for transport, from Jan 1928 to 1932 also minister of the interior. He opposed the Nazis and suppressed the *SA* and *SS*, proving himself a loyal servant of the *Weimar Republic*.

D Groener-Geyer: General Groener – Soldat und Staatsmann (1955).

Grossdeutsch. Term implying (contrary to *kleindeutsch*) the inclusion of Austria in a reformed *Deutscher Bund*. In 1848–49 the debate in the *Frankfurt National Assembly* on the boundaries of a future German empire was complicated by the nationality question, which involved the Czechs and Italians of Austria, the Poles in the Prussian Posen province, and the Danes of North *Schleswig*. The declaration on the protection of nationalities of 31 May 1848 provided for regional autonomy, free cultural activity and the recognition of their language as a second official language for the non-German part of the population. After the victory of the *Erbkaiserliche* at Frankfurt, the *grossdeutsch* alternative finally failed in 1866 (Seven Weeks' War). The ensuing separate development of Austria was later interrupted for seven years after the *Anschluss* of 1938. Followed up by the forcible inclusion of the Czechs (*Bohemia-Moravia*) and Poles (*Generalgouvernment*), *Hitler*'s 'Grossdeutsches Reich' meant a short-lived realization of the *grossdeutsch* conception.

G Wollstein: Das Grossdeutschland der Paulskirche (1977).

Grosse Politik. Short for 'Die grosse Politik der Europäischen Kabinette 1871–1914'. A collection of diplomatic records of the *Auswärtiges Amt*, compiled on its behalf by J Lepsius, A Mendelssohn-Bartholdy and F Thimme. It consists of 40 vols and a five-volume commentary, ed by B Schwerdtfeger. The collection appeared from 1922 to 1927 and was the first official comprehensive publication of documents by the government of a great power covering the period from the foundation of the German empire to the outbreak of World War I. It provided material for research on the 'war guilt question' which had been stimulated by the *war guilt clause*.

Gründerzeit. Period of promoterism following the foundation of the German empire in 1871. In 1871–73 a boom was caused by a combination of the French war contribution (Peace of *Frankfurt*) of which 2.2 million gold marks were spent on armaments; the redemption of state debts and war loans (increasing the circulation of money); and the standardization of the monetary and banking system on a federal basis (*Reichsbank*). The steep rise in the foundation of new enterprises was facilitated by joint stock companies and 49 new banks. Overall production rose by 30 per cent, that of steel even by 80 per cent. Overproduction led to the slump of 1873, when the number of credit banks was reduced from 139 to 73. The number of enterprises decreased far more than production itself (sinking by 5 per cent). This led to a business concentration, a development conspicuous in banking (*Deutsche Bank*) and heavy industry (*Cartels*).

H Rosenberg: Grosse Depression und Bismarckzeit (1967).

Gymnasium. Secondary (grammar) school preparing for university entrance by a special school-leaving examination ('Abitur', from 1834) in Prussia (from 1812) and later in the whole of Germany. The Gymnasium was a product of the new humanism as personified by W v *Humboldt*. The exclusive idealism of the Gymnasium preserved the advantage of higher education for a small section of society. The attendants of the Gymnasium came largely from upper middle class families, eg in 1885 out of 47 million inhabitants 7.5 million pupils attended a *Volksschule* and only 238,000 schoolboys went to a Gymnasium (133,000 in Prussia alone). From 1900 the 'classical' Gymnasium was challenged by modern schools which placed less emphasis on Latin (eg the 'Real'-Gymnasium, from 1908 also for girls), in line with the economic changes which transformed Germany into an industrial state.

K E Jeismann: Das preussische Gymnasium in Staat und Gesellschaft (1972).

Haase, Hugo (29 June 1863–17 Nov 1919); Social-Democratic politician. As Reichstag deputy for the *SPD*, 1887–1907 and 1912–18, he became one of the Party presidents in 1911 and leader of its parliamentary party from 1912 to 1915. During World War I he differed from the majority in the question of the war budget (*Burgfriede*). He was then regarded as the leader of the Left and joined the *USPD*. From 9 Nov to 29 Dec 1918 he shared the chairmanship of the *Rat der Volksbeauftragten* with *Ebert*. In this office Haase favoured measures injurious to the *November Revolution*. In 1919 he was elected to the *National Assembly,* but his membership was violently ended by assassination (*Feme murders*).

Halder, Franz (13 June 1884–2 Apr 1972); chief of the general staff of the army from 1 Sept 1938. He took part in the planning and execution of every *Blitzkrieg*. He was dismissed on 24 Sept 1942 after the failure of *Barbarossa* and succeeded by Zeitzler. His diaries are a major source for the study of World War II.

Hambach Festival. Political meeting of Liberals, Democrats and Republicans in the Castle of Hambach near Neustadt and der Haardt (Palatinate) on 27 May 1832. After the Bavarian government had revoked its prohibition of the festival about 30,000 persons took part in what was a demonstration of the will to fight for the unity and freedom of the German nation. The festival was the climax of the national movement. It proves that it was possible to mobilize the masses for revolutionary actions. But the disunity of the national forces allowed reactionary forces to take measures to prevent an eventual revolution, by complete suppression of freedom of assembly, associations and press. The speakers at the festival had to flee to escape arrest.

K Baumann (ed): Das Hambacher Fest (1957).

Hamburg Uprising. Communist rebellion from 22–24 Oct 1923. It received little support from the public and was brutally crushed. It was another Communist attempt to attain power in the *Weimar Republic* after entering governments in Saxony and Thuringia (*Reichsexekution*).

R A Comfort: Revolutionary Hamburg (1966).

Handelsgesetzbuch. Commercial code published on 10 May 1897 and enforced on 1 Jan 1900. It concluded the standardization of the law on a federal basis. Its four component parts deal with the business classes, trading companies, commercial transactions and maritime trade.

Handelskammern. Chambers of commerce in Germany which originated from medieval merchant corporations in the Baltic. In Napoleonic times chambers were founded in the *Rhineland* on the French model. These chambers survived after the restoration of the Prussian state and developed into representations of commercial interests. The first important chamber was at Cologne. Only in the 1840s did the Prussian government realize the necessity of further chambers of commerce and encourage new foundations. As a consequence of the industrialization of Germany the chambers became 'Industrie- und Handelskammern'.

W Fischer: Unternehmerschaft, Selbstverwaltung und Staat. Die Handelskammern in der deutschen Wirtschafts- und Staatsverfassung (1964).

Handelstag. Association of German Chambers of Commerce and of Industry and Trade (DIHT), founded in 1861 in response to the differences between protectionists (South German cotton-mills, West German steel industrialists) and free traders (manufacturing industry). The DIHT was dominated by liberal free trade attitudes up to 1876, when it was taken over by the Association of German Iron and Steel Industrialists (later the *Centralverband der deutschen Industriellen*).

Hansabund. League for trade, commerce and industry founded in 1905. It was conceived as a counterweight to the agrarian *Bund der Landwirte*. Its membership was recruited from the new middle classes and reached 1 million within a year; while the old middle classes from 1911 were organized in the 'Reichsdeutscher Mittelstandsverband'. In the *Reichstag* elections of 1912, 88 out of 200 Hansabund candidates were elected. This was regarded as a defeat by Social Democracy. In the *Weimar Republic* the Hansabund opposed most governments' financial policy, which burdened the trading petty bourgeoisie with costs for social legislation. The Hansabund revived its anti-agrarianism against the *Osthilfe*. It was dissolved in 1934.

S Mielke: Der Hansabund (1972).

Hansemann, Adolf (27 July 1826– 9 Dec 1903); financial magnate. He acquired a powerful position as director of the 'Disconto-Gesellschaft' and helped to finance the wars of 1886 (*Seven Weeks' War*) and 1870–71 (*Franco-Prussian War*). He also took over the 'New Guinea Co.' and other overseas transactions in Venezuela and China. He was chairman or member of the boards of directors of many enterprises. He had an annual income of 1,860 million marks and was the second richest man in Prussia after *Bleichröder*.

W Däbritz: David Hansemann und Adolf Hansemann (1954).

Hansemann, David (12 July 1790–4 Aug 1864); Rhenish entrepreneur. He was a member of the *Vereinigter Landtag* (from 1847) as a Liberal who regarded the reform of Prussia into a bourgeois liberal state as a pre-requisite for German unification under Prussian hegemony. The *Revolution of 1848* forced King *Friedrich Wilhelm IV* to appoint him minister of finance in *Camphausen's* cabinet. Hansemann was hampered in his economic activities by the restoration, though he became president of the *Handelstag*.

HAPAG (Hamburg-Amerikanische-Packetfahrt-Actien-Gesellschaft). Merchant shipping company founded in 1847 in Hamburg. Directed by A *Ballin* from 1886, the HAPAG developed into the world's greatest line before World War I, when it had 206 ships with 1.36 million BRT. It was reconstructed in 1920–26 in co-operation with United American Lines and the rival *Norddeutscher Lloyd*. In 1939 the HAPAG possessed 108 ships with a wide overseas service. The fleet was lost again in World War II.

Harden, Maximilian, real name: M Witkowski (20 Oct 1861–30 Oct 1927); publicist. In 1892 he founded the political weekly 'Die Zukunft' as a mouthpiece for the Bismarckians against the *Neuer Kurs* and the *Camarilla*. His accusations led to the scandalous trial of *Eulenberg* in 1906. Until 1914 Harden supported imperialist aims, but then adopted a pacifist position. After 1918 his espousal of Socialism led extreme nationalists to attempt to assassinate him (1922), whereupon Harden emigrated to Switzerland.

H F Young: Maximilian Harden Censor Germaniae (1959).

Hardenberg, Karl August Prinz v (30 May 1750–26 Nov 1822); Prussian statesman. Formerly a Hanoverian civil servant, he became Prussian foreign minister in 1804. Together with Count Haugwitz (1752–1832) he at first conducted a policy of neutrality towards France in the hope of gaining Hanover. He was responsible for the alliance with Russia in 1807 (*Bartenstein*), and was dismissed on Napoleon's behest. He re-entered Prussian service in 1810 with the task of restoring the state's finances. He wielded unlimited power as 'Staatskanzler', a position which combined the offices of prime minister and minister for the interior and for finance. He continued the reforms begun by *Stein* in a more liberal way. He decreed the *Regulierungsedikt* (1811), introduced freedom of trade and brought about the emancipation of *Jews*. He even thought of emulating the French example by some kind of *Nationalrepräsentation*. But after 1815 the climate was unfavourable to further reforms. In foreign affairs, he associated himself with the conservative policy of the Eastern powers (*Holy Alliance*). In 1813 he had adroitly postponed his consent to a national rising against Napoleon (*wars of liberation*). At the Congress of *Vienna* he achieved great gains in territory for Prussia. He then carried out the administrative reform of the enlarged Prussian state on the basis of a liberal-conservative civil service. His concept of law and liberalism greatly advanced the constitutional character of the state in Prussia.

P G Thielen: Karl August v Hardenberg 1750–1822. Eine Biographie (1967); E Klein: Von der Reform zur Restauration. Finanzpolitik und Reformgestzgebung des preussischen Staatskanzler Karl August v Hardenberg (1965).

Harkort, Friedrich (22 Feb 1793– 6 Mar 1880); Westphalian industrialist. He studied the industrial development of England at the beginning fo the 19th century and pleaded for its emulation by Germany. In 1818 he established a mechanical workshop for engineering, in 1826 a furnace using the puddling process and in 1832 an iron-foundry and a copper-smithery. He also paved the way for the German railway system. In his writings he called for a new financial and economic policy as a pre-requisite for German industrialization, which he only thought possible on the basis of a reformed Prussian state. As a member of the provincial diets he favoured the abolition of all feudal privileges. After 1848 he continued his pioneering role in the *Abgeordnetenhaus* and in the *Reichstag.* He emphasized public education as a means for solving social problems and was representative of enlightened Rhenish liberalism.

W Köllmann: Friedrich Harkort (1964).

Harzburg Front. Union of National Socialists, *DNVP* and other nationalist groups and industrialists to form a so-called national opposition to *Brüning*'s government. The front came into being at a meeting in Bad Harzburg on 11 Oct 1931. It accused Brüning of a rapprochement with the *SPD* and called upon the government 'to respond to the wishes of the people' (instead of governing by emergency decrees (*Notverordnungen*). The front was an essential stage on *Hitler*'s way to the seizure of power. It broke in 1932, when the DNVP failed to support Hitler's candidacy for the office of *Reichspräsident.*

Hassenpflug, Hans Daniel (26 Feb 1794–10 Oct 1862); Hessian politician. He attempted to promote reactionary government in Electoral Hesse. Appointed minister of justice by the Elector Friedrich Wilhelm I in 1832, he sought to undo the liberal constitution of 1831. He relied upon Austria and persuaded the elector to secede from the Prussian *Union Plan.* On 21 Sept 1850 he induced the *Bundestag* to decree an armed intervention against the Hessian Liberals. The military intervention by Austro-Hungarian troops of the *Deutscher Bund* almost ended in war with Prussia, but tension was relieved by the *Olmütz Punktation* in Nov 1850. In 1852 he introduced a new reactionary constitution. After his dismissal (10 Oct 1855) it took nearly seven years for the liberal constitution of the *Vormärz* to be largely restored on 21 June 1862.

Hecker, Friedrich (28 Sept 1811–24 Mar 1881); revolutionary. From 1842 he was a member of the second Baden chamber. Under the influence of Gustav v Struve (1805–1870) he changed from a Liberal to a Democrat, adopting

63

elements of English and French Socialism. In the *Revolution of 1848* he aspired for a federal German republic, which he tried to realize in South Germany during the first uprisings in *Baden*. After the failure of the putsch he and Struve fled to America. On a visit to Germany in 1873 he criticized conditions in Germany. His popularity is expressed in the tradition of the green Hecker hat as a democratic symbol.

Hegel, Georg Friedrich Wilhelm (27 Aug 1770–14 Nov 1831); philosopher. He first lectured at Jena and was later professor at Erlangen, Heidelberg and Berlin. In 1806–7 he published his greatest work 'Phenomenology of Mind', in which he interpreted the development of historical and individual thought from an objective-idealist position. His theory of Idealism, according to which all historical experience must be dominated by an abstract Spirit greater than material form, was expounded in 'The Philosophy of Right' (1821). Within his all-embracing system he elaborated his political thought. He postulated the construction of a socio-political order that satisfies the claims both of the universal law and the individual conscience. The synthesis of these two claims is a state resting on family and guild, institutions in which the individual finds satisfaction of his needs in co-operation. Hegel envisaged the state as a constitutional monarchy, quite different from the Prussia under Friedrich *Wilhelm III*. He wanted to demonstrate the unity of thought and reality in the entire universe. His systematic approach is also apparent in his philosophy of history, which presupposes the whole history of mankind as a process of spiritual and moral progress. Progress in thought resulted for Hegel in the interaction of two conflicting half-truths. This dialectical method was later adopted by Karl *Marx*. In his lectures Hegel began to attract a school of his own, *Neo-Hegelians*. Hegel's philosophy greatly influenced 19th-century political thought in Germany and abroad, eg the British New Idealists (Jowett, T H Green, Bosanquet).

F Wiedmann: G W F Hegel (1965); S Averini: Hegel's Theory of the Modern State (1972).

Helfferich, Karl (22 July 1872–23 Apr 1924); right-wing politician. In 1906 he became director of the Anatolian railway company (*Berlin-Baghdad Railway*). From 1908 a member of the governing body of the *Deutsche Bank*, he took over the leadership of German financial policy during World War I as secretary of state of the Treasury (1915) and Prussian minister of finance. He tried to cover the war costs with loans, thus initiating a development ending in inflation. In May 1916 he became secretary of state of the *Reichsamt* of the interior and vice-chancellor under *Bethmann-Hollweg* and *Michaelis* until the Left forced his resignation in 1917. In the *Weimar Republic* he was spokesman of the so-called 'national opposition' of the Right, attacking the policy of *fulfilment* and the *Dawes Plan* in the *Reichstag* (1920–24). His demagogic campaign led to the resignation of *Erzberger*. Helfferich was killed in a railway accident shortly after the election triumph of the *DNVP*, which would probably have nominated him for the chancellorship. He shares responsibility for poisoning the political atmosphere after 1918, but he helped to restore financial stability by means of the *Rentenmark*.

J G Williamson: Karl Helfferich, 1872–1924; Economist, Financier, Politician (1971).

Heligoland-Zanzibar Treaty. Anglo-German agreement of 1 July 1890 by which Germany accepted that Zanzibar should become a British protectorate, withdrew from Witu (north of *German East Africa*), and recognized Uganda to be within the British sphere. In turn Germany received the North Sea island of Heligoland (which had been ceded to Britain by Denmark in 1814). The treaty was concluded by *Caprivi* to promote an improvement of Anglo-German relations, but it was attacked by the colonial enthusiasts (*Kolonialverein*) as an 'exchange of a pair of trousers for a button'. However, in World War I the acquisition of Heligoland proved to be of an enormous strategical value for the German navy (*Flottenpolitik*).

Henckel von Donnersmárck, Count Guido (10 Aug 1830–19 Dec 1916); landed proprietor and industrialist. His Silesian factories became serious competitors of English iron. In 1908 his duty-paid income was only second to that of *Krupp*. He was a financial adviser to *Bismarck* and *Wilhelm II*, who made him a prince in 1901. Henckel von Donnersmarck helped to finance the colonial enterprises of *Lüderitz* and *Hansemann* and is notorious for his manipulation of the press during the first Moroccan crisis (*Tangier, landing in*). He was one of Germany's most active and versatile entrepreneurs in the late 19th century.

Henlein, Konrad (6 May 1898–10 May 1945); National Socialist. He was founder of the '*Sudetendeutsche* Partei' (1933), which, under his leadership, advocated the secession of Sudetenland from Czechoslovakia. After the dismemberment of Czechoslovakia (*Munich Agreement*) he was appointed *Reichsstatthalter* of the Sudetenland. He was sentenced to death in 1945 by the Czecho-Slovak Republic and committed suicide while a prisoner of the Americans.

Heppenheim Manifesto. Declaration of German Liberals at a meeting in Heppenheim on the Bergstrasse (Hesse-Darmstadt) in Oct 1847, when representatives of moderate Liberalism of the South German assemblies and West German Liberals (*Hansemann*, Mevissen) discussed the idea of a German Parliament. Judging by their manifesto they would have been content with the convocation of a customs congress. In this the Heppenheim Manifesto stood in marked contrast to the desire for a unified Jacobin state expressed a month earlier in the *Offenburg Manifesto*.

Herrenhaus. First chamber of the Prussian *Landtag* (1854–1918). It shared powers over budget and taxation with the *Abgeordnetenhaus*. Membership in the Herrenhaus was based on class privilege or royal appointment. Hence its reactionary character.

Hertling, Georg v, from 1914 Count (31 Aug 1843–4 Jan 1919); statesman.

Catholic deputy in the *Reichstag* from 1875–1912 (except during 1890–96), he belonged to the right wing of the *Zentrum*. In 1912 he became Bavarian minister-president and on 1 Nov 1917 he was appointed *Reichskanzler* and Prussian minister-president. He remained dependent on the *Oberste Heeresleitung* whose demands he fulfilled in the Treaty of *Brest-Litovsk*. He introduced the principle of ministerial responsibility to parliament, but failed to achieve common ground between the army and the Reichstag majority. He resigned on 29 Sept 1918.

Hess, Rudolf (26 Apr 1894–); leading National Socialist. He joined the *NSDAP* in 1920 and became a close confidant of *Hitler*. He took part in Hitler's *Munich (Bierkeller) Putsch* of 1923, for which he was sentenced to 18 months' imprisonment in a fortress, where the amanuensis was held together with his master, working on *Mein Kampf*. In Dec 1932 Hess succeeded G *Strasser* as chairman of the central political commission of the party, on 21 Apr 1933 he became Hitler's deputy in all party questions and on 1 Dec 1933 minister without portfolio. Hess helped to expand the Party apparatus and organized the 'Fifth Columns'. On 1 Sept 1939 he was declared to be second in line of succession to the *Führer* after *Göring*. On 10 May 1941 he parachuted to Scotland in the vain hope of negotiating a separate peace. The *Nuremberg Tribunal* sentenced him to life imprisonment.

E K Bird: Hess (1974).

Heydebrand und der Lasa, Ernst v (20 Feb 1851–15 Nov 1924); Silesian Junker and Conservative party leader, from 1888 in the Prussian *Abgeordnetenhaus*. He opposed the *Mittellandkanal* project and a revision of the *three-class suffrage*. The 'uncrowned king of Prussia', he also sat in the *Reichstag*, where he overthrew *Bülow* and opposed *Bethmann Hollweg*'s foreign and reform policy. Together with *Westarp* he was the outstanding Conservative parliamentarian in the last phase of the Wilhelmine empire.

Heydrich, Reinhard (7 Mar 1904–4 June 1942); leading National Socialist. He joined the *NSDAP* and the *SS* in 1931 and was commissioned by *Himmler* to organize the intelligence of the Nazi organizations. From 1934 he was in charge of the *Gestapo*, from 1936 also of the 'security police' and criminal investigation. On 27 Sept 1941 he was appointed 'Reichsprotektor' of *Bohemia-Moravia*. In his offices he ordered spectacular activities, eg the *Röhm Putsch* (1934), the *Crystal Night* (1938), and the raid on Radio Gleiwitz before the attack on Poland (1939). He signed the *Schutzhaft-Befehle* and helped in the creation of the *concentration camps*. On 24 Jan 1939 *Göring* entrusted him with the *final solution* of the Jewish question by evacuation and Heydrich fixed the schedule and methods of persecution, presiding over the *Wannsee-Conference* of 1942. On 27 May 1942 he was assassinated by the Czechoslovak resistance. His death resulted in an *SS* revenge massacre against the village of Lidice. He was typical of the National Socialist party official.

C Wighton: Heydrich, Hitler's Most Evil Henchman (1962); G Deschner: Reinhard Heydrich-Statthalter der totalen Macht (1977).

Hilferding, Rudolph (10 Aug 1877–12 Feb 1941); Socialist economic theorist. He was a Jew of Austrian birth who became editor of *Vorwärts*, 1907–17. In 1910 he was the first to assert that imperialism was the last stage of capitalism (in 'The Finance Capital'). In 1914 he joined the *USPD*, but returned to the *SPD* in 1920 after presenting his theory of 'organized capitalism' which would make possible socialism by democracy. Together with *Kautsky* he drew up the Heidelberg programme for the party's governing body, of which he was a member from 1922 to 1933. He was twice *Reichsminister* of finance in extreme financial crises (Aug–Oct 1923; 1928–29). His attempts to stabilize the *Reichsmark* and to balance the budget by increased taxation failed in the *Reichstag*. He drew up the Prague manifesto (1934), the most revolutionary programme of the *SPD*, while in exile. In 1941 the French authorities extradited him to the *Gestapo*.

Himmler, Heinrich (7 Oct 1900–23 May 1945); National Socialist leader. From 1923 member of the *NSDAP* and participant in the *Munich Bierkeller Putsch*, he joined the *SS* in 1925 and was appointed its 'Reichsführer' in 1929. In 1932, together with *Heydrich*, Himmler created the *SD*. After 1933 he held high police posts; in June 1936 he became head of the German police in the ministry of the interior and directed the terror at home. In 1939 he was entrusted with the consolidation of Germandom and was largely responsible for ruthlessness in the German occupied territories. During the last 2 years of World War II he was minister of the interior and commander of the reserve army. He was dismissed by *Dönitz* on 6 May 1945 and shortly afterwards committed suicide. Himmler was responsible for the bureaucratization of mass murder.

H Fraenkel and R Manvell: Heinrich Himmler (1965).

Hindenburg, Paul v (2 Oct 1847–2 Aug 1934); general and statesman. After the outbreak of World War I Hindenburg was made commander-in-chief of the 8th army in East Prussia which won the victory of *Tannenberg*, giving him a legendary reputation. In Nov 1914 he was promoted to the rank of field marshal and on 29 Aug 1916 he became chief of the *Oberste Heeresleitung*. He then practically commanded all German forces but was much under the influence of his nominal subordinate *Ludendorff*. His appointment restored morale but he had no remedy against trench warfare in the West (*Siegfried Line*). After the failure of Operation *Michael* on 8 Aug 1918 he had no choice but to agree to an armistice (*Compiègne*), after which he led the defeated army home and advised *Wilhelm II* to flee to the Netherlands. Hindenburg retired after the Treaty of *Versailles* and remained the most popular personality in Germany. His memoirs (published in 1920) gave rise to the *stab-in-the-back legend*. After *Ebert*'s death (1925) he was nominated by the parties of the right for the office of *Reichspräsident* and on 26 Apr 1925 was elected by 14,600,000 votes (as against 13,800,000 for W *Marx*). Although Hindenburg regarded himself as *Reichsverweser* for the monarchy, he was loyal to the *Weimar Republic* and approved of *Stresemann*'s policy. In the crisis of 1930 he appointed *Brüning* as *Reichskanzler* and allowed him to rule with

Notverordnungen. On 10 Apr 1932 Hindenburg was re-elected with the support of the *SPD* and *Zentrum*, who regarded the then 82-year old statesman as the last bulwark against *National Socialism*. But two months later Hindenburg dismissed Brüning, because he rejected his agrarian policy (*Osthilfe*). Hindenburg was then influenced by a lobby of generals and conservatives and appointed his personal friends *Papen* and (later) *Schleicher* to the chancellorship. In Jan 1933 Hindenburg reluctantly followed advice by his son Oskar to appoint the 'Bohemian corporal' *Hitler* as Reichskanzler (*Nazi seizure of power*). Hindenburg was treated with respect by the Nazis, but he was unable to prevent extremism (*Kirchenkampf, Röhm Putsch*) during his last days. His death marks the beginning of total dictatorship with Hitler succeeding as *Führer*.

W Hubatsch: Hindenburg und der Staat. Aus den Papieren des Generalfeldmarschalls und Reichspräsidenten von 1877 bis 1934 (1966); A Dorpalen: Hindenburg and the Weimar Republic (1964).

Hindenburg Programme. Economic and military effort in 1916 inspired by *Ludendorff* in the name of *Hindenburg*. The programme called for the increase of mechanization of army and industry; of labour manpower by disabled prisoners of war, women, and minors; Sunday work and the closing down of all industries which were unimportant for the war. Conscription was to be extended to 15-year old boys (preparatory service) as well as to men up to the age of 60. Forced labour was introduced in order to double the production of ammunitions and trench-mortars until spring 1917 and to treble the number of machine and heavy guns. The Hindenburg Programme was complemented by the establishment of new institutions like the Arms and Ammunitions Supplies Office ('Wumba'), the Supreme War Office (under *Groener*) and a *Reichsamt* for Economics in 1917. The effect of the programme was more moral than material. It was realized with the passing of the bill for the Patriotic Auxiliary Service on 2 Dec 1916 (by 235 to 19 votes), which established the obligation of all non-conscripts to serve either in war industry or in public service. But the questions of the labour shortage and army drafts remained unsolved, because applications for deferment increased. The Hindenburg Programme proved a dilettante interference of the *Oberste Heeresleitung* in the economic system. The real victors were the trade unions who secured the workers' interest in an arbitration board.

G D Feldman: Army, Industry, and Labor in Germany 1914–1918 (1966).

Hirsch-Dunckersche Gewerkvereine (trade associations). Oldest German trade unions, for which the basis was developed in 1868 by M Hirsch (*d.* 1905). In 1869 the 'Union of German Trade Unions' was founded with the assistance of F Duncker and H *Schulze*-Delitzsch. The Hirsch-Dunckersche Gewerkvereine tried to emulate the British principle of self-help by creating supporting organizations. They seldom called strikes; instead they stressed the common interest of workers and entrepreneurs. Their demands were as moderate as their attraction for the workers. In 1910 they had 122,000 members. After 1919 they joined the pro-Republican 'Gewerkschaftsring', which was submerged in the *DAF* in May 1933.

Hitler, Adolf (20 Apr 1889–30 Apr 1945); *Führer* of the National Socialist movement. Of Austrian birth, Hitler left school prematurely and settled in Vienna to become a painter. Here he took interest in politics and became acquainted with the ideas of *Pan-Germanism* and *Anti-Semitism*. In 1913 he moved to Munich to evade military service in the Austrian army, but he volunteered for the German army in 1914, served as a messenger in the rank of corporal and was awarded the *Iron Cross*. After the *November Revolution* the *Reichswehr* employed him as an agent against the revolutionary left and Hitler therefore joined the 'Deutsche Arbeiterpartei', the later *NSDAP*. He developed the party into a home for nationalists in Bavaria with whom he achieved public prominence in 1923 in the abortive *Munich (Bierkeller) Putsch*, for which he was sentenced to 5 years' imprisonment in a fortress. He only had to serve one year during which he wrote *Mein Kampf*, the platform of *National Socialism*. During the following years he reinforced his claim for the party leadership and increased his contacts with the bourgeois nationalist establishment, with which he concluded the *Harzburg Front*. By his personal charisma and demagogic oratory he increasingly gained the support of wide sections of the German people, especially the petty bourgeoisie, whose dissatisfaction during the crisis of the *Weimer Republic* he managed to convert into a protest movement against the existing political and social system. In the elections for *Reichspräsident* in 1932 Hitler obtained 36.8 of the votes, second only to *Hindenburg,* who finally appointed him *Reichskanzler* on 30 Jan 1933 at the head of a cabinet of the right. After the *Nazi seizure of power*, Hitler consistently undertook the erection of a Fascist dictatorship. By the *Enabling Act* he eliminated the non-National Socialist forces and effected the *Gleichschaltung* of almost all of the political, social and cultural institutions. After the elimination of rival elements inside the party and the state in 1934 (*Röhm Putsch*) he left the further demands of interior affairs to his party apparatus and turned towards foreign policy. He not only envisaged a *Revisionspolitik* against the clauses of the Treaty of *Versailles* but aimed at the creation of a *Grossdeutsches Reich*. He wilfully included the risk of war for the realization of his aims (*Hossbach Minutes*) on the path from the *Anschluss* of his native homeland via the *Munich Agreement* to the attack on Poland. The diplomatic basis for the conduct of World War II was given by the *Ribbentrop-Molotov Pact*, which Hitler, the firm anti-Bolshevik, never intended to respect. He started his crusade against Marxism with operation *Barbarossa* on 22 June 1941. After the unfavourable turn at *Stalingrad* he increasingly assumed all military leadership. Only when German defeat seemed unavoidable did military circles of the resistance movement attempt Hitler's assassination on 20 July 1944 (*July Plot*). When the Red Army stormed *Berlin*, Hitler, whose nerves were overstrained in the end, committed suicide on 30 Apr 1945, after condemning the German people and international Zionism for his failure.

Hitler had successfully exploited the psychological vacuum among the masses after World War I. He responded to a widespread craving among the German people for rescue from social chaos and the extension of *Lebensraum*. His policy resulted in the loss of Germany's national greatness.

A Bullock: Hitler: A Study in Tyranny (1952); W Maser: Adolf Hitler, Legende, Mythos, Wirklichkeit (1971); J C Fest: Hitler (1973); J Toland: Adolf Hitler (1976).

Hitler-Stalin Pact. See *Ribbentrop-Molotov Pact*.

Hitler Youth. National Socialist youth organization founded in 1926 to assist the agitation of the *NSDAP*. After the *Nazi seizure of power* Hitler Youth, under its leader *Schirach*, became the only official youth organization by the law of 1 Dec 1936. Membership became obligatory for youth from 1939. Boys between 10 and 14 years were enrolled in the 'Jungvolk'. After swearing an oath to the *Führer* they entered the Hitler Youth proper which prepared them for the *Reichsarbeitsdienst* and military service. The girls (Jungmädel, 'Bund deutscher Mädel') were prepared for their task of motherhood; many had to perform an obligatory year of domestic service. Hitler Youth was a uniformed, para-military body which instilled Nazi ideology into the young Germans. In 1938 it comprised almost 8 million youths.

A Klönne: Hitlerjugend. Die Jugend und ihre Organisation im Dritten Reich (1960); H W Koch: The Hitler Youth (1975); P D Stachura: Nazi Youth in the Weimar Republic (1975).

Hohenlohe, Prince Chlodwig zu Hohenlohe-Schillingsfürst (31 Mar 1819–6 July 1901); statesman. South German aristocrat of liberal-conservative and *kleindeutsch* views; Bavarian minister-president, 1866–1870. In 1871 Hohenlohe advocated Bavaria's integration into the new German empire. In 1874 he was ambassador in Paris, from 1885 a tactful governor of *Alsace-Lorraine*. Hohenlohe succeeded *Caprivi* as *Reichskanzler* in 1894. His chancellorship marked the relapse from *Sozialpolitik* to *Sammlungspolitik*, as illustrated by the *Umsturzvorlage* (1894) and the *Zuchthausvorlage* (1899). Hohenlohe showed little understanding for the social questions of his time. In foreign policy he pursued a pro-Russian course. His East Asian policy resulted in the acquisition of *Kiaochow* (1897) and increased the estrangement with Britain, which reached a climax with the *Krüger-Telegram* in 1899. As chancellor Hohenlohe was too old and feeble to direct policy. With little power over events and no influence in the *Reichstag*, he acquiesced in the decisive steps towards *Weltpolitik* until his retirement in 1900.

Hohenzollern Candidacy. Claim of Prince Leopold of Hohenzollen-Sigmaringen to the vacant throne of Spain. In May 1869 *Bismarck* sent envoys to Spain to promote the candidacy. By 19 June 1870 Leopold was persuaded to accept the candidacy, securing the support of King *Wilhelm I* of Prussia on 21 June. The announcement of the candidacy caused an outcry in the French press which had fears concerning France's security. Under pressure from Wilhelm, Leopold withdrew the candidacy on 12 July, but Bismarck still made use of it in the *Ems Telegram*.

L D Steefel: Bismarck, the Hohenzollern Candidacy, and the Origins of the Franco-Prussian War of 1870 (1962).

Holstein, Friedrich v (24 Apr 1837–8 May 1909); diplomat. Influential official in the *Auswärtiges Amt* from 1876. He disapproved of *Bismarck*'s policy of alliances but after Bismarck's fall he played a key role in shaping German foreign policy, though he never rose beyond the rank of Director of the Political Section. He advised the inexperienced *Caprivi* and *Marschall* to adopt the *Neuer Kurs*. His belief in Germany having a 'free hand' in the choice of a partner proved mistaken by the emergence of the entente cordiale, which led him to provoke the Moroccan crisis, even at the risk of war. Bülow made him a scapegoat for the failure of the *Algeciras* conference. Holstein was forced to resign on 6 Apr 1906. Regarded as an éminence grise by contemporaries, he was assumed to be the decisive force behind German foreign policy. This view seems exaggerated in the light of his private papers, which demonstrate his part in the miscalculations of the *Wilhelmstrasse*.

N Rich: Friedrich von Holstein: Politics and Diplomacy in the Era of Bismarck and Wilhelm II, 2 vols (1965).

Holy Alliance. Document signed by Czar Alexander I of Russia, the Austrian Emperor and the King of Prussia at the Czar's invitation on 26 Sept 1815 in Paris. The Holy Alliance was gradually enlarged by the entry of almost every European ruler (except the Pope, the Prince Regent and the Sultan). The alliance stated that 'the precepts of Justice, Christian Charity and Peace ... must have an immediate influence on the Councils of Princes and guide all their steps'. The Holy Alliance soon became a catchword for the conservative reactionary policy of the Metternich system as exemplified by the *Carlsbad Decrees*. The Holy Alliance had been designed as a permanent security factor against revolution and the country of its origin. The signatories agreed to meet at regular conferences, but in practice this was rarely done. The *Quadruple Alliance* became politically more important.

Hossbach Minutes. Minutes of a conversation between *Hitler*, *Neurath*, *Blomberg*, and the supreme commanders of the three branches of the *Wehrmacht* on 5 Nov 1937, kept by Hitler's personal adjutant, Hossbach. The memorandum records Hitler's exposition of conquest to secure *Lebensraum* as the aim of German policy, which implied an armed conflict. He envisaged an outbreak of war not later than 1943–45, possibly earlier if France was hampered by interior or exterior tensions. The first blow was to be struck against Austria (*Anschluss*) and Czechoslovakia; Poland was also to be eliminated, while Russia was kept in check by Japan. The memorandum demonstrates that Hitler never gave up the aims formulated in *Mein Kampf* and expected his policy to lead to war in spite of appeasement by the Allies.

71

Hugenberg, Alfred (19 June 1865–12 Mar 1951); industrialist and right-wing politician. He was chairman of the governing body of *Krupp's*, 1909–1918. His press empire developed into one of the greatest propaganda organizations which influenced public opinion in the inter-war years. It included the Ufa film company, the Scherl publishing house, Ala advertising, and a telegraphic union. He was a founder of the *Alldeutscher Verband*, and a member of the *DNVP* from its foundation in 1918. He became president of the DNVP in 1928. He stood for a nationalist policy and opposed parliamentary democracy. His opposition to the *Young Plan* united him with *Hitler* in the *Volksbegehren* of 1929, which led to the *Harzburg Front* (1931). After discords over the election of the *Reichspräsident* he preferred *Papen* and *Schleicher*, before he supported Hitler's appointment as *Reichskanzler* and entered the latter's cabinet as *Reichsminister* of Economics and Food. In June 1933 he gave up his offices and withdrew from politics. He played a decisive part in the rise of *National Socialism*.

D Guratzsch: Macht durch Organisation; Hugenberg's Presseimperium (1974).

Hultschin territory. Territory in Upper Silesia which belonged to Prussia from 1742. In 1919, by art. 83 of the Treaty of *Versailles*, Germany ceded it to the new Czechoslovak Republic. In spite of the census of 1930, according to which 95 per cent of its population was Czech, the Hultschin territory was returned to Germany by the *Munich Agreement* of 1938. In 1945 it again became part of Czechoslovakia.

Humboldt, Wilhelm Freiherr v (22 June 1767–8 Apr 1835); Prussian diplomat and man of letters. He entered the Prussian civil service in 1801, directed the educational system in 1809–10 and created the humanist *Gymnasium*. He was an adherent of the ideals of classical humanism. In 1810 he founded the *Berlin University*. In 1814–15 he accompanied *Hardenberg* to the Congress of *Vienna*, where he tried in vain to support the cause of German unity. After his dismissal in 1819 for his criticism of Prussian reactionary policy (*Carlsbad Decrees*), he devoted himself to academic studies (philology and linguistics). Like *Stein* he failed to complete his reforms of the Prussian educational system.

S Kaehler: Wilhelm von Humboldt und der Staat (2nd ed., 1963); J H Knoll and H Siebert; Humboldt, Politik und Bindung (1969).

Huns Speech (Hunnenrede). Speech of *Wilhelm II* on 27 July 1900 at Bremerhaven to the German contingent which was leaving for China to participate in the suppression of the Boxer rising. In the speech Wilhelm II exhorted the German soldiers to acquire a reputation like that of the 'Huns a thousand years ago under the leadership of Attila'. Although the word 'Huns' ('Hunnen') did not appear in the official text (which had been purified by Bülow), it was printed by the local press and spread abroad, where it roused a scandal. During World War I it provided the catchword for Allied propaganda which denounced the German soldiers as Huns.

IG Farben. Interest group ('Interessengemeinschaft') of the German dye-stuffs industry, formed by a combination of BASF ('Badische Anilin und Sodafabrik'), Bayer AG and Farbwerke Hoechst in 1925. The founding of the IG Farben was facilitated by a *Kartell* of the dye-stuffs industries that had existed from 1904 and had been expanded in 1916. The main initiator of the union was C *Duisberg*. The turnover of IG Farben was enlarged by the annexation of plants in the German occupied territories. In summer 1945 the Allies confiscated the entire property of IG Farben, which was dissolved by law No 9 of the Control Council on 30 Nov 1945. Members of the board of directors of IG Farben were tried by the *Nuremberg Tribunal* for the exploitation of the German-occupied territories and the employment of slave labour (*Fremdarbeiter*).

Indemnity Bill. Bill moved by *Bismarck* in the Prussian *Abgeordentenhaus*, asking parliament for the endorsement of the expenses incurred during the period of the *constitutional conflict*, when taxes had been unconstitutionally collected. After Prussia's victory in the *Seven Weeks' War* (1866) it was hoped that the bill would appease the opposition in Prussia and gain the support of the non-Prussian Liberals in the *North German Confederation*. On 3 Sept 1866 the bill was passed by 230 votes to 75. The Conservatives voted for it en bloc, although their majority disapproved the surrender to the opposition; the Liberals split into a pro-Bismarckian *Nationalliberale Partei* and an anti-Bismarck *Fortschrittspartei*. The compromise over the bill by many Liberals meant the renunciation of their ambition to transform Prussia into a parliamentary monarchy. The middle class ceased to insist on control of the state in exchange for a 'liberal' administration by the Junkers and the prospect of German unity.

Industrial Accident Act. Second act of *Bismarck's* social legislation (*social insurance*) passed in 1884 to introduce insurance against labour accidents. When the act was proposed in 1881, it met the opposition of the Liberals who refused state subsidies for it. The act of 1884, which was amended in 1900, required the entrepreneurs to pay the whole premium. In 1911 the act was integrated into the 'Reichsversicherungsordnung.'

Insurrektionspolitik. Instigation of subject races devised to crack the home front of the Allied powers in World War I. In 1914–1918 the *Auswärtiges Amt* cooperated with conspirators from parts of the British Empire (Egypt, Middle East, India), appealing to Pan-Islamic and national sentiments. Contacts with the Irish underground (R Casement) could not be successfully coordinated for the Easter Rising in 1916. An Irish army was created out of prisoners of war in Germany, but it did not become combatant. The policy failed to fulfill *Wilhelm II's* dream of causing revolution in the British Empire, because the Germans underestimated British opposition and organization. It achieved more positive results in Russia with the aid of Russian revolutionaries (Parvus Helphand). A chain of buffer states (Finland, the Ukraine, Transcaucasia) was set up in 1918, temporarily bridging the gap between *Mitteleuropa* and Central Asia, thereby opening up vast resources of raw materials (oil), whereas the policy was ambiguously applied in the Baltics and Poland, where it conflicted with the aim of a germanized *Lebensraum*.

Interfraktioneller Ausschuss. Joint committee of the parliamentary groups of the four parties of the *Reichstag* majority (National Liberals, *Fortschrittspartei, SPD, Zentrum*). It originated on 6 July 1917, when the questions of suffrage (*three-class-suffrage*) and the budget for the fourth year of war were deliberated. The committee prepared the *peace resolution* and marked the beginning of parliamentary government in Germany.

K Epstein: 'Der Interfraktionelle Ausschuss und das Problem der Parlamentarisierung 1917–1918', in Historische Zeitschrift 191 (1960); U Bermbach: Vorformen parlamentarischer Kabinettsbildung in Deutschland. Der Interfraktionelle Ausschuss 1917–18 und die Parlamentarisierung der Reichsregierung (1967).

Iron Cross. Prussian war decoration for all military ranks, founded by King *Friedrich Wilhelm III* on 10 Mar 1813 to commemorate the birthday of the late Queen Luise. It was revived for the duration of the wars in 1870 and 1914 and adopted by the *Wehrmacht* in 1939. Higher classes of the Iron Cross were the 'Eisernes Kreuz I', the 'Ritterkreuz' and the 'Grosskreuz'.

Jagow, Gottlieb v (22 Jan 1863–11 Jan 1935); diplomat. From 1909 he was ambassador in Rome, where he worked for the renewal of the *Triple Alliance*. On 11 Jan 1913 he succeeded *Kiderlen-Wächter* as secretary of state of the *Auswärtiges Amt*. During the July crisis of 1914 he shared responsibility for policy which deliberately took the risk of war, because he regarded the situation as advantageous for Germany. In the war he refused a peace on the basis of the status quo and demanded the weakening of Russia by the creation of buffer states on its western frontier. On 22 Nov 1916 Jagow was replaced by A *Zimmermann*.

Jahn, Friedrich Ludwig (11 Aug 1778–15 Oct 1852); founder of the patriotic sports movement. He was a teacher in Berlin, where he established the first sports ground in 1811. He did not regard physical education (*Turnen*) as an end in itself but as part of patriotic indoctrination. In 1813 he served in the *Lützow-Korps* and had a major share in the foundation of the Burschenschaften. In 1819 he fell victim to the persecution of the *demagogues* and was sentenced to imprisonment in a fortress until 1825. In 1848 he was elected to the *Frankfurt National Assembly*. His book on physical education 'Deutsche Turnkunst' (1816) is a classic work.

January Strike. See *Spartacist Uprising*.

Jena-Auerstedt. Twin battle in the war between Prussia and Napoleon on 14 Oct 1806. At Jena Napoleon defeated the Prussians led by Prince Hohenlohe; at Auerstedt, a few miles further north, the main Prussian army under Duke Karl

74

of Brunswick was destroyed by Marshal Davout. The victories of Jena-Auerstedt led to the fall of Berlin and marked the temporary end of Prussian military power.

Jesuit Law. Law of 4 July 1872 prohibiting all establishments of the Society of Jesus (Jesuits) within the German empire. The law was passed after vehement parliamentary debates during the *Kulturkampf*. It infringed the constitutional principles of liberalism but was only opposed by a few Liberal leaders (*Bamberger, Lasker*). The law was repealed in 1917.

Jews, boycott of. Boycott of Jewish-owned shops, organized by the *NSDAP* leadership for 1 Apr 1933. The boycott was propagated by *Streicher* and actively supported by the *SA*, which prevented people from entering the shops, although National Socialist propaganda tried to make it appear as if the boycott expressed public feeling. The economic and social discrimination of the Jews was soon further promoted by the *Aryan Clause*, the *Nuremberg Laws*, and the *Crystal Night*.

H Genschel: Die Verdrängung der Juden aus der Wirtschaft des Dritten Reiches (1966); U D Adam: Judenpolitik im Dritten Reich (1972).

Jews, emancipation of. The emancipation of the Jews in Prussia was promulgated by the edict of 11 Mar 1812. Thereby the Jewish citizens were placed on an equal footing with their fellow citizens, if they chose a permanent family name and employed the German language in legal and commercial affairs. The Jews were admitted to all trades in town and country and could freely exchange goods and acquire property. However, they remained ineligible for legal and administrative posts and higher posts in the army. These restrictions only applied to followers of the Jewish religion and not to Jewish converts to Christianity. In the Prussian provinces acquired after 1812 the emancipation of the Jews was even more far-reaching. There were special regulations for Posen with its Jewish Poles. In 1848–49 equal citizenship was granted to all Prussian subjects. The Jewish emancipation aimed at christianizing the Jews and integrating them into the nation.

R Rürup: Emanzipation und Antisemitismus (1976).

Jodl, Alfred (10 May 1890–16 Oct 1946); general. He entered the general staff in 1929 and became head of the home defence department under *Blomberg*. In 1939 he rose, as chief of the *Wehrmacht*'s operations staff, to become *Hitler*'s main adviser on strategic questions. Jodl directed the planning of the operations against Austria and Czechoslovakia as well as the attacks on Denmark, Norway (*Weserübung*), the *Blitzkrieg* in the West and the Balkans, and the conduct of war in North Africa (*Afrika Korps*) and Italy (*Axis*). He approved of the tactics of scorched earth (*Nero-Order*), organized the infiltration of the army with Nazi supporters, and was an advocate of total warfare. On 7 May 1945 he signed the *unconditional surrender* to the Western Powers in Reims. He was sentenced to death by the *Nuremberg Tribunal* and was executed in 1946.

July Plot, 20 July 1944. Attempted coup d'état by a group of officers and resistance fighters, who wanted to overthrow the National Socialist regime after killing *Hitler*. The army's resistance to Hitler was revived by his faulty conduct of war and the increasing subordination of the *Wehrmacht* to the *SS*. The officers were supported by members of the bourgeois establishment who recognized the uselessness of continuing the war. The organizers of the plot wanted to conclude a separate peace with the Western Allies. Their social concept for post-war Germany was reactionary, despite contacts with the *Kreisau Circle*. Dominating personalities of the plot were *Beck, Goerdeler, Rommel* and *Stauffenberg*, who attempted both to assassinate the *Führer* and to organize the putsch in Berlin as chief of staff of the home reserve (*Walküre*). The near miss of the bomb plot and the inconsistency of the army resulted in the failure of the conspiracy. Several participants were executed the same day, others fell victim to the terror judgments of the *Volksgerichtshof*.

P Hoffmann: The History of the German Resistance, 1933–1945 (1977).

Junges Deutschland. Group of liberal-revolutionary writers, formed after the French July revolution of 1830. They were without close personal connections, but were regarded as a group because of their common approach. Led by H Heine (1797–1856) and L Börne (1786–1837), they attempted to make art an instrument for social, political and moral revolution. They championed freedom of the spirit; emancipation of the individual, of women and Jews; and democratic constitutionalism. On 10 Dec 1835 their works were prohibited by the decree of the *Bundestag*; in late 1837 the Prussian government prohibited the writings of their exponents K Gutzkow (1811–1878), L Wienberg (1802–1872), Th Mundt (1808–61) and H Laube (1806–84).

Jutland, Battle of. Principal naval battle in World War I off the Danish coast between the German High Seas Fleet and the British Grand Fleet, 31 May–1 June, 1916. Since German inferiority in dreadnoughts (*Flottenpolitik*) did not permit a decisive battle, Vice-Admiral Scheer (1861–1928) aimed at a continuous weakening of the British fleet by a number of sorties, of which Jutland was to be the first (and only one). As the British had intercepted the German signals, they mobilized the entire Grand Fleet. The extent of the ensuing encounter surprised both sides. At first Rear-Admiral Hipper (1863–1932)'s vanguard lured Admiral Beatty into a precipitous attack, then the Germans were trapped by Commander-in-Chief Jellicoe, who had been lining up between the Germans and the Jadebusen coast. The Germans were, however, able to extricate themselves by difficult manouvering and returned to port. They lost one battleship, one battle-cruiser, four cruisers and five smaller vessels; the British lost three ships more. The German escape from a superior British fleet was given triumphant publicity in Germany, but in fact Jutland was a British victory, because the balance of power in the North Sea remained unchanged and the British continued their blockade. The German navy saw no chance in another major engagement with the British and increased pleas for an unrestricted *U-Boat Warfare*, while the fleet remained in harbour until the *Kiel Naval Mutinies*.

D Macintyre: Jutland (1957).

Kaas, Ludwig (23 May 1881–15 Apr 1952); Roman Catholic politician. Kaas represented the *Zentrum* in the National Assembly and the *Reichstag* from 1919–20. In 1928 he took over the leadership of his parliamentary party and in 1929 the party leadership. This meant a strengthening of the liberal-conservative tendencies within the Zentrum. He supported Brünig and refused his party's support for *Papen*. In 1932 he pleaded for a majority government of the Zentrum and *NSDAP*. After the *Nazi seizure of power* he voted for the *Enabling Act*. In 1933 he emigrated to Rome.

A Wynen: Ludwig Kass (1953).

Kahr, Gustav Ritter v (29 Nov 1862–30 June 1934); Bavarian politician. He became Bavarian minister-president in 1920–21 (after the *Kapp-Putsch*). His right-wing policy strengthened Bavarian particularism. In 1923, after the proclamation of a state of emergency, he was appointed 'general commissioner' with executive power. He then came into conflict with the central government when he bound the Bavarian part of the *Reichswehr* by oath. This measure was exploited by *Hitler* for his putsch in 1923. Kahr was murdered by the National Socialists during the *Röhm Putsch* in 1934.

Kaiser, deputation to. Delegation to King *Friedrich Wilhelm IV* of Prussia, whom the *Frankfurt National Assembly* had elected on 28 Mar 1849 by a narrow majority as hereditary emperor of a future German empire. Thereupon the delegation, headed by the speaker of the National Assembly, E v Simson, travelled to Berlin, where it offered the imperial crown to the Prussian ruler. On 3 Apr the delegation was informed that it had neither the right to bestow a crown nor to pass a constitution. The Hohenzollens' refusal to take the lead in the movement for German unification on a parliamentary basis doomed the *Revolution of 1848* to failure, for, like Prussia, the other important German states were not prepared to co-operate with the delegation.

Kaiserproklamation. Proclamation of the King of Prussia, *Wilhelm IV*, as German Emperor (*Deutscher Kaiser*), on 18 Jan 1871. This ceremony took place in the hall of mirrors at Versailles, symbolizing the connection between France's defeat in the *Franco-Prussian War* and the realization of a German national state. It was attended by princes, diplomats and courtiers. But the proclamation was an indirect response to the wish for unification of the majority of the German nation and was generally regarded as the foundation act of the new German empire.

Th Schieder and E Deuerlein (eds): Reichsgründung 1870–71 (1911); E Deuerlain (ed): 'Gründung des Deutschen Reiches 1870–71' in Augenzeugenberichten (1971).

Kaltenbrunner, Ernst (4 Oct 1903–16 Oct 1946); leading National Socialist. An Austrian-born lawyer, Kaltenbrunner joined the *NSDAP* and the *SS* in 1932. On 11 Mar 1938 he organized the encompassment of the Viennese chancery. After the *Anschluss* he became secretary of state for public order and leader of the police in Austria. On 29 Jan 1943 he succeeded *Heydrich* as head of the security police and as secretary of state in the ministry of the interior. From 1944 he directed the espionage service. In his official capacity he had a great share in the crimes committed in the *concentration camps* and the *final solution* of the Jewish question, for which he was sentenced to death by the *Nuremberg Tribunal*.

Kapp Putsch. Coup d'état by the American-born ex-civil servant and founder of the *Vaterlandspartei* Wolfgang Kapp (1858–1922) with the military assistance of General v Lüttwitz (1859–1942). On 13 Mar 1920 the *Marinebrigade Erhardt* entered Berlin and Kapp was proclaimed *Reichskanzler*. The government escaped to Dresden and Stuttgart, from where it organized a general strike of the *Gewerkschaften*. The passive resistance of the workers and the ministerial bureaucracy forced Kapp to flee to Sweden on 17 Mar, only to appear in court in 1922, when he died in imprisonment on remand before he could be tried for high treason. Though the putsch failed, its significance lay in revealing the ambiguous relationship between the *Weimar Republic* and the *Reichswehr*, which stood aside uncommitted.

J Erger: Der Kapp-Lüttwitz-Putsch (1967).

Kardorff, Wilhelm v (8 Jan 1828–21 July 1907); industrialist and politician. He was a member of the *Abgeordnetenhaus* from 1868 to 1903. As an admirer of *Bismarck* he founded the *Freikonservative Partei*. From 1868 also in the *Reichstag*, Kardorff belonged to those Junker circles which represented industrial interests. He was a member of the board of directors of various firms and founder of several industrial enterprises. After the *Gründerzeit* (1873) he demanded protection of German industry (*protective tariff*). In 1887 he took the lead in the party coalition of National Liberals and Conservatives, the 'Kartell' (*Sammlungspolitik*). He was the central figure who integrated reactionary agrarian and industrial conservative interests.

Karl I (1823–1891); King of Württemberg. Son of *Wilhelm I*, he came to the throne in 1864, and took Austria's side in 1866. After Württemberg's defeat Karl I had to pay an indemnity of 8 million gulden. His chief minister Varnbüler then concluded a secret alliance with *Bismarck*. After siding with Prussia in 1870–71 (*Franco-Prussian War*), Karl I led his country into the German empire. His new chief minister Mittnacht secured certain *reserved rights* for Württemberg. Under Karl I's reign the kingdom's manufacturing industry (automobiles, precision machinery) was successfully developed in Württemberg.

Kartell. Term first used for a business combination by E Richter in 1879 to denounce a group of iron producers who had mutually agreed to keep their domestic prices high. The impetus for cartelization came in the 1870s, when the slump of 1873 (*Gründerzeit*) and the introduction of a *protective tariff* in 1870 led to the formation of many cartels, especially in the heavy industries, eg the Rheinisch-Westfälisches Kohlensyndikat (1893) and the Stahlwerksverband (1904) which made possible an immense rise in production before 1914, when Germany conquered the world markets by its cartel policy, often by dumping. In 1893 Germany first beat Britain in steel production, in 1904 also in pig iron, which stirred public opinion in Britain. During World War I, the government furthered the cartel system because of its importance to the armament industry. By 1926 it dominated 75 per cent of the coal output and 79 per cent of the steel (Vereinigte Stahlwerke) production. The share was even greater in the electrical industry (*Siemens*) and in chemicals (*IG Farben*), where the special cartel form of profit pools (Interessengemeinschaften) flourished. In 1935 a cartel decree against the misuse of monopoly power did not lead to much dissolution. The Nazis favoured the cartel to facilitate their war production (*Reichswerke*). In 1945 the Allied occupation powers outlawed the cartels.

Kathedersozialisten. Term first used in 1871 by the Liberal H B Oppenheim for a group of social reformers opposed to rigid Manchester Liberalism demanding a public social policy. The Kathedersozialisten regarded the protection of the working class as an ethical duty of the state, which they saw in the role of an arbiter in the struggle between capital and labour, mitigating class conflicts and promoting social improvement for the workers. From 1872 they were organized in the 'Verein für *Sozialpolitik*'. Their most prominent representatives were A Wagner, L Brentano and G. Schmoller, who held chairs in the socio-economic faculties of the German universities and influenced a whole generation of higher civil servants and politically involved academics in their social attitudes.

F Völkerling: Der deutsche Kathedersozialismus (1959).

Kautschukparagraphen. Proposed amendments of the *Strafgesetzbuch* moved by *Bismarck* in 1875–76, tightening up penal regulations against newspapers and unions of Catholic and Social Democratic tendencies . They were rejected by the *Reichstag* on 10 Feb 1876. A similar bill was laid before parliament with the first draft of the *Sozialistengesetz*.

Kautsky, Karl (16 Oct 1854–17 Oct 1938), German-Austrian Socialist theorist. He was private secretary to *Engels* in London (1881) and became the most recognized authority on Marxist theory, propagating his ideas of orthodox Marxism in 'Die Neue Zeit'. He held that the collapse of capitalism was imminent and any revolutionary action was superfluous. He believed that the *SPD* should concentrate on obtaining a parliamentary majority. His ideology of passive radicalism had a decisive influence on the Erfurt programme (1891). Before 1914 he was the spokesman of the Marxist centre, opposing the revisionists (*Bernstein, David*) and the radical left (*Luxemburg*). Convinced of

Germany's responsibility for World War I, he joined the *USPD* in 1917. After 1918 he was briefly secretary of state in the *Auswärtiges Amt* and was commissioned to compile the 'German Documents on the Outbreak of War' (*war guilt clause*). He returned to the SPD in 1922 but without regaining influence.

W Blumenberg: Karl Kautskys literarisches Werk (1960).

Keitel, Wilhelm (22 Sept 1882–16 Oct 1946); field marshal. He sympathised with the pro-National Socialist section in the *Wehrmacht*. In 1933 he became head of the army office and in 1938 chief of the new armed forces (*OKW*). He was a faithful servant of *Hitler* during World War II, his administrative talent making him a central figure of the army bureaucracy. He played a leading role in the exploitation of the occupied territories. On 8 May 1945, with the appearance of a Prussian Junker, he signed the *unconditional surrender* to the Russians at Berlin-Karlshorst. The *Nuremberg Tribunal* sentenced him to death.

W Goerlitz: Generalfeldmarschall Keitel; Verbrecher oder Offizier? (1961).

Ketteler, Wilhelm Imanuel von (25 Dec 1811–13 July 1877); Bishop of Mainz. The main representative of *political Catholicism*, he grasped the social problems created by the industrial revolution. He advocated a social Catholicism and urged employers and government to pass social legislation (*Sozialpolitik*). He intended to solve the social problem by co-operation between the Roman Catholic Church, welfare organizations and the economy, thereby undermining the appeal of Social Democracy.

A Birke: Ketteler und der deutsche Liberalismus (1972).

Kiaochow. District in the Shantung area of North-East China, which was occupied on 14 Nov 1897 in retaliation against the assassination of German missionaries. By the German-Chinese treaty of 6 Mar 1898 the Reich leased Kiaochow for 99 years and acquired railway and mining concessions. It was administered by the naval office (*Reichsämter*) and expanded into a naval base. Its port Tsingtao became the trading centre of the coastal region. Japan declared war on Germany on 15 Aug 1914 and Kiaochow surrendered on 7 Nov 1914. In 1922 Japan ceded Kiaochow to China, and Germany renounced its rights to it in 1923.

Kiderlen-Wächter, Alfred v (10 July 1852–30 Dec 1912); diplomat. He became representative of the secretary of state of the *Auswärtiges Amt*, von Schön, in 1908 and foreign secretary in 1910. He succeeded in overcoming the Bosnian crisis (1908) in co-operation with Britain. He aimed at a 'triple entente' with the Western European powers, but he believed that Germany's prestige had first to be raised. Hence he sympathized with moderate *Pan-Germanism*. He pursued a hard line in the second Moroccan crisis. The minute colonial gains of the *Moroccan Agreements* did not satisfy nationalistic public opinion, which he had tried to distract from Eastern Europe to prevent a conflict with Russia. He could not solve the dilemma of German foreign policy by his sophisticated diplomatic methods. See also *Panther's Spring*.

Kiel Canal (Nord-Ostsee-Kanal or 'Kaiser-Wilhelm-Kanal'). Maritime canal built in 1887–95, linking the North Sea with the Baltic near Kiel. It facilitated Baltic sea trade (via Hamburg) but was mainly of strategic importance for the German navy. When it proved too small for the new dreadnought class, the Navy Bill of May 1906 (*Flottenpolitik*) granted the money for the extension of the canal in 1909–14.

Kiel naval mutinies. Insurrections of the marines in 1917–18. The first revolt of summer 1917 originated in social discontent of the sailors and was suppressed by means of the imposition of death sentences on their ringleaders. The new uproars in Oct–Nov 1918 were also political in their aims. The mutiny was caused by the naval command's orders of 30 Oct for a battle with the Royal Navy. The sailors refused to obey and demanded the abdication of the Kaiser. The government appointed *Noske* as governor of Kiel and he succeeded in soothing the mutineers. But the unrest spread to other ports (*Bremen,* Hamburg) and the first German Soviets were formed (*Workers' and Soldiers' Councils*). The mutinies were symptomatic of the revolutionary mood among disillusioned soldiers at the end of World War I.

D. Horn: The German Naval Mutinies of World War I (1969).

Kirchenkampf (Church Struggle). Strife between the National Socialist state and the Churches. After seizing power, *National Socialism* – despite its anti-Christian mysticism – sought an understanding with the Churches by professing a vague positive Christianity. On 20 July 1933 the government concluded the *Reichskonkordat* with the Vatican. The Protestants at first welcomed the *Nazi seizure of power*. A pro-Nazi group, the 'Deutsche Christen' (German Christians) had been formed by 1932, but after 1934 the majority of Protestants gathered in the 'Bekennende Kirche' ('Confessing Church'), which opposed the application of the *Aryan Clause* to the Church and declared a state of emergency. The Bekennende Kirche, led by Pastors Niemöller and Bodelschwingh, offered resistance until 1938, when its influence was eclipsed by the terror of the totalitarian state, which then also hit Roman Catholic clergy.

F Zipfel: Kirchenkampf in Deutschland, 1933–1945 (1965); F H Littell and H G Locke (eds): The German Church Struggle and the Holocaust (1974).

Kirdorf, Emil (8 Apr 1847–13 July 1938); industrialist. As general director of the 'Gelsenkirchen Mining Co.' (1892) he developed it into the Rhenish Westphalian Coal Syndicate (1893), which by 1906 was the biggest mining enterprise in Germany. A leading member of the *Centralverband deutscher Industrieller*, he demanded the suppression of all trade union and political activities of the labour movement. From 1927 he sponsored the *NSDAP* (*Freundeskreise*), which earned him the honorary title of 'Staatsrat' in 1937.

Kissinger Diktat. Memorandum of 15 June 1877, in which *Bismarck* laid down his ideas about the solution of the Eastern question and the position of

Germany towards the other powers: Britain and Russia should come to an agreement giving the former preponderance in Egypt, the latter in the Black Sea. Both should have the same interest in the preservation of the status quo as Germany, for whom Bismarck held no territorial acquisitions desirable. But too close an understanding among the others could bring pressure on Germany. Thus he wished to maintain some rivalry among them, so that all except France would need Germany and abstain from forming a coalition against her. In Bismarck's view this flexible policy was a result of Germany's central position, and he acted accordingly at the Congress of *Berlin*. The memorandum is so called because it was dictated at Bad Kissingen.

Kleindeutsch. Term which came into use in 1848 during the debate in the *Frankfurt National Assembly* on the territorial extent of the future German empire. As opposed to *grossdeutsch*, the word implied the exclusion of Austria from Germany and Prussian domination in the Reich. The kleindeutsch idea was enforced by the *Erbkaiserliche* who, after the rejection of the *Kaiserdeputation*, supported the Prussian *union plan*. The way for the kleindeutsch solution was paved by *Bismarck* with the defeat of Austria in the *Seven Weeks' War* of 1866.

Kolonialpolitik. Policy inaugurated by *Bismarck* in the early 1880s to protect German overseas trade, after the system of chartered companies (following the British example) had failed. The formal annexation of territories in Africa and the Pacific created the *Schutzgebiete*. Kolonialpolitik became feasible because of Britain's diplomatic isolation in the Egyptian question. In home policy it helped to influence the Reichstag elections of 1884 (*Sammlungspolitik*). But neither Bismarck nor *Caprivi* shared the enthusiasm of the colonial movement (*Kolonialverein*). In 1896 *Wilhelm II* proclaimed a German world empire, but Kolonialpolitik still lacked a concrete programme. Being latecomers in the scramble for colonies, Germany's rulers nevertheless claimed a 'place in the sun'. *Weltpolitik* urged a change in the colonial status quo, in spite of conflicts with imperial rivals. Kolonialpolitik was not a direct cause of World War I, under whose impact colonial aspirations reached a new peak (*Mittelafrika*) until the Treaty of *Versailles* excluded Germany as a colonial power. The aftermath of *Kolonialpolitik*, the colonial *Revisionspolitik* was abandoned by *Hitler* in 1939, when he discarded the idea of compensation in Africa.

W O Henderson: Studies in German Colonial History (1962); H U Wehler: Bismarck und der Imperialismus (1969); K Hildebrandt: Hitler, NSDAP und die koloniale Frage 1919–1945 (1969).

Kolonialrat, Advisory body to the government in 1890–1908 in questions of *Kolonialpolitik*. In 1895 its membership was increased from 15 to 25, half of whom were representatives of the financiers of German colonization, who dominated the Africa merchants and colonial enthusiasts (*Kolonialverein*).

Kolonialverein. Propaganda organization founded by colonial enthusiasts in 1882 to promote German *Kolonialpolitik*. It succeeded in winning the support of prominent junkers and statesmen (*Miquel*). In 1884 *Peters* founded the 'Gesellschaft für deutsche Kolonisation' to finance the acquisition of the first *Schutzgebiete*. In 1887 it united with the *Kolonialverein* to form the 'Deutsche Kolonialgesellschaft' (KG), whose 18,000 members increased to 42,000 in 1914, of which 40 per cent were merchants and entrepreneurs. To spread the colonial idea the KG organized a colonial exhibition (1896) and founded a colonial museum. From 1898 the KG began to rival the *Flottenverein*'s naval propaganda. In World War I, in spite of the setback of the *Schutztruppe*, the KG demanded the expulsion of Britain and France from Africa to enable the creation of a German *Mittelafrika*. After 1919 the KG fought for the return of the German colonies (*Revisionspolitik*). After 1933 the KG was merged into the 'Reichskolonialbund' which mobilized the *Volksdeutsche* overseas to support *National Socialism*.

Kolping, Adolf (8 Dec 1813–4 Dec 1865); Roman Catholic priest. From 1846 he devoted himself to the establishment of clubs for Roman Catholic journeymen. With the sponsorship of the Roman Catholic Church, he succeeded in rapidly increasing the number of clubs. These clubs aimed at providing social and moral security to craftsmen and workers, thereby removing grievances which could have aroused Socialist sympathies among Catholics.

Königgrätz (Sadowa). Site in Bohemia of the chief battle between Austria and Prussia in the *Seven Weeks' War* on 3 July 1866. Executing the strategic plans of the elder *Moltke*, the Prussian corps invaded Bohemia in three separate armies, which united only on the battle-field. In one day the Austrians lost 24,000 men while 13,000 were taken prisoner. At Königgrätz Prussia profited by the recent economic and technological changes (railway, telegraph) and by the increased effectiveness of her army after the reforms of *Roon*. An armistice was concluded on 26 July 1866. The battle represents the beginning of Prussian hegemony in Europe (*kleindeutsch, Mitteleuropa*); therefore 'revanche pour Sadowa' became the catchword of French anti-Prussian policy.
G A Craig: Königgrätz (1966).

Konsumvereine. Retail co-operative societies first established in the 1860s (preceded by the savings societies of the 1850s). They were founded by philanthropic middle class reformers instead of by workers. They were closely associated with urban co-operative banks ('Volksbanken' of *Schulze-Delitzsch*). By 1873 there were 189 Konsumvereine, half of them affiliated to the German Co-operative Union which had 87,000 members.

KPD (Kommunistische Partei Deutschlands). Communist party founded in Dec 1918 under the leadership of R *Luxemburg* and K *Liebknecht* out of dissenters from the Independent Social Democrats (*USPD*), emerging from the *Spartakus-Bund*. The KPD boycotted the elections for the National Assembly in Jan 1919. The Communists worked illegally in civil war strifes (*Spartacist uprising*), and directed the Soviet Republics in *Munich* and *Bremen*. The KPD polled only

441,000 votes in the *Reichstag* elections of 1920, but it increased its strength by splitting the left wing of the USPD and merging it with its own party in Oct 1920. In Mar 1921 and Oct 1923 (*Hamburg Uprising*) the Communists rose in armed insurrections against the *Weimar Republic*. They proclaimed the Social Democrats as chief enemy of the workers, denouncing them as 'social fascists', and continued their fight against the *SPD* when the Nazis rose to power in the 1930s. After 1924 the KPD was transformed into a disciplined bureaucratic party dependant on Stalinist directives which were obeyed under the leadership of *Thälmann*. Its membership rose to 360,000 in 1932. Its recruits came from the working class in industrial areas, where it partly overtook the SPD. In Nov 1932 the KPD won 17 per cent of the votes, making it the third strongest party. After the *Reichstag* fire of 27 Feb 1933 the KPD was outlawed by the Nazis, who arrested their leaders and murdered many of them. The remainder organized themselves illegally to resist *National Socialism* (*Anti-Fascists*). From 1935 the KPD propagated a popular front of all Socialists, which was realized in 1945 by the formation of a united front under Communist domination in East Germany.

W T Angress: Die Kampfzeit der KPD 1921–1923; O K Flechtheim: Die KPD in der Weimarer Rapublik (repr. 1969).

Kraft durch Freude. Recreational organization of the *DAF* founded on 27 Nov 1933. It was propagated by the National Socialist leadership as the practical realization of socialism and a gigantic cultural achievement of *National Socialism. Kraft durch Freude* resumed trade unionist traditions (eg adult education, theatre attendances at reduced prices). It became popular by a subsidized mass tourism from which 40 million profited by 1939. 750,000 cruised the Mediterranean or North Sea with vessels owned by the Kraft durch Freude. It helped to compensate workers through the *Arbeitsordnungsgesetz* and assisted rearmament by organizing *Volkswagen* savings.

Kreisau Circle (Kreisauer Kreis). Circle of opponents of *National Socialism*, founded in 1940 by the descendants of the elder *Moltke* at their manor house in Silesia. It consisted of officers and bourgeois democratic politicians, who discussed the problem of a post-Nazi state and social order. They envisaged a democratic society and incorporated some socialist thinking. The circle tried to contact the *Anti-Fascists* through J *Leber*. It was linked to the *Goerdeler* group and the conspirators of the *July Plot* (1944) and was dissolved after the failure of that plot.

H Rothfels: Die deutsche Opposition gegen Hitler (1957); G v Roon: Der Kreisauer Kreis innerhalb der deutschen Widerstandsbewegung (1967).

Kreisordnung. District regulations for the six Eastern provinces of Prussia, proclaimed on 13 Dec 1872. They abolished the junkers' authority over the police and the hereditary village mayor ('Erbschulze'), which became an elective office. The regulations transferred a number of administrative functions from the local government authorities to the 'Landkreise' (rural districts). Hence the 'Landrat' (district magistrate) had to be a civil lawyer instead of a local squire holding that office for life, thereby making it a temporary post in the career of a higher civil servant. The Landrat was supported by a district council elected from among the members of the 'Kreistag' (local council meeting), in which the junkers continued to predominate, but the Kreisordnung reduced their preponderance by limiting them to a quarter or a third of the seats. Between Kreis and village community a new administrative institution, the 'Amt' (bailiwick), was established. An Amt comprised several villages and manors with about 6,000–8,000 inhabitants. It was headed by an 'Amtsvorsteher' (bailiff), appointed by the *Oberpräsident*, and in most cases a local landlord, who was entrusted with the police authority. The Kreisordnung was first opposed by the *Herrenhaus* but it was adopted after *Wilhelm I's* creation of 25 new peers. The Kreisordnung brought about closer contact between ministerial bureaucracy and rural self-government.

Kreuzzeitung. Popular name for the 'Neue Preussische Zeitung' because of the *Iron Cross* as its emblem. It was founded in 1848 by L *Gerlach* and supported the *Camarilla* and the extreme right in the Prussian *Abgeordnetenhaus*, the so-called Kreuzzeitung party, which stood in opposition to *Bismarck*.

Krüger Telegram. Telegram of 3 Jan 1896 from King Wilhelm II to President Krüger of the Transvaal Republic, congratulating him on his success in defending the independence of his country without the aid of allied countries. The telegram (which had been suggested by *Marschall* to prevent an even stronger action on the part of the Kaiser, such as a declaration of a German protectorate over Transvaal) was an affront to Britain, as it meant that Germany declared herself a friend of the Boers, who were an integral part of the British Empire. In Britain the telegram caused a wave of anti-German feeling and it was a worthless gesture to the Boers, because Germany was in no position to assist them.

Krümper-System. Short-service training which was applied in the Prussian army from 1808 to 1812 to circumvent the limitation placed by the *Paris Convention*. The system, invented by *Scharnhorst*, provided for a continuous change of recruits, making it possible to draw on wide circles of the population for military service. It allowed Prussia to create a reserve force.
W O Shanahan: Prussian Military Reforms 1786–1813 (rep. 1966).

Krupp. Family of steelwork owners in Essen. Their firm was founded by Friedrich Krupp (17 July 1787–8 Oct 1826) in 1811. In 1826 Alfred Krupp (26 Apr 1812–14 July 1887) took over his father's firm and turned the small domestic workshop into a large industrial undertaking. In 1838–39 he toured England and inspected the steelworks there. The rise of the firm began in the 1850s with the increasing demand for railway materials. In 1859 Krupp received the first order for cannon barrels by the Prussian government, soon to be followed by many orders for armaments by foreign governments. In 1871 Krupp was a mammoth enterprise, called the 'arsenal of the empire' for its performance in the war against France (*Franco-Prussian War*). The number of employees rose from 6,000 in 1864 to 21,000 in 1887. For his workers Alfred Krupp created a comprehensive welfare scheme (1836: sickness and burial fund; 1855: pension fund; 1861: housing settlements for his employees) which served as a model for the social legislation (*social insurance* enacted under *Bismarck*). The firm further expanded under Alfred's son Friedrich Alfred (1854–1902). In 1902 the many-sided, vertically organized concern had 43,000 employees. In 1909 Bertha Krupp's husband Gustav Krupp von Bohlen und Halbach (7 Aug 1870–16 Jan 1950) took over its leadership. In World War I Krupp played a major role in developing the artillary used by Germany, being especially famous for long range guns. Krupp again contributed to the German military machine in World War II. For this and the employment of prisoners of war and the inmates of concentration camps Gustav's son Alfried (13 June 1907–30 July 1967) was sentenced by the *Nuremberg Tribunal* on 29 July 1948 to 12 years' imprisonment and his entire property was forfeited. (The judgment was reviewed in 1951, when he was released and his fortune restored to him.)

W Manchester: The Arms of Krupp (1968).

Kühlmann, Richard v (17 May 1873–16 Feb 1948); diplomat. He served in various foreign missions before becoming counsellor of the German embassy in London (1908–14) where he drafted the treaties for colonial understanding with Britain (*Angola Treaty*, *Berlin-Baghdad Railway*). In World War I, Kühlmann became minister at the Hague (1915) and ambassador in Istanbul (1916). On 6 Aug 1917 he was appointed secretary of state in the *Auswärtiges Amt*. He tried to bring about a compromise peace with Britain, but his answer to Pope Benedict XV's peace appeal dodged the issue of Belgian sovereignty and so his secret initiative via Spain fell through in London. In 1918 he led the German delegation at *Brest-Litovsk*, where he camouflaged annexionist aspirations with slogans of self-determination for the non-Russian peoples. When, on 24 June 1918, he declared in the *Reichstag* that a peace dictated by military victory was beyond achievement, the *Oberste Heeresleitung* forced his resignation on 8 July.

L. Namier: 'Men who Floundered into the War. Herr von Kühlmann', in Vanished Supremacies (1958).

Kulturkampf. Expression coined by *Virchow* for the conflict between *Bismarck* and the Roman Catholic Church during the period 1871–1891. The Syllabus of Errors and the dogma of papal infallibility were regarded as intolerable papal claims of authority over the Roman Catholic population of the new German empire. The Roman Catholic Church was anti-Prussian by tradition and geography and thus sympathized with particularist and *grossdeutsch* forces. Its political organizations (*Zentrum*, Verein deutscher Katholiken, founded on 22 May 1872) were strong enough to menace the stability of Bismarck's system. *Kulturkampf* originated in a struggle over the clerical control of education and turned into a general attack on the independence of the Roman Catholic Church, which Bismarck, supported by the Deutscher Verein, fought with unnecessary vehemence. The first move was the abolition of the Catholic department in the Prussian ministry of culture on 8 July 1871, followed by the *School Supervision Law*. Penal measures against the clergy included: the *Pulpit Clause* and the *Jesuit Law*, and culminated in the *May Laws* of 1873, which were supplemented by the introduction of civil marriage (*Registry Offices*) in Prussia. Papal protest against these laws was countered by the *Expatriation Act* (1874). But then the resources of the state were exhausted and the changes in the parliamentary situation (*Sammlungspolitik, Sozialistengesetz*) and in foreign policy the disappearance of the danger of the formation of an ultramontane bloc (France and Austria-Hungary) persuaded Bismarck to relax the tension in the early 1880s. In 1886–87 Bismarck made his peace with the Roman Curia and by 1891 much of the Kulturkampf legislation was suspended, although some (state school supervision, pulpit clause, obligatory civil marriage) remained in force. The Kulturkampf, which was waged more heavily in Prussia than in the other *Länder* of Germany, failed to deprive the Roman Catholic Church of its liberty and independence and deferred the integration of the Roman Catholic population into the new nation state.

E Schmidt-Volkmar: Der Kulturkampf in Deutschland 1871–1890 (1962).

Labour, regulation of national (Gesetz zur Ordnung der nationalen Arbeit). Act passed on 20 Jan 1934 regulating the relations between the employer, the employee and the state. The employer became head of the workshop, the employees his subordinates, who were urged to work faithfully for the employer, who in turn was to care for their welfare. Shop stewards merely advised the works manager; their majority could appeal to one of the 13 trustees. The trustee was generally a National Socialist appointed by the *DAF* (from 19 May 1933); he was the real agent for the state and sided mostly with the entrepreneur. In reality the act was far from being progressive. It did not create a national community (*Volksgemeinschaft*) in the workshop.

Labour, protection of. Law for the protection of workers, promulgated on 1 June 1891, amending the *Gewerbeordnung* of 1869. The law was intended to protect the workers from injuries to their health caused by long working hours. Grievances in industrial conditions had been dealt with from 1839–53 in Prussia by factory inspectors, who – following the British example – were appointed to supervise sanitary and technological installations and the length of working hours. The law greatly improved upon previous regulations, prohibiting work on Sundays, and for children under the age of 13 and restricting the working day for children under the age of 16 to 10 hours and for women to 11 hours. Further amendments in 1903, 1905 and 1908 brought new improvements for women (10 hours) and children, whereas a maximum working day for men was only tentatively realized before 1918 (*Eight-Hour Day*).

Länder. Term used for the member states of the *Deutsches Reich* in the *constitution* of 1919. From 1871 to 1918 the states had been called 'Staaten'.

The Länder of the *Weimar Republic* preferred the term 'Freistaaten' for themselves as the German equivalent for republic to demonstrate their constitutional status. Since 1945 the term Länder has been continued in the Federal Republic of Germany.

Landstände. Representations of the German states (1815–48). The Landstände, based on § 13 of the federal act of the *Deutscher Bund*, were formed by the estates and organized in a bicameral system. They were increasingly displaced by the national representative system. After 1848 they were superseded by the *Landtage*.

Landtage. Originally assemblies of the estates in the territories of the *Deutscher Bund*, eg the *Vereinigter Landtag* in Prussia. As a result of the *Revolution* of *1848*, constitutions were decreed, which inaugurated the Landtage; as bicameral representation in Prussia: *Herrenhaus* and *Abgeordnetenhaus*. From 1919 Landtage denoted the state parliaments of the *Weimar Republic*. The Nazis abolished the Landtage by the law of 30 Jan 1934 (*Gleichschaltung*) and replaced state governments by *Reichsstatthalter*. Landtage were restored in the Federal Republic of Germany founded in 1949.

Landvolk. Rural resistance movement in *Schleswig-Holstein*. It prevented forfeits and auctions during the agrarian crisis of the *Weimar Republic*.

G Stoltenberg: Die politischen Strömungen des schleswigholsteinischen Landvolks 1918–1933 (1963).

Landwehr. Territorial reserve (militia) set up in Prussia by the decree of 17 Mar 1813, initiated by the insufficient combative force of the standing army in the *wars of liberation*. All healthy men from the age of 17 to 40, irrespective of whether they had served or not, were obliged to serve in the Landwehr, unless they were already in the line. The introduction of the Landwehr was an essential contribution of the Prussian army reform (*Wehrpflicht*).

Langemarck. On 11 Nov 1914, four reserve corps, consisting mainly of volunteers, among them many gymnasium and university students, were thrown into the battle of *Flanders* at Langemark. Their armament and equipment were insufficient, when they charged the Anglo-French lines singing *Deutschland, Deutschland über alles*. The regiments suffered severe casualties. A large number of the future officers were killed at Langemark.

Langensalza. Place in Thuringia where on 29 June 1866 the Hanoverian troops fighting on Austria's side in the *Seven Weeks' War* surrendered to a Prussian corps under Falckenstein.

Lasker, Eduard (14 Oct 1829–5 Jan 1884); parliamentarian. Entered the *Abgeordnetenhaus* as deputy for the *Fortschrittspartei* in 1865. He voted for the *Indemnity Bill* and laid the foundation of the *Nationalliberale Partei* in 1866.

From 1867 he was a member of the *Reichstag*. He supported the approach made by the South German states to the *North German Confederation*. After 1871 he helped to bring about the legal and economic unity of the new German empire. During the *Gründerzeit* (1873) he was a critic of economic mismanagement. He broke with *Bismarck* over the *Sozialistengesetz* and the issue of *protective tariff*. In Mar 1880 he left his party. In 1881 he joined the Liberale Vereinigung, where his influence was superseded by *E Richter*.

Lassalle, Ferdinand (11 Apr 1825–31 Aug 1864); founder of the Social-Democratic movement. Influenced by the *Neo-Hegelians* he became a radical democrat and was co-editor (with *Marx*) of the Neue Rheinische Zeitung. Lassalle's agitation aimed at a separation of the working class from the middle class. He opposed *Schulze-Delitzsch's* project of forming co-operative societies. Lassalle taught that only 'productive associations', subsidized by the state, could break the 'iron ring of wages', adopting the wages theory of Ricardo. But he respected the state and did not preach class-conflict. His attitudes brought him into contact with the Workers' Unions. On 23 May 1863 their Leipzig congress welcomed his programme and founded the *ADAV*, of which he became president. Before he could develop it into a real mass organization, however, he fell in a duel.

H Oncken: Lassalle zwischen Marx und Bismarck (repr 1960).

League. See under *Bund*.

Lebensraum. Essential part of the programme of National Socialism, providing for the expansion of the German people. It was preceded by *Pan-Germanism*, which the doctrine of the Lebensraum combined with the Aryan racial doctrine: in the framework of a 'new world order' the predestined German master race was to gain Lebensraum (living space) at the cost of the allegedly inferior races, the Slavs and the Jews. The creation of the *Grossdeutsches Reich* led to the temporary acquisition of land in the East. As in 1918 (*Brest-Litovsk*), these aspirations came to naught because of the failure of Operation *Barbarossa*. Germany's defeat in World War II reversed the process and led to the expulsion (*Vertreibung*) of Germans from Eastern Europe.

Leber, Julius (16 Nov 1891–4 Jan 1945); Social Democrat member of the resistance movement. An officer in the *Reichswehr* until 1920, he entered the *Reichstag* as representative of the *SPD* in 1924. He was arrested in 1933 and kept in detention till 1937. From 1940 he was in close touch with *Stauffenberg* and the *Kreisau Circle*. He strove for a union with the *Anti-Fascists*. On 4 July 1944 he was again arrested by the *Gestapo* and subsequently hanged.

Legien, Carl (1 Dec 1861–26 Dec 1920); trade union leader. He was president of the 'Generalkommission' of the *Freie Gewerkschaften* from 1890. He co-operated with the entrepreneurs for a wage scale and promoted the integration of the workers into the state. From 1919 president of the *ADGB*, he demanded trade unionist influence on economic and social policy, but when *Ebert* offered him the succession to *Bauer* as *Reichskanzler* he declined the experiment of a trade union government. He wrecked the *Kapp Putsch*, when he proclaimed a general strike on 13 Mar 1920.

H J Varain: Freie Gewerkschaften, Sozialdemokratie und Staat. Die Politik der Generalkommission unter der Führung C Legiens 1890–1920 (1956).

Legion Condor. Name of the German military units which intervened on the Fascist side in the Spansih Civil War from Nov 1936. The Legion Condor mainly consisted of elements of the *Luftwaffe* but also included tank formations. Its strength fluctuated between 5,000 and 10,000 men. The Legion Condor provided for most of the instructors of the Nationalists and, together with the Italian interventionists, had great influence on the outcome of the war. It used the Spanish scene for testing material and tactics of the Luftwaffe. Its name is inseperable from the first carpet bombardment in history (Guernica).

Leipzig, Battle of (Völkerschlacht). Battle near Leipzig from 16 to 19 Oct 1813, in which the allied forces of Prussia, Russia and Austria won a decisive victory over Napoleon in the *wars of liberation*. On 17 Oct Napoleon offered in vain an armistice to fresh enemy troops which were pursuing him. On 18 Oct Saxony deserted him. The battle was ended by the conquest of Leipzig by the coalition troops, who lost 52,000 men to 70,000 of Napoleon's. The victory in the battle inaugurated the final phase of the liberation of Germany.

G Loh: Die Völkerschacht bei Leipzig. Eine bibliographische Übersicht (1963).

Leuschner, Wilhelm (15 June 1890–29 Sept 1944); trade unionist. In 1928 he was minister of the interior in the provincial government of Hesse. From 1933 in the governing body of the *ADGB*, he opposed the *Gleichschaltung* of the trade unions and was arrested in 1933/34. From 1938 he was in close contact with *Leber* and from 1942 active in the *Kreisau Circle*. He was considered for inclusion in the *Goerdeler* cabinet, although he did not share Goerdeler's reactionary attitudes. Again arrested after the failure of the *July Plot* in 1944, Leuschner was sentenced to death by the *Volksgerichtshof* and hanged.

H Esters and H Pelger: Gewerkschafter im Widerstand (1967).

Ley, Robert (15 Feb 1890–25 Oct 1945); National Socialist politician. He joined the *NSDAP* in 1924 and became *Gauleiter* in the *Rhineland* in 1925. In 1924 he became a member of the Prussian *Landtag* and in 1930 of the *Reichstag* and succeeded G *Strasser* as leader of the political organization of the party in 1932. After the *Nazi seizure of power* he played a leading part in the destruction of the trade unions and from Mar 1933 he built up the *DAF*. As its leader he propagated the idea of the *Volksgemeinschaft*. After the German defeat in World War II, he committed suicide in his cell at Nuremberg.

Lichnowsky, Karl Max Prince v(8 Mar 1860–27 Feb 1928); diplomat. As ambassador in London (1912–14) he worked for Anglo-German understanding and co-operation, but his reports did not prevent the misinterpretation of British intentions in Berlin. In 1918 he published a memorandum on his mission to London, attacking the *Auswärtiges Amt* for its conduct in the July crisis of 1914. In Britain his description was taken as evidence for Germany's responsibility for the outbreak of World War I (*War Guilt Clause*); in Prussia he was excluded from the *Herrenhaus*.

H F Young: Prince Lichnowsky and the Great War (1976).

Liebknecht, Karl (13 Aug 1871–15 Jan 1919); Socialist politician. The son of Wilhelm Liebknecht, he helped to initiate the Socialist youth movement. From 1908 a member of the *Abgeordnetenhaus* and from 1912 in the *Reichstag*, he belonged to the extreme left wing of the *SPD*. He was a radical pacifist and organized the anti-war demonstration on 1 May 1916 in Berlin. The *Spartakus* letters by him and his partner R *Luxemburg* were the prelude to the formation of the *KPD*. Liebknecht championed a radical course and tried to exploit the *November Revolution* for the setting up of a Soviet republic. During the disturbances of January 1919 he and R Luxemburg were detained and shot without trial by government troops.

W Kerff: Karl Liebknecht 1914–16 (1967); E Hanover-Drück and H Hanover: Der Mord an Rosa Luxemberg und Karl Liebknecht (1967).

Liebknecht, Wilhelm (29 Mar 1826–7 Aug 1900); Socialist leader. He took part in the *Baden uprisings* of 1848–49 (*Revolution of 1848*), after which he emigrated to England, where he became a disciple of *Marx* and *Engels*. On his return in 1862 he joined the *ADAV*, from which he was expelled by *Lasalle*. After being expelled from Prussia, Liebknecht founded the Sächsische Volkspartei in 1886. He took an extremely anti-authoritarian attitude and was tried for treason in 1872. In 1869 he helped to found the 'Sozialdemokratische Arbeiterpartei', whose merger with the ADAV was largely due to his initiative. The Gotha programme of May 1875 reflected the usual democratic stand of Liebknecht whose leading role in the *SPD* soon passed to *Bebel*. Liebknecht was chief editor of *Vorwärts* and a fervent speaker for his party in the *Reichstag*.

List, Friedrich (6 Aug 1789–30 Nov 1846); political economist. As a deputy in the Württemberg chamber he was sentenced for alleged high treason and only released when he agreed to emigrate to America. In 1833 he returned as US Consul. He advocated the planning of an all-German railway system centred on Berlin (*Reichsbahn*). In the 1840s he propagated the idea of a customs union (*Zollverein*), but he simultaneously demanded tariff protection for Germany's national economy until it could successfully compete in the world market. This theory is expounded in his book 'The National System of Political Economy' (1846).

F Bülow: Friedrich List (1959).

Locarno. Place in Tessino (Switzerland), where the agreements on a West

European security system were negotiated in Oct 1925. The main treaty (Locarno Pact) was signed (by *Stresemann* for Germany) in London on 1 Dec 1925. Germany pledged not to change the existing frontiers in western Germany by force and to observe the demilitarized zone of the *Rhineland* (which was guaranteed by Britain and Italy). Locarno implied Germany's recognition of the western frontiers as fixed by the Treaty of *Versailles*, but it left open the door for a *Revisionspolitik* in the east. The coming into force of Locarno facilitated Germany's entry into the League of Nations in 1926. As a reaction to Locarno the *DNVP* left *Luther*'s government, but the treaties easily won parliamentary approval with the support of the Democrats and Social Democrats. On 7 Mar 1936 *Hitler* declared the Locarno Pact null and void and reoccupied the Rhineland.

C Höltje: Die Weimarer Republik und das Ost-Locarno Problem, 1919–34 (1958); J Jacobson: Locarno Diplomacy: Germany and the West 1925–1929 (1972).

Lohmann, Theodor (1831–1905); civil servant. He played a prominent part in *Bismarck*'s *Sozialpolitik*. As under-secretary of state in the ministry of commerce he was responsible for the drafting of important bills. In contrast to Bismarck he recognized the motives of the 'political' workers' movement and was prepared to reconcile them within the existing order. While his ideas were thwarted by Bismarck, *Wilhelm II*'s initiative enabled him to pursue his aims together with *Berlepsch*. Lohmann's endeavours, which led to the 'February decrees' of 1890, were ended by the 'era of *Stumm*'.

London Naval Agreement. Agreement on mutual naval strength between Germany and Britain, concluded on 18 June 1935 by an exchange of notes between Hoare and *Ribbentrop*. The proportion in war-ship tonnage was fixed at 100 to 35, but Germany was permitted 45 per cent (in emergency even full parity) in submarine tonnage. The agreement meant the scrapping of the naval clause of the Treaty of *Versailles*. In spite of Allied protest against the introduction of conscription (*Wehrpflicht*), the agreement sanctioned German naval rearmament. The British policy of appeasement hoped to avoid a naval race comparable to that prior to World War I. *Hitler* interpreted this compromise as a sign of weakness and was hence convinced that his policy of *fait accompli* would score further successes. But in 1939 the Germans had not even rearmed up to the level permitted by the London Naval Agreement (*Z-Plan*).

E H Harazzt: Treaty Breakers or 'Realpolitiker'? The Anglo-German Naval Agreement of June 1935 (1974).

London Ultimatum. Period of six days fixed on 5 May 1921 by the London conference on *reparations* for receiving German payments. The Allies threatened Germany with the occupation of the *Ruhr* region and another blockade to enforce German payments, which were fixed by a commission at 132 million Goldmark. After receiving the ultimatum, the *Fehrenbach* cabinet resigned and was succeeded by *Wirth*, who accepted the ultimatum (policy of *fulfilment*). The ultimatum was accepted by parliament against the votes of the *DVP* and the *DNVP*.

Ludendorff, Erich (9 Apr 1865–20 Dec 1937); general. On 21 Aug 1914 he was appointed *Hindenburg*'s chief of staff and was one of the heroes of the Battle of *Tannenberg*. On 29 Aug 1916 he was promoted by the *Oberste Heeresleitung* to first general quarter master, in which capacity he determined Germany's war policy. He advocated unrestricted *U-Boat warfare*, initiated the *Hindenburg Programme* and the Patriotic Auxiliary Service to mobilize the home front. His strategy of 'hammer-strokes' in the west did not force victory, but he boycotted the quest for a negotiated peace in 1917 (*peace resolution*), contriving the replacement of *Bethmann Hollweg* by his puppet *Michaelis*. When Russia collapsed Ludendorff dictated the terms of *Brest Litovsk* and shifted troops for the decisive offensive in the west in spring 1918 (*Michael*). After Allied victory had become apparent Ludendorff peremptorily demanded negotiations on 29 Sept 1918 for an armistice (*Compiègne*). He was dismissed by Prince *Max von Baden* on 26 Oct 1918. His military dictatorship was contrary to the urgent needs for parliamentary democracy and peace and thus contributed to the *November Revolution*. After 1919 he helped to spread the *stab-in-the-back legend*, took part in the *Kapp-Putsch* and together with *Hitler* directed the *Munich (Bierkeller) Putsch*. From 1924 to 1928 a member of the *Reichstag*, he was the *NSDAP*'s candidate for the *Reichspräsident* elections of 1925 but won only 1.1 per cent of the votes.

D J Goodspeed: Ludendorff – Soldier, Dictator, Revolutionary (1966).

Lüderitz, Adolf (16 July 1834–24 Oct 1886); German colonialist. In 1883 he bought the Bay of Angra Pequena and its hinterland in South-West Africa from native chiefs to establish a trading post there (since 1886 known as Lüderitz Bay). On his demand the territory became the first of the German *Schutzgebiete* as *German South-West Africa* on 24 Apr 1884. But *Bismarck*'s reluctance and British objections prevented the realization of Lüderitz's plan to extend the possessions up to St Lucia Bay on the eastern coast to provide for the settlement of German immigrants. His activities gave a strong impetus to the German colonial movement (*Kolonialverein*). He was drowned during an expedition in the Oranje river. The port founded by him was named after him in 1920.

Ludwig I (25 Aug 1786–29 Feb 1868); King of Bavaria. On 13 Oct 1825 he succeeded his father *Maximilian I Joseph*. His early reign was marked by a reformist spirit, but the revolutionary wave of 1830 drove him into the arms of reactionary clericals. In 1837 he appointed as minister-president the Ultramontane K v Abel (1788–1859), who suppressed the Protestants and censored Liberalism. Ludwig's affair with the Irish dancer Lola Montez led to demonstrations by radicals in 1847–48. Ludwig then abdicated in favour of his eldest son, *Maximilian II*.

E C Conte Corti: Ludwig I (repr. 1960).

Ludwig II (25 Aug 1845–13 June 1886); King of Bavaria. The son of *Maximilian II*, he acceded to the throne on 10 Mar 1864. In the *Seven Weeks' War* in 1866 Ludwig sided with Austria on the advice of his chief minister Pfordten, who was replaced by Prince Hohenlohe-Schillingsfürst after the Bavarian defeat. Ludwig then moved closer to Prussia (alliance of 1867) but safeguarded Bavaria's sovereignty. In the *Franco-Prussian War* of 1870 Ludwig at once took Prussia's side. In Dec he was persuaded by *Bismarck* to address a letter to the King of Prussia asking him to become German Emperor. As a reward Ludwig received secret donations from *Welfenfonds* and a number of *reserved rights* were allotted to Bavaria in the *November Treaties*. Dissatisfied with the solution of the German question and his constitutional position, Ludwig morbidly excluded himself from the world after 1882. He concentrated on the building of romantic castles, which put a heavy strain on the Bavarian treasury. Finally, his ministers had him declared insane and on 10 June his uncle, Prince Luitpold, assumed the regency. Ludwig drowned himself in Lake Starnberg three days later.

W Blunt: The Dream King (1970).

Luftwaffe, German air force. Its rearmament, which violated the clauses of the Treaty of *Versailles*, had been started in the *Weimar Republic*, with part of the aircraft production and flight training taking place in Soviet Russia. On 9 Mar 1935, in connection with the introduction of conscription (*Wehrpflicht*), *Göring* unmasked the Luftwaffe whose armament was then speeded up. The Luftwaffe was conceived as support for the *Blitzkriege*. It mainly consisted of light fighters (dive-bombers), whereas long-distance bombers were neglected. The Luftwaffe played a prominent part in the campaigns against Poland in the west, but failed in the *Battle of Britain (Adlerangriff)*. The Luftwaffe subsequently lost its air supremacy. It carried out the first carpet bombings on civil targets (such as Rotterdam), thereby provoking Allied attacks on German cities (eg Dresden), which inflicted heavy casualties on the civilian population.

D Irving: The Rise and Fall of the Luftwaffe (1973); E L Homze: Arming the Luftwaffe. The Reich Air Ministry and the German Aircraft Industry 1919–39 (1977).

Luther, Hans (10 Mar 1879–11 May 1962); statesman. Without being a member of any political party, he was appointed *Reichsminister* for Food and Agriculture in *Cuno*'s government (1922). Under *Stresemann*, Luther served as minister of finance and his endeavours led to the stabilization of the monetary system. In 1925 he was called upon to form a government. His first cabinet tended towards the right, including *Zentrum*, *DVP* and *DNVP*. His tenure of office saw the tax reform of 1925 and the treaties of *Locarno*, after which the DNVP withdrew and Luther tried to rule Germany with a minority government. He favoured an administration by expert ministers against the influence of parliament. His resignation in May 1926 was caused by the *Flag Decree*. From 1930 to 1933 he was president of the *Reichsbank* and his inflationary credit policy contributed to *Hitler*'s programme for the provision of labour. Luther was replaced by *Schacht* and sent to Washington as ambassador (1933–37).

K B Netzband and H P Widmaier: Währungs- und Finanzpolitik der Ära Luther (1964); K H Minuth: Die Kabinette Luther I und II, 1925–26 (1977).

Lützow-Korps. Guerrilla troops ('Freikorps') formed by Major Lützow (1782–1834) to operate against Napoleon in the *wars of liberation* of 1813–15. The Lützow Korps comprised 3,000 members of all ranks, including many students and well-known personalities (*Jahn*, Friesen, Eichendorff). The corps' operations in Napoleon's rear before June 1813 were of little military significance. After being massacred by French troops which disregarded the armistice, the corps were finally dissolved when Lützow was wounded in 1814. The Lützow-Korps's colours (black coat with red lapels and yellow buttons) were adopted by the *Burschenschaften* and recognized as German colours from 1818.

Luxembourg Question. Question of the status of the Duchy of Luxembourg which arose in 1886–67, when Luxembourg was claimed by France. Hitherto it had belonged to the *Deutscher Bund*, but it remained outside the *North German Confederation*. French annexionist demands caused an acute danger of war. The conflict was settled by the London conference of 11 May 1867, at which the European powers guaranteed Luxembourg's neutrality. Economically, Luxembourg continued to be a member of the *Customs Union*.

Luxemburg, Rosa (5 Mar 1870–15 Jan 1919); German-Polish Socialist. The founder and leader of the Social-Democratic party in the 'Polish Kingdom' (1893), she settled in Germany in 1898 and became a member of the *SPD*. In 1905 she took part in the Russian revolution. She belonged to the radical wing of German social democracy and opposed revisionism. She made significant contributions to the development of Marxist theory, eg 'The Accumulation of Capital' (1913). During World War I she and K *Liebknecht* founded the *Spartakus* and attacked the *Burgfriede*, for which she was imprisoned for most of the wartime, writing her famous 'letters from prison'. After the *November Revolution* she joined the *KPD* and in January 1919 took part in the Communist uprising, for which she was detained and, together with K Liebknecht, shot without trial by government troops.

P Nettl: Rosa Luxemburg (1967).

Manteuffel, Otto Freiherr v (3 Feb 1805–26 Nov 1882); Prussian Conservative. Spokesman of the *Camarilla* in the *Vereinigter Landtag* in 1847. After the *Revolution of 1848* he became a member in *Brandenburg*'s cabinet: in 1850 he became minister-president. Under his rule the reactionary constitution of 5 Dec 1848 was decreed; in 1849 the *three-class suffrage* was introduced. Manteuffel remained in office until 1858, the year of the *New Era*.

Marinebrigade Erhardt. A *Freikorps* founded by Cpt Herrmann Erhardt in 1919.

Part of the preliminary *Reichswehr*, it helped to put down Communist uprisings and had a major share in the *Kapp-Putsch*, after which it was dissolved.

G Krüger: Die Brigade Erhardt (1971).

Marinekabinett. See *Naval Cabinet*.

Marne, Battle of the. Franco-British counter-attack along the entire western front led by Joffre from 5 to 19 Sept 1914 against the right wing of the German armies (under Kluck and Bülow) invading North-East France. Overestimating the Allied forces, the Germans, under orders from H v *Moltke* (the younger), retreated north of the Marne. This 'miracle of the Marne' meant the failure of the *Schlieffen-Plan*, but Allied progress was also checked and the war of movement gave way to trench warfare on French soil, with one tenth of France in German hands. This front was later modified by the *Siegfried Line* and only in the spring of 1918 did the Germans again break through to the Marne (operation *Michael*).

R Asprey: The First Battle of the Marne (1962).

Marschall von Bieberstein, Baron Adolf (12 Oct 1842–24 Sept 1912); diplomat. In 1890 he succeeded *Bismarck*'s son Herbert as secretary of state of the *Auswärtiges Amt*. At first he pursued a policy of understanding with Britain but soon after followed the advice of *Holstein* for a policy of the 'free hand'. He disapproved of *Wilhelm II*'s 'personal rule' and resigned in 1897. He then became ambassador to Constantinople and helped develop closer German-Turkish relations prior to World War I. After the failure of the Haldane mission of 1912 (*Flottenpolitik*), he was posted to the embassy in London, where he died a few months later.

Marx, Karl (5 May 1818–14 Mar 1883); philosopher and economist. He sympathized with the *Neo-Hegelians* in his youth, but turned away from *Hegel*'s idealism and, under the influence of Feuerbach, became an adherent of Socialism. From 1843 he lived in Paris, and then in Brussels, where he developed the fundamental propositions of his economic theory of history, seeing each principle of social organization represented by class. In 1847 he helped to found working-class associations and in 1848, in collaboration with his life-long friend and sponsor Friedrich *Engels*, he drew up the *Communist Manifesto*. Marx returned to Cologne during the *Revolution of 1848* to revive his journalistic activities with the 'Neue Rheinische Zeitung'. He was expelled from Prussia in 1849 and emigrated to London, where he spent the rest of his life, at first as a correspondent for the 'New York Tribune', later mainly absorbed in research in the British Museum. The first volume of his 'Das Kapital' appeared in 1867. In this book he developed a theory of the capitalist system and its dynanism, with emphasis on its self-destructive tendencies. In 1864 he had founded the First International, which he led until 1876. Marx's doctrine became the creed for various Socialist and Communist movements, notably German Social Democracy (*SPD*). His achievement lies less in the enunciation of a real programme than in the creation of a consciousness of the socio-economic aspects of industrial society.

I Berlin: Karl Marx. His Life and Environment (1963); F J Raddatz: Karl Marx. Eine politische Biographie (1975).

Marx, Wilhelm (15 Jan 1863–5 Aug 1946); Roman Catholic politician. He represented the *Zentrum* in the *Reichstag* from 1910. In 1921 he became party president and leader of the parliamentary party. In Dec he was appointed *Reichskanzler* and formed a minority cabinet tolerated by the *SPD*. His policy was strongly influenced by his foreign minister *Stresemann* by means of state control. Marx achieved a certain stabilization of the economy, which he continued with his second cabinet of July 1924 with the help of the *Dawes-Plan*. After the elections of Dec 1924 he resigned and in 1925 he was defeated by *Hindenburg* in his candidature for *Reichspräsident*. After belonging to *Luther's* cabinet as minister of justice, he formed his third minority government in May 1926, but accepted a vote of no confidence following the criticism of the *Reichswehr's* secret co-operation with the Red Army. In Jan 1927 he secured a majority for the first time by including the *DNVP*. The opening towards the right came to an end in July 1928, when it was succeeded by *Müller's* grand coalition. Marx resigned the party presidency and retired in 1933.

H Stehkämpher (ed): Der Nachlass des Reichskanzlers Wilhelm Marx, 4 vols (1968).

Märzrevolution. See *Revolution of 1848*.

Master Race Theory. See *Aryan racial doctrine*.

Mathy, Karl (17 Mar 1807–3 Feb 1868); Liberal politician. He was forced into exile from 1835 to 1840. On his return he became a deputy in the Baden chamber and a member of the *Frankfurt National Assembly*, where he supported the *Erbkaiserliche*. In *Baden* Mathy opposed the Democrats in the uprisings of 1848–49. From 1860 he held high government posts and, being friendly towards Prussia, paved the way for a *rapprochement* of Baden with the *North German Confederation*.

Matriculated contributions (Matrikularbeiträge). Annual contributions of the federal states of the Reich to its expenses 1871–1918. They were calculated per capita of the population.

Max von Baden, Prince (10 July 1867–6 Nov 1929); heir presumptive to the Grand Duchy of Baden from 1907. On 3 Oct 1918 he was appointed *Reichskanzler* and Prussian foreign minister with a commission to introduce parliamentary government and to begin peace negotiations. He headed a reform ministry of the later *Weimar coalition*. He opened armistice negotiations with the USA and secured the dismissal of *Ludendorff*. At the outbreak of the

November Revolution he tried to preserve the monarchy. In vain did he advise the voluntary abdication of *Wilhelm II*, which he announced on his own responsibility on 9 Nov. He then resigned his office to *Ebert* and refused the latter's offer of the post of a *Reichsverweser*.

E Matthias/R Morsey: Die Regierung des Prinzen Max von Baden (1962).

Maximilian I Joseph (27 May 1756–13 Oct 1825); Elector (1799–1806) and King (1806–25) of Bavaria. Intending to make Bavaria a sovereign state independent of Austria, he made a separate treaty with Napoleon in 1801. Indemnified for the cessions to France on the left bank of the Rhine by the *Reichsdeputationshauptschluss* (1803), he acquired Swabian and Franconian territories that made Bavaria the largest German middle state. In 1806 he adopted the title of King. Membership in the Confederation of the Rhine gave him full sovereignty and new territories. His minister Montgelas (1759–1838) reorganized Bavaria by means of anti-clerical reforms, sweeping away traditional privileges in the constitution of 1 May 1808. On 1 Feb 1817 Montgelas was dismissed for his reluctance to concede a liberal constitution, which Maximilian I Joseph proclaimed on 26 May 1818. It introduced a bicameral parliament with a lower house elected on a narrow franchise. Maximilian I Joseph ruled as a model constitutional monarch until his death. He was succeeded by his son *Ludwig I*.

Maximilian II (28 Nov 1811–10 Mar 1864); King of Bavaria. He succeeded his father *Ludwig I* in 1848. Maximilian II tried to prevent Bavaria from being crushed by Prussian hegemony in a united Germany. Therefore, he did not support the offer of the Imperial Crown to *Friedrich Wilhelm IV* (*Kaiserdeputation*). Maximilian II also refused to join the *Three Kings' Alliance* (1849). On 2 Feb 1850 he concluded an Alliance of the Four Kings with Württemberg, Hanover and Saxony, suggested by his minister L v d Pfordten (1811–80) with the aim of establishing a range of medium states (*Trias*). From 1854 Maximilian II struggled with parliament and in 1859 dismissed Pfordten in favour of K v Schrenck. Meanwhile Maximilian II had made Munich a centre of Germany's cultural life, furthering science and history at the Bavarian Academy of Sciences. He was succeeded on 10 Mar 1864 by his son *Ludwig II*.

May Laws. Climax and principal item of the *Kulturkampf* legislation in Prussia, issued 11–14 May 1873, subjecting the Church to state laws. They concerned the academic education and employment of the clergy, ecclesiastical disciplinary authority, application of ecclesiastical measures, and secessions from the Church. The laws met with the passive resistance of the Roman Catholic clergy, which the Prussian minister of culture, Falk, tried to overcome with new penal measures. But the May Laws failed to attain their objective and were suspended at the end of the *Kulturkampf*.

Mehring, Franz (27 Feb 1846–28 Jan 1919); journalist and historian. From 1891 a member of the *SPD*, Mehring was chief editor of the 'Leipziger Volkszeitung' from 1902 to 1907. In World War I he was one of the founders of *Spartakus* and the *USPD* and in 1919 he participated in preparations for the foundation of the *KPD*. He wrote a four-volume history of Social Democracy (1897–98) based on historical materialism.

W Kumpmann: Franz Mehring als Vertreter des historischen Materialismus (1966).

Mein Kampf. Book written by *Hitler* in co-operation with *Hess*, when they were arrested in the fortress of Landsberg after the *Munich (Bierkeller) Putsch* (1924). *Mein Kampf* explains the programme and essence of *National Socialism*. It propagates the hierarchic *Führer*-state, racialist and expansionist ideas, the *Lebensraum* theory and a war of conquest. Economic and social questions are hardly tackled in it. It only became a bestseller after the *Nazi seizure of power* with its Führer-cult. Six million copies of the book had been sold, but it is doubtful whether its many purchasers actually read it.

Ch Zentner: Hitlers Mein Kampf (1974).

Memelland. Northernmost territory of East Prussia, which Germany had to cede without plebiscite in 1919 (Treaty of *Versailles*). On 16 Feb 1920 France took over the administration. In 1923 Lithuanian guerrillas invaded the Memelland and the Memel statute of 14 Nov 1924 made it an integral part of Lithuania. After the rise of *National Socialism*, resistance of the German majority (87 per cent) in Memelland was voiced in the election of Dec 1938 and forced its retrocession on 22 Mar 1939. After the evacuation of Memelland by German troops in 1944–45 it became part of the Lithuanian SSR.

E A Plieg: Das Memelland, 1920 bis 1939 (1962).

Michael. Code word for the final German offensive in World War I launched by *Ludendorff* on 21 Mar 1918. The 'Operation Michael', also termed 'Emperor's Battle', was expected to bring a decisive victory to the Central Powers before the advent of the Americans on the western front in large numbers. The *Oberste Heeresleitung* (OHL) sought to deal a surprise blow and feigned attacks all along the western front. Altogether 62 German divisions prepared to attack. On 26 Mar the 5th British army was split, but on 27–28 March the German attack weakened before reaching Amiens. Michael had failed because of the lack of fresh reserves and ammunition and in inferiority in tanks, though Ludendorff attributed his failure to lack of discipline in the army (*stab-in-the-back legend*). The Allied counter-attack succeeded from 18 July, and on 8 Aug, the 'black day' of the German army, achieved a breakthrough. The OHL had to withdraw the forces to the *Siegfried Line* and precipitately asked the government to sue for an armistice via US President Wilson (*Compiègne*).

Michaelis, Georg (8 Sept 1857–24 July 1936); politician. As Prussian state commissioner for food supplies he suggested an 'economic general staff' headed by a military leadership. This was practically realized with his appointment as Reichskanzler on 14 July 1917. He accepted the *Peace Resolution* of the *Reichstag* 'as he understood it' and approved of annexionist war aims in the

East at the Kreuznach conference (19 Aug 1917). He was a mere puppet of the *Oberste Heeresleitung*. On 24 Oct 1917 the majority parties demanded his resignation and on 1 Nov the Kaiser replaced him by *Hertling*.

Military Cabinet (*Militärkabinett*). Administrative military office for the personal affairs of officers in Prussia, 1808–1919, which was directly subordinated to the King as supreme warlord. After 1850 it often stood in opposition to the War Ministry from whose control it was freed in 1883 under its ambitious chief general E L v Albedyll (1871–1887). Under *Wilhelm II* the military cabinet served as an instrument of 'sub-government' for the Kaiser and the military party.

G A Craig: The Politics of the Prussian Army (1955).

Miquel, Johannes (19 Feb 1828–8 Sept 1901). National Liberal parliamentarian; one of the founders of the *Nationalverein*. As Prussian minister of finance (1891–1901) he reformed the tax system, introducing on 24 June 1891 a progressive income tax instead of the previous class tax which lowered the rate for lower incomes and raised it for medium and higher ones, starting with 0.62 per cent for annual incomes of 900–1050 marks, and rising to 4 per cent for those above 100,000 marks. His reform improved the financial basis of the Prussian state but favoured the Junkers and industrialists who were the pillars of his *Sammlungspolitik*. From 1897 also vice-president of the *Staatsministerium*, Miquel failed to placate Conservative objections to the *Mittelland Canal* and was overthrown in May 1901.

Mittelafrika. Conception of a coherent German colonial empire in Central Africa in the 1890s, speculating on the acquisition of the Belgian and French Congos and the Portuguese possessions, over which negotiations were carried out before 1914 (*Berlin [Congo] Conference, Moroccan Agreements, Angola Treaty*). In World War I Mittelafrika became part of the German war aims (*September Programme*) and in late 1916 *Solf* even demanded an enlargement of Mittelafrika into 'Tropical Africa', which was to include great parts of West Africa. The quest for Mittelafrika was founded on power-political and economic reasons, but after the military loss of all colonies except East Africa, the *Oberste Heeresleitung* regarded Mittelafrika as useless, because it would always be at Britain's mercy, and preferred the *Mitteleuropa* expansionism, though the political leadership never opted out of *Mittelafrika*, if only as a compensation for renunciations in Europe. This idea was revived in the age of appeasement but appealed only to ex-colonialists (Schnee) and was discarded by *Hitler*.

Mitteleuropa. Political catchword expressing the desire for a reorganization of Central Europe after the downfall of the oldest empire in 1806. Mitteleuropa received an economic significance due to *List*'s concept of an industrial and commercial expansion of Germany towards the South-East into the Danube and Balkan region. C Franz (1817–91) propagated the idea of Mitteleuropa as a federation to reconcile Prussian preponderance with Habsburg interests. The *Triple Alliance* provided the diplomatic foundation for Mitteleuropa under German leadership. In 1904 J Wolf founded the 'Central European Economic Society' to promote the Mitteleuropa idea, which was popularized in F *Naumann's* book 'Mitteleuropa' (1915), by which time Mitteleuropa had become an integral part of Germany's war aims (*September Programme*). The conception was revived in Hitler's *Lebensraum* ideology.

H C Meyer: Mitteleuropa in German Thought and Action (1951).

Mittelland Canal. Canal system between the Rhine, Weser, Elbe and Berlin. Construction began in 1905 after controversies over the project in 1899–1901, when the Conservative Mittelland Canal 'rebels' opposed it in the Prussian *Abgeordnetenhaus* to preserve agrarian interests. They feared a reduction in price of the transport costs for overseas grain and voted twice against the Canal construction bill, after *Miquel's* failure to win them over by promising tariff revision of the Reich's trade policy. When the rebels went as far as to obstruct the *Reichstag* (May 1901–Dec 1902), *Bülow* sacrificed the first section, Hanover–Elbe. Thus the Canal remained a torso until World War I, and was only opened in its full length (325 km) in 1938.

H Horn: Der Kampf um den Bau des Mittellandkanals (1964).

Moltke, Helmuth Graf v, the elder (26 Oct 1800–24 Apr 1891); Prussian field marshal. He was appointed chief of the Prussian general staff in 1858, which had been a mere subordinate office until then. In 1866 he received the command over all troops and army staff. He became responsible for the strategic planning of Prussia in the *Seven Weeks' War* (1866) and held the same position in 1870–71 in the *Franco-Prussian War*. In the following years he built up the first modern general staff which was able to co-ordinate war on a mass scale. Moltke was an outstanding military theorist and writer. He made use of new scientific, technological and economic knowledge. His concept was realized perfectly at *Königgrätz*. In politics Moltke, who was a member of the *Reichstag*, stood for German unification under Prussian leadership. Sceptical of the possibility of durable peace, he wanted the German army to be always ready for a preventive war. He resigned in 1888.

K Stadelmann: Moltke und der Staat (1950).

Moltke, Helmuth v, the younger (25 May 1848–18 June 1916); chief of the general staff. The nephew of the elder Moltke, he succeeded *Schlieffen* in 1906. In trying to adapt his plan to changed circumstances, Moltke left the right flank of the German forces too weak in 1914 and had to resign after German defeat in the Battle of the *Marne*. He had been an advocate of preventive war, believing that the strength of Germany and her allies was diminishing in comparison with that of the entente. In July 1914, by encouraging Austria's mobilization against Russia, he contributed to the outbreak of World War I.

Mommsen, Theodor (30 Nov 1817–1 Nov 1903); historian. As member of the

Prussian *Abgeordnetenhaus* he was an opposition speaker against *Bismarck*. From 1863 to 1866 he represented the *Fortschrittspartei*, from 1873 to 1879 the National Liberals. In 1880 he opposed *Treitschke*'s *Anti-Semitism* in Berlin. From 1881 to 1884 Mommsen was a Reichstag deputy for the radical Liberals. In 1902 he was awarded the Nobel prize for literature for his researches in ancient history.

A Heuss: Theodor Mommsen und das 19. Jahrhundert (1956); A Wurcher: T Mommsen – Geschichtsschreibung und Politik (1956).

Monumenta Germaniae Historica. Collection of sources of German medieval history, edited by an association founded in 1819 by *Stein*. The first volume was published in 1826. The motto of each volume ('Sanctus amor patriae dat animum') reflects the patriotic character of the editors, for they hoped to achieve German unity by promoting the recollection of the nation's history. The project was suspect to the German states, who mistrusted Stein and only financed it after his death. The work then flourished under the direction of G Waitz (1813–1886).

Moroccan Agreements. Two treaties concluded on 4 Nov 1911 between Germany and France. They gave France a free hand to establish a protectorate over Morocco; in return Germany, while ceding a strip of territory in the northeastern *Cameroons* to the French, received tracts of the French Congo giving the German colony access to the Ubangi and Congo rivers. In the talks at Kissingen the German negotiator *Kiderlen*, who had previously sparked off the *Panther's Spring* to Agadir, wanted to obtain all of the French Congo between the Atlantic and the River Sanga as a compensation for recognition of France's position in North Africa. Because of British opposition to German *Mittelafrika* aims, Kiderlen had to content himself with the so-called 'duck's bill' arrangement, which was denounced by the right-wing opposition in the *Reichstag* as a 'few acres of swamp'. National public opinion (*Alldeutscher Verband*, *Kolonialverein*) was aggrieved and once more convinced of an *encirclement* plot. Hitherto Germany had remained satisfied with colonial gains, but after the Moroccan Agreements she was to make a bid for European hegemony (*Weltpolitik*, *Pan-Germanism*).

Müller, Herrmann (18 May 1876–20 Mar 1931); Social-Democratic politician: from 1916 *SPD* member of the *Reichstag*, and from 1920 leader of the parliamentary party. In June 1919, as foreign minister in *Bauer*'s cabinet he was forced to sign the Treaty of *Versailles*. After the *Kapp-Putsch* (Mar 1920) he formed the provisional government, which resigned after the elections of 6 June 1920 and was succeeded by the first of the bourgeois governments of the *Weimar Republic*, whose tolerance Müller promoted. In May 1928 he formed his second government, integrating 5 parties ranging from SPD to *DVP*. This coalition failed over the financing of the *unemployment insurance* at the beginning of the world economic crisis. He resigned on 27 Mar 1930. He was the last Social Democratic *Reichskanzler*. His failure foreshadowed the doom of democracy.

Munich Agreement. Agreement between Britain, France, Italy and Germany concluded at Munich on 29 Sept 1938. It forced Czechoslovakia to cede the *Sudeten* territories to Germany. Earlier *Hitler* had issued the threat of war to win the Czech stepping-stone of his *Revisionspolitik* (*Hossbach-Protokoll*). He was helped by Allied appeasement, as expressed by N Chamberlain on his visits to Hitler in Berchtesgaden (16 Sept) and Godesberg (22–24 Sept). But Hitler, who preferred a solution by war, escalated his demands. On Mussolini's initiative a conference was convened in Munich on 29 Sept, at which Hitler, Chamberlain, Mussolini and the French Premier Daladier sealed the fate of Czechoslavakia, which was not even represented. For her cessions to Germany, Poland and Hungary the Czechoslovak Republik was promised a guarantee for her existence, which she never got (*Bohemia-Moravia*). The agreement determined the evacuation of the districts claimed by Germany by 10 Oct 1938. The agreement, which was almost immediately broken by Hitler, was a vain attempt by the western powers to keep the peace in Europe by giving way to Nazi pressures. The Munich Agreement is illustrative of great power diplomacy at the expense of smaller nations.

B Celovsly: Das 1938 (1958); K Robbins: Munich 1938 (1968).

Munich (Bierkeller) Putsch. Attempted coup d'état of 8–9 Nov 1923 by *Hitler* in co-operation with *Ludendorff*. The putschists tried to exploit the rift between Bavaria and the Reich over the *Republikschutzgesetz*. Hitler succeeded in capturing some members of the Bavarian government (*Kahr*) in a Munich beer hall and then announced the 'national revolution'. Hitler was to be the political and Ludendorff the military leader. But a demonstration headed by the two on the next day at noon collapsed under the fire of a police cordon. Hitler was sentenced to five years' imprisonment in a fortress but was released in 1924.

H J Gordon jr: Hitler and the Beer Hall Putsch (1972).

Munich Soviet Republic (Münchner Räterepublik). Soviet Republic of Munich, established on 7 Apr 1919 after the assassination of *Eisner*, who had called out the Republic on 8 Nov 1918. The 'people's delegation', which was formed to govern the republic, consisted of independent anarchists including intellectuals, such as Toller and Landauer. The elected Bavarian government (under Hoffmann, *SPD*) fled to Bamberg. On 13 Apr 1919 a second republic was instituted by the Communists led by Leviné and Lenien. On 1 May 1919 the republic was liquidated by the *Reichswehr* and the *Freikorps*.

A Mitchell: Revolution in Bavaria 1918–1919 (1967).

Nachtigal, Gustav (23 Feb 1834–20 Apr 1885); colonial pioneer. From 1869 to 1874 he travelled through unknown parts of the Sahara and the Sudan. In 1884 he was sent to Upper Guinea by *Bismarck* as a Reichskommissar to place *Togo* and the *Cameroons* under German protection (*Schutzgebiete*). Nachtigal died at sea on his voyage home.

National ... See *Reichs—*

Nationalkomitee Freies Deutschland. Organization founded on 12–13 July 1943 at Krasnogorsk near Moscow to collect all *Anti-Fascists* among the *Wehrmacht* prisoners of war in Russia. The organization was directed by Communists headed by E Weinert. In Sept 1943 it merged with the 'Bund deutscher Offiziere', which included several generals after mid-1944, among them Gen Paulus, the loser of *Stalingrad*. The organization appealed to German front-line fighters and sponsored the political instruction of the prisoners of war. It tried to build up a predominantly Communist popular front for the development of an anti-Fascist post-war Germany.

B Scheurig: Freies Deutschland. Das Nationalkomitee und der Bund deutscher Offiziere (1960).

Nationalliberale Partei. Liberal Party founded in 1867 out of the *Fortschrittspartei*. It was the party of the propertied and educated bourgeoisie and became the main pillar of *Bismarck's* policy, eg in the *Kulturkampf*. It approved the *kleindeutsch* solution of German unification and in 1871 achieved its highest election with c 30 per cent of the votes. In 1880 the free traders in the party seceded in protest against the protectionist legislation favoured by the majority in the party. While the secessionists organized themselves as the 'Liberale Vereinigung', the party was reduced to medium size, its votes in the *Reichstag* elections having dwindled to c 13 per cent. Important leaders included *Bennigsen*, E *Bassermann* and *Stresemann*. Before 1914 the Nationalliberale Partei championed an imperialist *Weltpolitik* and co-operated with the *Alldeutscher Verband*. In World War I it approved of unrestricted *U-Boat Warfare* and annexionist war aims. The demand for interior reforms (introduction of parliamentary democracy) led to the split of the party in 1919; the greater part joined the *DVP*, others the *DNVP* and *DDP*.

Nationalrepräsentation. Aspired constitutional reform within the framework of the reforms of *Stein* and *Hardenberg*, aiming at the introduction of an elected national Prussian representative body (also called 'Reichsstände' in contrast to *Landstände*). The reform was expected to form a link between society and state and bring about the identification of state and nation. The possibility of a constitutional system on a representative basis alarmed the reactionary forces, which ruined the project.

National Socialism. German variation of Fascism. It was characterized by rigid anti-Liberalism which demanded the surrender of individualism for the integration of citizens into the state; it was dominated by a racial élite and organized according to the *Führer*-principle. Its roots can be found in Prussian militarism as well as the neo-romanticism of *Wagner* and *Nietzsche*. The ideology of National Socialism attempted the unqualified application of what it regarded as the laws of nature to human social life; it received its clearest expression in the *Aryan racial doctrine*. The master race theory manifested itself in the aspirations for a *Third Reich* with *Lebensraum* for the German people. After World War I the disillusion and impoverishment of many Germans made possible the rise of National Socialism as a political force which became identified with the national movement for a *Revisionspolitik*. As a movement opposed to international Communism, it attracted support from the petty bourgeoisie and from traditional Conservatives. It originally regarded itself as a revolutionary movement fighting against the exploitation of the *Volksgenossen* and for the realization of the *Volksgemeinschaft*, but to attain power it soon made compromises with other social groups and after the seizure of power gave up all aspirations for social revolution (*Röhm Putsch*, 1934). From then until 1945 National Socialism, represented by its leader and the party organizations (*NSDSP*), governed Germany on the principle of totalitarianism (*Gleichschaltung*). It permeated German society by propaganda, intensive organization and terror (*SA, SS, SD, Gestapo, concentration camps*). These features were intensified during World War II. Resistance was ineffective and was destroyed after the *July Plot* (1944). The system only collapsed with Hitler's death (30 Apr 1945). The movement was destroyed by the denazification policy of the Allies after World War II (*Nuremberg Tribunal*).

W Hofer: Der Nationalsozialismus (1957); H Grebing: Der Nationalsozialismus (1959); E Nolte: Der Nationalsozialismus (1972); M J Thornton: Nazism, 1918–1945 (1966).

National Socialist schools. Schools in National Socilaist Germany for the education of the rising generation of party and state officials. These schools recruited the most promising members of the *Hitler Youth* at the age of 12 and prepared them for matriculation, subjecting them to very strict discipline. In addition to the National Socialist schools there existed the 'National-Political Educational Institutes' (Napola), which emulated the Prussian military academies, educating their pupils in a militarist spirit. While the National Socialist schools were supervised by the *Hitler Youth*, the Napola were controlled by the *NSDAP* and the *SS*, which recruited the best school-leavers for their *Ordensburgen*.

H Scholtz: NS-Ausleseschulen. Internatsschulen als Herrschaftsmittel des Führerstaates (1973).

Nationalsozialer Verein. Political union founded in 1896 under the leadership of F *Naumann*. It propagated a national socialism within the Hohenzollern monarchy that would enjoy the approval of the bourgeoisie and the consent of the working class. Its members came from among the intellectuals and the urban middle classes. After the *Reichstag* elections of 1903, in which it only won one seat, the union was dissolved, whereupon most of its members joined the *Freisinnige Vereinigung*.

D Düding: Der Nationalsozialer Verein 1896–1903 (1972).

Nationalverein. National society founded in Sept 1859 in Frankfurt, inspired by an assembly of *kleindeutsch* Democrats and Liberals in Eisenach and Hanover. Leading members of the society were *Schulze-Delitzsch* and *Bennigsen*. It tried to stimulate Prussia to resume her *union plan* and developed vague ideas about a parliament and a central government. At its peak in 1862 it had 250,000 members. It was dissolved after the formation of the *North German Confederation*.

Naumann. Friedrich (25 Mar 1860–24 Aug 1919); politician and theorist. From 1890 he was a member of the *Evangelisch-sozialer Kongress*. Under his influence 'The Young' split from the Conservatives (*Stoecker*). In 1896 he founded the *Nationalsozialer Verein*. He wanted to win over the working class for a socially reformed monarchy. In 1903 he joined the *Freisinnige Vereinigung* and from 1907 to 1918 he sat in the *Reichstag*, promoting the union of the *Fortschrittliche Volkspartei*. During World War I he envisaged central European economic integration under German leadership ('*Mitteleuropa*', 1915). In 1918 he helped to found the *DDP*, whose chairman he became in July 1919, when he was a member of the *Weimar National Assembly*. His vague concept of a synthesis of Nationalism, Socialism and Liberalism failed to bridge the gap between working class and bourgeoisie in Wilhelmine Germany.

Th Heuss: Friedrich Naumanns Erbe (1959); K Oppel: F Naumann (1961).

Naval Cabinet (Marinekabinett). Administrative naval office for the personal affairs of naval officers. It was instituted according to the model of the *military cabinet* under *Wilhelm II* to suit his personal ambitions in *Flottenpolitik*.

W Görlitz (ed), Georg Alexander v Müller: Regierte der Kaiser? Kriegstagebücher, Aufzeichnungen und Briefe des Marinekabinetts 1914–1918 (1959).

Nazi. See *National Socialism* and *NSDAP*.

Nazi seizure of power (Machtergreifung). Seizure of power by the National Socialists from the appointment of *Hitler* as *Reichskanzler* (30 Jan 1933) to the consolidation of Nazi power. Hitler's 'cabinet of national concentration' included *NSDAP* ministers (*Frick, Göring*) in key positions (internal security). Other members were *Papen* as vice-chancellor, *Hugenberg* (*DNVP*) and Seldte, the leader of *Stahlhelm*. Since his government lacked a parliamentary majority and was dependent on *Notverordnungen*, Hitler announced new elections for 5 Mar 1933. Meanwhile the *Schutzhaftbefehle* of 4 Feb initiated an organized terror against political opposition, which increased after the *Reichstag Fire*. The elections resulted in a narrow majority for the coalition of the right (NSDAP: 43.9 per cent; DNVP: 8 per cent) and induced Hitler to table the *Enabling Act*. Its acceptance by the *Reichstag* on 23 Mar laid the basis for the erection of total dictatorship. The seizure of power was completed by the *Gleichschaltung* of all political and social institutions during the remainder of 1933. It had been enabled by the miscalculation of all other political forces: the half-hearted resistance of the *Weimar Coalition*, the dogmatism of the *KPD* and particularly by the sleeping partnership of the conservatives who hoped to use Hitler as their 'drummer'. After the seizure of power there remained only the alternative of either accommodation with the Nazis or of withdrawal from public life. *National Socialism* had achieved unparalleled domination.

K D Bracher, W Sauer and G Schultz: Die nationalsozialistische Machtergreifung (1960).

Nazi-Soviet Pact. See *Ribbentrop-Molotov Pact*.

Neo-Hegelians. Group consisting of disciples of the philosopher *Hegel*. They were also called 'Left Hegelians' because of their radical political position. Prominent members were D F Strauss, A Ruge, B and E Bauer, and Stirner. Others like L Feuerbach and Moses Hess used the Neo-Hegelian dialectic to prove the need for communism. The young Hegelians interpreted their master's doctrine as a philosophy of revolutionary action. In their desire for rational progress they turned against religion and the state, particularly the Prussian state. Their chief organ, the 'Hallische Jahrbücher', was repeatedly prohibited in Prussia. The Neo-Hegelians were overconfident that the power of their minds could change realities, but they lacked the support of a clearly defined social class. Hence the importance of this radicalism during the last years of the *Vormärz* should not be overestimated.

Neo-Rankeans (Jung-Rankianer). Historians who modelled their historical writing on L v *Ranke* in opposition to both the political historiography of *Treitschke* and the social history of Lamprecht. The neo-Rankeans wanted to recognize the tendencies ('ideas') which really moved an historical period. Their leader was M Lenz (1850–1932), other neo-Rankeans being H *Delbrück*, Giesebrecht, Sybel and E Marcks.
H H Krill de Capello: Die Rankerenaissance. Max Lenz und Erich Marcks (1962).

Nero-Order. Order issued by *Hitler* on 19 Mar 1945 to destroy all military, industrial and logistic facilities which the enemy could make use of in the war. The order was not fully implemented, thanks partly to non-observance by *Speer* and other party officials in co-operation with industry.

Neuer Kurs. Term for the foreign policy as pursued after the fall of *Bismarck* in 1890 by *Wilhelm II* and his Chancellor *Caprivi*, who renounced the *Reinsurance Treaty* with Russia. The *Neuer Kurs*, contrary to the precautions of *Realpolitik*, disregarded the danger of a Franco-Russian *rapprochement* without balancing it by a permanent understanding with Britain.
J C G Rooehl: Germany without Bismarck (1967).

Neurath. Konstantin Baron v (2 Feb 1873–14 Aug 1956); diplomat. He was ambassador in London (1930–32) and *Reichsminister* for foreign affairs in the cabinets of *Papen* and *Schleicher*, retaining his post under *Hitler*. He joined the *NSDAP* in 1933. During his term of office Germany left the League of Nations, introduced conscription (*Wehrpflicht*), concluded the *London Naval Agreement*, and reoccupied the Rhineland. On 4 Feb 1938 he was replaced by *Ribbentrop* but remained minister without portfolio and was chairman of the *Geheimer Kabinettsrat*. In Mar 1939 he became 'Reichsprotektor' of *Bohemia-Moravia*, in which capacity he was responsible for terrorism and germanization. On 27 Sept 1941 he resigned because of old age. The *Nuremberg Tribunal* sentenced him to 15 years' imprisonment. He was released in 1954.
H A Jacobsen: Neuraths Aussenpolitik 1933–38 (1968).

107

New Era (Neue Ära). Change of course in Prussian policy in autumn 1858, acknowledging the growing importance of the liberal bourgeoisie. The 'New Era' was introduced by the future Emperor *Wilhelm I*, who was installed as Prince Regent for his brother *Friedrich Wilhelm IV* against strong opposition by the *Camarilla*. Wilhelm sought a certain understanding with the Liberals who had triumphed in the elections for the *Abgeordnetenhaus*. On 7 Nov he replaced the reactionary *Manteuffel* cabinet by a government of moderately liberal aristocrats (including Karl Anton, R v Auerswald), mostly belonging to the *Wochenblattpartei*. In an address to them the prince raised hopes for reforms and an active national policy, but he also referred to the need of an army reform. This led to the *constitutional conflict*, which ended in 1861 what had been prematurely hailed as a new era of liberal rule.

New Order (of Europe). National Socialist propaganda slogan voiced after the victory over France in 1940. The New Order was the outline of *Hitler*'s war aims: domination of the European continent from the Atlantic to the Ural Mountains by a 'Germanic Empire of the German Nation' with direct (in the east) or indirect (in the west) rule of Germany over the various parts, whose exact role was to be left undecided until after the war. The implication of a united European campaign against 'Bolshevism' was subordinated to the *Lebensraum* ideology. The unfavourable course of the war from 1942 on prevented the full realization of the New Order as envisaged in the 'Generalplan Ost' for the *resettlement* in Eastern Europe. The New Order had to give way to the defence of the 'Fortress of Europe'.

L Gruchmann: Nationalsozialistische Grossraumordnung (1962).

Nibelungentreue. Political catchword first used in the Bosnian crisis of 1908–09. It denoted the unconditional faithfulness of Germany to her ally Austria-Hungary regardless of her own interests, because Germany was otherwise afraid to lose her only ally. It was instrumental in the drawing of the *blank cheque* of 1914.

Nietzsche, Friedrich Wilhelm (15 Oct 1844–25 Aug 1900); philosopher. Influenced by Schopenhauer and R *Wagner* in his youth, he concluded his psychological observations by contending that all human behaviour could be reduced to a single basic drive, 'The Will to Power' (posthumously published in 1906). The highest state to be reached by man was that of 'superman', who could enjoy the exercise of power unrestrained by moral considerations. Nietzsche's aphoristic writings were contemptuous of bourgeois Liberalism and Christianity. They provided the catchwords for the master race theory of *Pan-Germanism* and *National Socialism*, under which the essence of his thought was deliberately perverted to serve as a justification for a ruthless power policy. In fact, Nietzsche's complex philosophy had tried to trace the deepest roots of human nature and gave expression to the cultural crisis of the late 19th century.

K Jaspers: Nietzsche (3rd edition, 1950).

Night-and-Fog-Decree. Decree issued personally by *Hitler* on 7 Dec 1941 to arrest all persons who endangered German security in the German-occupied territories in Western Europe. If not immediately shot, they were to be deported under the cover of 'darkness and fog'. No information on their whereabouts and fate was to be given. The decree, which was carried out by the *SD*, was the German reaction to increased activities of the French resistance.

Night of the Broken Glass. See *Crystal Night*.

Non-Aggression Pact, German-Polish. Non-aggression pact between Germany and Poland concluded on 26 Jan 1934. It aroused great surprise, because the German *Revisionspolitik* was largely directed against Poland, which had profited from two-thirds of the German losses due to the Treaty of *Versailles*. By means of this pact German diplomacy sought to forestall Franco-Polish preventive action. The purely tactical character of the pact became evident in 1939, when Germany launched the first of her *Blitzkriege* against Poland.

Norddeutsche Allgemeine Zeitung. Daily newspaper founded in 1861 in Berlin. It was regarded as the mouthpiece of *Bismarck*, a fact which gave it a semi-official character. From 1919 it changed its name to *Deutsche Allgemeine Zeitung*. In 1920 it was taken over by the *Stinnes* concern, and in the 1930s by the government. From 1939 it was published by the Nazi successor to the *Ullstein* Co ('Deutscher Verlag'). It then became important for publishing (semi-official) articles on foreign policy.

Norddeutscher Lloyd. Merchant shipping company founded in 1857 in Bremen. From 1876 it served all important ports on the American east coast. In 1884 it won its first 'Blue Ribbon'. Postal service with East Asia and Australia was started in 1886, freight service in 1905. After Allied confiscations in 1919 it reconstructed its fleet and in 1938 had 85 vessels with 618,000 BRT, which was again lost in World War II.

North German Confederation (Norddeutscher Bund). Confederation of Prussia and 17 smaller German states, established by *Bismarck* after the Prussian victory over Austria in the *Seven Weeks' War* (1886). The constitution of the confederation was accepted by the constituent North German *Reichstag* on 16 Apr 1867, endorsed by the allied states on 17 Apr and enforced on 1 July. Its main ideas were thought out by *Bismarck*. The *Bundesrat* was the supreme organ and representative of the sovereignty of the confederation; it was appointed by the 'Bundespräsidium' (federal presidency), which was hereditary and lay in the hands of the Prussian King, who exercised command over the army and appointed the *Bundeskanzler*. All other executive tasks were executed by Prussian offices. The constitution of the confederation guaranteed the total hegemony of Prussia and favoured the Bonapartist regime of Bismarck. It was enlarged and became the *Deutsches Reich* by the *November*

Treaties (1870), which modified the constitution to suit the entry of the German states south of the River Main (Bavaria, Baden, Württemberg), but the institutions of the confederation were essentially continued throughout the German Empire (*Constitution* of 1871).

R Dietrich (ed): Europa und der Norddeutsche Bund (1968).

Noske, Gustav (9 July 1868–30 Nov 1946); Social-Democratic politician. A *Reichstag* deputy from 1906, Noske became a member of the *Rat der Volksbeauftragten* after the retreat of the *USPD*. Noske who had quelled the *Kiel Naval Mutinies* in Nov 1918, put down the *Spartakus* uprisings of 1919 with the help of government troops and *Freikorps*. From 1919 to 1920 he was the first *Reichswehr* minister of the *Weimar Republic*. After the *Kapp Putsch*, during which he showed little authority towards the generals, Noske was forced to resign by his party comrades. Lacking a competent successor to the controversial Noske, the *SPD* had to cede his post to the bourgeois parties in the second *Weimar coalition*.

U Czisnik: Gustav Noske; ein sozialdemokratischer Staatsmann (1970).

Notverordnungen. Emergency decrees enacted under art. 48 of the *Constitution* in the *Weimar Republic*. They enabled the *Reichspräsident* to abrogate some of the human rights in the event of danger to security and order. They also made provision for the employment of armed forces and gave monarchical power to the president, who was obliged to give notice to the *Reichstag* (which could initiate the revision of an emergency decree). The decrees were applied by *Ebert* during the *Kapp Putsch* and the *Munich (Bierkeller) Putsch*. *Brüning's* government largely depended upon them.

November Revolution. Overthrow of the Hohenzollern monarchy in Nov 1918. The revolution had its roots in the denial of constitutional reforms (*Constitution of 1871, three class suffrage*), the rise of the socialist movement (*SPD*) and the growing radicalization of the proletariat during World War I. The imminent collapse of the German empire in Sept 1918 sparked off the naval mutiny of 3–4 Nov (*Kiel Naval Mutinees*), which was the beginning of the revolution which spread to other large towns (*Bremen, Munich Soviet Republic*) including the capital, Berlin (*Spartacist Uprising, Spartakusbund*). To stop the revolution, the last imperial Chancellor, *Max von Baden*, announced the Kaiser's abdication and appointed the Social Democrat *Ebert* as *Reichskanzler*. On 9 Nov, at 2 pm, *Scheidemann* proclaimed the Republic; two hours later K *Liebknecht* proclaimed the Socialist Republic. The Kaiser emigrated to Holland; all princes abdicated. All over Germany workers' councils were formed (*Workers' and Soldiers' Councils*). Their national conference in Berlin (16–20 Dec) settled the question of a Soviet or parliamentary system in favour of the latter. The *Rat der Volksbeauftragten* acted as an interim government. The elections for the *National Assembly* on 19 Jan 1919 inaugurated the *Weimar Republic*.

A J Ryder: German Revolution of 1918 (1967).

November Treaties. Treaties between the *North German Confederation* and the South German states (Baden, Württemberg, Bavaria, Hessen) concluded in Nov 1870. They were negotiated by *Bismarck*, who succeeded in treating each South German delegation separately at Versailles and isolated Bavaria from Baden and Hessen, which signed treaties on the basis of the North German constitution on 15 Nov. These were the basis for the November Treaties with Bavaria (23 Nov) and Württemberg (25 Nov), which only preserved certain prerogatives (*reserved rights*), but could not achieve a more federal structure of the new German state. The treaties were the constitutional basis for the foundation of the *Deutsches Reich* as manifested in the *Kaiserproklamation*.

NSDAP (Nationalsozialistische Deutsche Arbeiterpartei). Party of the *National Socialist movement*. Its leader was A *Hitler*. The predecessor of the NSDAP, the 'Deutsche Arbeiterpartei' (DAP), was founded in 1919. The 25 points of the party programme of 24 Feb 1920 became the unchanged basis of the NSDAP. It agitated against the Treaty of *Versailles*, demanded *Lebensraum* and contained anti-Semitic polemics. Socialist items (eg confiscation of war profits, land reform) were purely demagogical. In its beginnings the *NSDAP* was supported by military and industrial circles in Munich. Until 1923 the party was so powerful as to organize the *Munich (Bierkeller) Putsch*, after which it was temporarily prohibited. In the stable years of the *Weimar Republic* the vociferous agitation of the NSDAP (*Völkischer Beobachter*) remained without influence upon German politics, but after its revival the NSDAP became a national party. Hitler secured his leadership against the left-wing (*Strasser*). Only during the world economic crisis of 1928–29 did the party win political relevance. From 1930 the NSDAP increased its share of votes and entered provincial state governments. Now the party drew growing support from big business circles (Freundeskreise), which helped to finance the electoral campaigns. In July 1932 the NSDAP further advanced and became the largest parliamentary party in the *Reichstag* (37.4 per cent, 230 seats). Despite the setback of Nov 1932 (33.1 per cent) the NSDAP became the ruling party on 30 Jan 1933. After the *Nazi seizure of power* the NSDAP was the only party in the state and soon controlled the whole political and cultural life (*Gleichschaltung*). Its all-embracing power was visibly demonstrated at annual party rallies in Nuremberg. The NSDAP was structured according to the *Führer* principle. Hitler enjoyed unchallenged authority. From his closest collaborators (*Hess, Bormann, Göring*) the hierarchy extended to the *Gauleiter*, the local branch leaders and the 'block wardens', who watched over their fellow-citizens.

This pyramid had its equivalent in the numerous sub-organizations (*SA, SS, DAF, Hitler Youth*, unions for trades and professions). This party apparatus secured totalitarian rule over the German people. The *Nuremberg Tribunal* declared the hard core of the NSDAP a criminal organization.

D Orlow: History of the Nazi Party, 2 vols (1973).

Nuremberg Laws. Racial laws of 15 Sept 1935. They consisted of a 'national citizens law' (Reichsbürgergesetz) and a law for 'the protection of German blood and honour'. The former divided all German citizens into national citizens and subjects, giving full political rights only to the citizens. Jews were excluded from citizenship. The regulations of 14 Nov 1935 arbitrarily defined a Jew by his religious profession (or that of his ancestors). The second part of the Nuremberg Laws prohibited inter-marriage between Jews and non-Jews as well as sexual intercourse, which was branded as 'racial shame'. The laws caused the systematic exclusion of Jews from the national community. By 1939 they could no longer associate with non-Jews, use no public amenities (schools, parks, libraries) and were ordered to live in ghettos; by 1941 they were forbidden the use of public transport; all over 6 years of age had to wear a yellow badge. Jewish communities lost their legal basis. The laws and their supplements were a practical application of the *Aryan racial doctrine*.

J Wulf: Die Nürnberger Gesetze (1960).

Nuremberg Party Rallies. See *NSDAP*.

Nuremberg Trials. See *Nuremberg Tribunal*.

Nuremberg Tribunal. International court at Nuremberg in 1945–46 which tried 24 leading members of the *NSDAP*, the Nazi government and the *Wehrmacht* as well as 6 Nazi organizations. The charges – conspiracy and crimes against peace and crimes against humanity – were based on the statute of the Nuremberg Trial which made these offences punishable. The Nuremberg Tribunal passed 12 death sentences, of which 10 were executed: *Ribbentrop*, *Kaltenbrunner*, *Frank*, *Frick*, *Streicher*, *Seyss-Inquart*, *Rosenberg*, *Keitel*, *Jodl* and Sauckel (*Fremdarbeiter*). *Göring* and *Ley* committed suicide; *Bormann* was sentenced to death in absence. Those sentenced to imprisonment (eg *Neurath*, *Hess*, *Dönitz*, *Schirach*, *Speer*) were brought to the war criminals' jail at Berlin-Spandau. The trial was followed by 12 further trials in 1947-49 by an American court at Nuremberg which dealt with concentration camp surgeons and industry (*IG Farben*).

S S Glueck: Nuremberg Trial and Aggressive War (1946); W E Benton and G Grimm (eds): Nuremberg, German Views of the War Trials (1955); W Maser: Nürnberg, Tribunal der Sieger (1976).

Oberpräsident. The highest civil servant of a *Provinz* in Prussia from 1815 to 1945.

Oberste Heeresleitung (OHL). Supreme German command in World War I. According to the constitution of 1871 (*Reichsverfassung*, 1), the armed forces were neither subordinated to the *Reichstag* nor to the government. While the first and second OHL (*Moltke*, *Falkenhayn*) did not attempt to exercise political power from their military positions, the third OHL under *Hindenburg* and *Ludendorff* from 1917 increasingly forced the government to comply with its wishes for military conduct irrespective of diplomatic consequences (*U-Boat Warfare*) and also interfered in questions of war and peace policy (*Peace*

Resolution). The ascendancy of the OHL to political power led to the dismissal of *Bethmann Hollweg* and the appointment of *Michaelis*. In 1918 the OHL was also largely responsible for the annexionist terms of the treaty of *Brest-Litovsk*.

G Ritter: Staatskunst und Kriegshandwerk, vols III–IV (1964–68).

Offenburg Manifesto. Claims of the South-West German radical Democrats, passed on 12 Sept 1847 at a meeting presided over by *Hecker* and Struve. The programme demanded the equality of all citizens instead of the system of privileges: equal taxation by a progressive income tax; access of all to educational institutions. It also included the 'fundamental laws' (individual freedom etc). The open demand for a republic was avoided but the overthrow of all monarchist regimes in Germany was the final aim of the authors of the programmes which called for a parliament constituted on the basis of universal suffrage and administrative self-government instead of the old civil service regime. Juries, a militia, and (for the first time) the equality between capital and labour were advocated. The Offenburg Manifesto signified a clear break of the Democrats with the Liberals.

OKW (Oberkommando der Wehrmacht). Military staff of the *Führer* placed under his direct command. The OKW was formed in Feb 1938, after the *Fritsch Plot* and the dismissal of *Blomberg*, by transforming the *Wehrmacht* office in the war ministry. It also embraced the War Economy and Armament Office of the Armed Forces ('WiRuAmt'). The OKW co-ordinated and directed the three branches of the Wehrmacht with special emphasis on planning. It was headed by *Keitel* and his close assistant *Jodl*.

Old-Age Insurance Act. Third act of Bismarckian social legislation (*social insurance*) passed in 1889. It provided for old-age pensions for the workers, the amount of which – partly subsidized by the state – was paid out at a common rate in the entire Reich from 1899. The 'Reichsversicherungsordnung' of 1911 extended the scope of the act to include provisions for dependants (widows' and orphans' pensions).

Olmütz Punktation. Agreement of 29 Nov 1850, concluded between Prussia and Austria in Olomouc (Moravia). It regulated the relationship of the two powers and signified the abandonment of the Prussian *Union Plan*. The development leading to the Olmütz Punktation was sparked off by the conflict in Electoral Hesse. Here the Elector Friedrich Wilhelm I (1802–75), after violating the constitution signed by his father Wilhelm II in 1831 (*Hassenpflug*), applied for support to the Frankfurt *Bundestag*. Thereupon Austrian and Bavarian troops entered Hessian territory on 31 Oct 1850. To defend the roads that linked Prussia with her territories in the Rhineland, Prussian troops also marched into Hesse. This led to an imminent danger of war between Austria and Prussia which were estranged over the *Union Plan*. But as Russia stood behind Austria, Prussia had temporarily to give up its hegemonial aspirations. Its diplomatic defeat also embittered Conservative circles (*Camarilla*).

Ordensburgen. Top category in the National Socialist school system. They were supervised by the *NSDAP* and controlled by the *SS*, which also provided the staff. They were modelled on the castles of the Teutonic Order and provided the education of a new elite. Their pupils were recruited from the most reliable of the *National Socialist schools* and the 'Napola'.

Organisation Consul. Secret terrorist right-wing organization, which was formed out of ex-members of the *Marinebrigade Erhardt* after the *Kapp-Putsch* (1920). It was anti-republican and fought for a violent abolition of parliamentary democracy. It was pledged to anti-Communism and Teutonic racialism. Led by Captain Erhardt, it had 5,000 members and was responsible for numerous political murders including those of *Rathenau* and *Erzberger*.

Organisation Todt. Organization founded by F Todt in 1938 to carry out construction work. Recruited from the ex-unemployed, it built the *Autobahnen* and the *Westwall*. In World War II Todt became minister of armaments and munitions. The ranks of the organization were filled up with *Fremdarbeiter*, who helped to construct military defence installations such as air-raid shelters and the Atlantic wall.

Ossietzky, Karl v (3 Oct 1889–4 May 1938); pacifist journalist. He attacked militarism, rearmament and opportunism in the politics of the *Weimar Republic*. From 1927 he edited the 'Weltbühne', a periodical giving him international reputation. In 1931 a German court sentenced him to 18 months' imprisonment for alleged military espionage. From 1933 he was imprisoned in several concentration camps. World-wide protest and the bestowal of the Nobel Prize for Peace in 1936 secured his transfer to a hospital. He and all other Germans were forbidden to accept any Nobel Prize in the future by *Hitler's* decree of Jan 1937.

Osthilfe. Relief programme for the Eastern provinces. It was started as East Prussian Aid in 1928; on 31 Mar 1931 it was extended to all East Elbian districts. It was intended to promote the financial healing of agriculture in the East, but it failed because of irregularities in the distribution of funds. In 1932 a budget committee enquiring into the 'Osthilfe scandal' failed to reach any conclusion before the dissolution of the *Reichstag*.

Ostmarkenverein. Propaganda organization founded in 1894 to promote germanization in the Eastern provinces of Prussia. Its members were often called 'Hakatisten' after the initials of their three founders *Hansemann*, Kennemann and Tiedemann. They never became a mass movement (c 50,000 members in 1911), but their rigid anti-Polish attitude influenced German public opinion and the negative image of Germany's Polish policy abroad. After the German-Polish *Non-Aggression Pact* of 26 Jan 1934 the organization was dissolved by the *Gestapo* and replaced by the 'Bund Deutscher Osten'.

A Galos, F H Gentzen and W Jakobczyk: Die Hakatisten. Der Deutsche Ostmarkenverein 1894–1934 (1966).

Pan-Germanism. Term mainly used outside Germany for the German nationalist movement. It was first employed during the *wars of liberation* by patriotic writers (*Arndt*, Fichte, *Jahn*) who overstated the value of German national consciousness in contrast to Western European civilization. The ideal Germany of Pan-Germanism was to include all German-speaking peoples and some of the neighbours (Dutch, Flemish, Swiss), for all peoples of Teutonic origin were attributed a common 'tribal consciousness'. The Rhine from source to mouth was regarded as purely German. Many writers also claimed the Nordic peoples of Scandinavia and *Lebensraum* in the East for the German 'cultural mission'. These trends were supported by the master race theory and the *Mitteleuropa* idea. After 1848–49 Pan-Germanism underwent an anti-democratic and xenophobic development. In the 1890s its supporters became organized in the *Alldeutscher Verband*. While Pan-Germanism was not official German policy before 1914, its claims (*Kolonialpolitik*) influenced *Weltpolitik*. In 1918 the Treaty of *Brest-Litovsk* seemed to realize much of the dream of Pan-Germanism which did not acknowledge the defeat of World War I and passed into the *Weimar Republic*, where, intellectually supported by *geopolitics*, it merged with *National Socialism*. In 1945 the *Vertreibung* deprived Pan-Germanism of its *Volksdeutsche* (ethnic Germans), whose claim for a 'right to the homeland' together with the will for German reunification formed the postwar relics of Pan-Germanism until the late 1960s.

H Pross: Die Zerstörung der deutschen Politik (1959).

Panther's Spring. Arrival of the German warship 'Panther' in the Moroccan port of Agadir on 1 July 1911. The Panther Spring was ordered by *Kiderlen*, who declared the French occupation of Fez in May 1911 to be a violation of the Act of Algeciras. Germany demanded new negotiations with a view to achieving economic co-operation in Morocco. Though the Panther Spring demonstration accelerated the conclusion of the *Moroccan Agreements*, the *Auswärtiges Amt* had misjudged the international reaction to its gunboat diplomacy, which caused the second Moroccan crisis during which the British, stirred by German *Flottenpolitik*, held together with the French against a redistribution of power in Germany's favour. Thus the Panther's Spring, instead of shattering the entente cordiale, strengthened Allied solidarity against Germany (*Encirclement*).

I C Barlow: The Agadir Crisis (1947).

Papen, Franz v (29 Oct 1879–2 May 1969); statesman. Formerly an unimportant Prussian *Landtag* deputy of the right wing of the *Zentrum*, he was appointed *Reichskanzler* by *Hindenberg* on 1 June 1932. A monarchist at heart, he formed the *Cabinet of Barons* without any parliamentary backing, although he accomplished the cancellation of the *reparations* payments for which the way was paved by his predecessor *Brüning*. The deposition of the Prussian *Braun-Severing* government on 20 July, and his assumption of office as 'Reichskommisar' of Prussia (until 7 Apr 1933), was a coup d'état to impress the Nazis, who became the strongest party on 31 July. Papen failed to satisfy *Hitler*'s thirst for power by offering him the vice-chancellorship. Papen's plans for an authoritarian constitutional reform were thwarted by *Schleicher*'s resignation as *Reichswehr* minister, which in turn forced that of Papen on 3 Dec 1932. Papen then strove for the appointment of Hitler, whose cabinet he joined as vice-chancellor, hoping to control him. This proved illusory when the *Röhm-Putsch* took place (30 July 1934), after which Papen resigned. But he continued to serve the Reich as ambassador in Vienna until the day before the *Anschluss* (10 Mar 1938) and in Turkey (1939–44). Acquitted by the *Nuremberg Tribunal*, he was sentenced to 8 years' imprisonment by a German court in 1947 but released in 1949.

Paris Convention. Treaty between Prussia and France concluded on 8 Sept 1808. It laid down the amount of the Prussian war contribution at 140 million francs (which was reduced to 120 million on 5 Nov by the intervention of the Czar). The money was to be paid in monthly instalments of 4 million francs. In return, the evacuation of the Prussian territory, except certain strong points on the River Oder, within 40 days was granted. The size of the Prussian army was limited to 42,000 men for ten years. In the event of a war against Austria, Prussia was to support France with 16,000 men. The payment agreed upon proved an unbearable burden for Prussia, which was soon in arrears and thus could not observe the Paris Convention.

Paulskirche. See *Frankfurt National Assembly*.

Peace Offer (1916). See *Central Powers*.

Peace Resolution. Peace appeal drafted on 13 July 1917 by members of the *Interfraktioneller Ausschuss* and passed by the *Reichstag* on 19 July 1917 (by 212 against 126 votes with 17 abstentions). It was supported by the *SPD*, *Zentrum, Fortschrittspartei* and other Liberals. The peace resolution demanded a peace of 'no annexations and no indemnities' and aimed at a compromise peace with the Allies. The *Oberste Heeresleitung* used it to force the resignation of *Bethmann Hollweg* and the nomination of *Michaelis*, who accepted it 'as I understand it'. But the Reichstag majority of the future *Weimar Coalition* remained united over the resolution and opposed to the military group.

Peasants' Liberation. Liberation of the Prussian peasants within the framework of reforms by *Stein* and *Hardenberg*. After increasing pressure from peasants, the liberation was accomplished in three stages. The edict of 9 Oct 1807 provided for the abolition of serfdom and forced domestic service. The 'Regulierungsedict' of 14 Sept 1811 regulated the hitherto unresolved questions of property right and mortgages: the landlord could be compensated for the abolition of statute-labour by the cession of a third to half of the peasant land or by payment of a rent. But the declaration of 26 May 1816 limited this to peasants able to provide draught animals. The liberation was a protracted process; it was only completed in mid-19th century (edict of 2 Mar 1850). The freedom of the peasants remained limited until the abolition of patrimonial jurisdiction in 1877.

116

People's ... See *Volks—*.

Peters, Carl (27 Sept 1856–10 Sept 1918), German colonialist. Full of admiration for the British Empire after two visits to London, he founded the Gesellschaft für deutsche Kolonisation (*Kolonialverein*) in 1884. The same year he went to East Africa where he made 'treaties' with the native chiefs, which formed the basis of *German East Africa*, for which he received *Bismarck*'s placet in 1885. In 1887 Peters led an expedition to expand German influence into Central Africa (*Mittelafrika*) and to the Upper Nile, but his endeavours were thwarted by the *Heligoland-Zanzibar Treaty* of 1890, which annulled Peters's treaties with the King of Buganda. In 1891 Peters became Reichskommissar for Kilimanjaro, but was dismissed in 1897 for maltreatment of the Africans.

Plebiscite Districts. German border districts where a plebiscite was held according to the Treaty of *Versailles* (1919) to determine the future national affiliation of the area. In Northern Slesvig only the southern zone voted for Germany. Eupen-Malmedy fell to Belgium after an irregular, non-secret ballot. East and West Prussia voted for the Reich with an overwhelming majority. In Upper Silesia 60 per cent voted for Germany, but the pro-German districts were not adjacent to one another. The Allies allotted a third of the territory and half of the population to Poland. A decision in the *Saar District* was postponed until 1935.

Polish Circles. Polish parliamentary parties in the Prussian *Landtag* and the *Reichstag*, 1849 to 1918. They originated in the national associations that sprang up during the *Revolution of 1848*. While the 'Liga Polska' was prohibited in 1851, other associations continued to secure the organizational unity of all Polish deputies. Their programme of 1849, which hardly changed until 1918, propagated the preservation of national rights (as assured by the Congress of *Vienna*), of civil rights for Polish nationals and of Polish national characteristics and institutions against the anti-Polish Prussian-German policy (*Ansiedlungskommission*) and propaganda (*Ostmarkenverein*). The majority in the Polish Circles was aristocratic-Roman Catholic, from the late 1890s bourgeois-national intelligentsia. They then held 14–20 seats in the Reichstag, 12–17 in the *Abgeordnetenhaus* and 10 votes in the *Herrenhaus*. Here the Poles were loyal, whereas the Polish Circles in the Landtag fought for the introduction of Polish as a teaching language. In their opposition to the expropriation bill of 1907–08, the Polish Circles in the Reichstag were supported by the *Freisinnige Partei* and the *Zentrum* and other national minorities. In 1914 the Polish Circles joined the *Burgfriede* for Russophobe motives; in 1917 they opposed the *Peace Resolution* as unfavourable for the realization of national self-determination, which they openly asked for in their last appearance in Oct 1918.

Posadowsky Wehner, Count Arthur (3 June 1845–23 Oct 1932); politician. He was secretary of state of the 'Reichsschatzamt' (treasury) in 1893 and of the

Reichsamt of the interior in 1897, and representative of the *Reichskanzler* and Prussian minister until 1907. He was appointed as a 'strong man' against the labour movement, but when he did not find a *Reichstag* majority for a repressive policy (*Zuchthausvorlage*), he introduced new reforms continuing the *Sozialpolitik* of *Berlepsch* and *Lohmann* without sharing their view of an equal partnership of the working class in society. His measures included an extension of the *social insurance* (1901–03), the establishment of labour courts for employers, and daily payments for deputies. He determined German domestic policy from the turn of the century till *Bülow's* break with the *Zentrum* in autumn 1906.

Potsdam Agreement. Agreement concluded on 2 Aug 1945 between the USA, the Soviet Union and Great Britain concerning the preparation of a peace treaty with, and the treatment of, Germany after her defeat in World War II. The agreement established an Allied Control Council in Berlin to deal with the administration of Germany. Claims for reparations were to be satisfied by the dismantlement of industrial plants. A unitary economic system for Germany was to be revived. Germany's eastern provinces (East Prussia, Pommerania, Silesia) were placed under Soviet and mainly Polish administration. The *Vertreibung* of the German population from there was to be carried out as humanly as possible. In its territorial stipulations, Potsdam fixed a status quo for Central Europe pending a future peace conference.

Princes, compensation for. Compensation of the deposed princes, whose fortunes had been confiscated in the *November Revolution* of 1919. The German states concluded agreements with the ex-monarchs in 26 separate treaties, the first of which was signed in Württemberg (Nov 1918) and the last with the Hohenzollerns on 6 Sept 1926. (The Hohenzollerns were granted about 250,000 acres of land and 15 million *Reichsmark*.) The compensation was controversial and led to a campaign by parties of the left (*SPD*, *KPD*), who failed in their referendum to win a decision for expropriation without compensation.

Protective Tariff (Schutzzoll). Protective tariff introduced in 1879. Toward the end of the 1870s German agriculture was challenged by US wheat and Bismarck was determined to protect it for reasons of Social Conservatism (*Sammlungspolitik*). Industry, hit by the great depression of 1873 (*Gründerzeit*), needed protection too and Bismarck was determined to protect a great iron and steel industry so as to ensure German strength in wartime (*Krupp*). Thus agricultural tariff was to satisfy the Junkers, and industrial tariff the capitalists: it was opposed by the National Liberals, who split in two in 1880. The protective tariff bill was passed on 12 June 1879 and hence Germany was a protectionist country. An economic appreciation of the tariff policy must, however, take into consideration the trend in all other countries except Britain, the British competition for the German iron industry, and the oncoming crisis in agriculture due to imports from Russia and overseas.

I Lambi: Free Trade and Protection in Germany 1868 to 1879 (1963); K W Hardach: Die Bedeutung der wirtschaftlichen Faktoren bei der Wiedereinführung der Eisen- und Getreidezölle in Deutschland 1879 (1967).

Provinz. Administrative unit in Prussia from 1815. Since the decree of the *Provinzialordnung* (1875) a *Provinz* was also a territorial corporate body ('Provinzialverband'). Head of the administration was the *Oberpräsident*; the authority competent for resolutions concerning public duties was the 'Provinzialrat'; organs of the Provinz were the 'Provinziallandtag', which elected a provincial committee and a 'Landesdirektor' or 'Landeshauptmann', whose duty was to deal with the daily business and the representation of the Provinz. In 1933 provincial self-government was abolished.

Provinzialordnung. Regulations for the relation between the executive organ and the elected legislature in the structure of provincial government, on 29 June 1875. The latter was given the care for highways, road construction and water conservation; welfare duties (institutes for the blind and for the deaf and dumb etc) and cultural duties (monuments, museums). The 'Landesdirektor' (or 'Landeshauptmann') became head of the provincial legislature (*Provinz*). The Provinzialordnung was not immediately introduced in the provinces most affected by the *Kulturkampf* (Rhineland, Westphalia, Posen), but it was generally effective by 1888.

Provinzialstände. Representative corporate bodies of a *Provinz*, which were re-established (after their decay in the era of Absolutism) with limited competence in Prussia in 1823. The concept of estates as practised in the Provinzialstände was incompatible with modern constitutionalism. After the *Provinzialordnung* of 1875 they were superseded by provincial 'Provinziallandtage'.

Pulpit Clause (Kanzelparagraph). The 'pulpit clause' of 10 Dec 1871 was an addition to the *Strafgesetzbuch* (para 130a) as a legal precaution to remove ecclesiastical influence from politics. The clause prohibited priests to discuss public affairs in a manner prejudicial to public peace. It originated during the *Kulturkampf* in Bavaria, whose minister of culture had moved it in the *Bundesrat*. It was later used by the National Socialist dictatorship to suppress church resistance (*Kirchenkampf*).

Puttkammer, Robert v (5 May 1828–15 Mar 1900); Prussian minister. From 1879 minister of education, he was appointed to mitigate the effects of the *Kulturkampf*. In 1881 he became minister of the interior and vice-president of the *Staatsministerium*. His home policy was marked by police measures against the *SPD* and a militarization of the administration. In the 'era of Puttkammer' civil servants were chosen only from Conservative quarters and by a decree of 4 Jan 1885 they were obliged to be loyal to the government. After the accession of *Friedrich III* Puttkammer was dismissed in June 1888. His administrative policy laid the foundations for the reactionary spirit in the Prussian bureaucracy.

Quadruple Alliance. Treaty between Prussia, Austria and Britain, concluded on 20 Nov 1815 in Paris. It was based on the war alliance against France and designed for mutual assistance against the country of origin of revolution. The alliance lost its importance when France joined it (pentarchy of 1818).

Quidde, Ludwig (23 Mar 1858–5 Mar 1941); historian and politician. Before World War I he played a prominent part among the South German democrats. He was a pacifist and drafted a plan for international disarmament in 1913. From 1914 to 1929 he presided over the German Peace Society. In 1927 he became the second German to receive the Nobel Prize for Peace, one year after *Stresemann.*

Raeder, Ernst (24 Apr 1876–6 Nov 1960); admiral. He became chief of the naval high command in 1928. Raeder favoured an Atlantic war of supplies, which would cut off the enemy's sea-lines by quick formations. After differences with *Hitler* over the role of heavy surface vessels he resigned in 1943. The *Nuremberg Tribunal* found him guilty of conducting Germany's sea warfare and sentenced him to life imprisonment. He was, however, released in 1955.
C A Gemzell: Raeder, Hitler und Skandinavien (1965).

Raiffeisen, Friedrich Wilhelm (30 Mar 1818–11 Mar 1888); founder of rural co-operative banks. He met the needs of smallholders, rural craftsmen and village shopkeepers, enabling them to purchase potatoes and bread. Most of the capital was provided by philanthropically disposed wealthy farmers. Their property was sufficient as security for members of the Raiffeisen societies. By 1890 there existed 1,729 Raiffeisen banks, mainly centred in southern Germany.

Ranke, Leopold v (21 Dec 1795–23 May 1886); historian. His 'History of the Latin and Teutonic Peoples' (1824) secured him a chair at the *Berlin University*, where he was the first to establish a historical seminar. He taught there for 50 years. Ranke united the 18th-century concept of universal history with the Romanticist doctrine of individualism and organic development. He set up the maxim that a historian ought not to judge but to demonstrate 'how things really were'. He tried to accomplish this by means of a critical analysis of the sources. He concentrated on political order and discounted socio-economic forces. He is the founder of modern historiography and shaped historical-political thinking in 19th-century Germany (see *Neo-Rankeans*).
T H v Laue: L Ranke. The Formative Years (1950).

Rapallo. Place in Switzerland where Germany and Soviet Russia concluded a treaty on 16 Apr 1922. The treaty aimed at the normalization of Russo-German relations by a *rapprochement* for commercial, military and diplomatic reasons. The treaty provided for the immediate establishment of diplomatic and consular relations and the initiation of close economic relations on the basis of the most-favoured-nation clause. It was negotiated by *Wirth* during the Geneva conference on *reparations* and only hesitantly by his foreign minister *Rathenau*. Rapallo was criticized by the western powers as a counterpoise to *Locarno*. Rapallo initiated a phase of cordial relations between Germany and Russia which was confirmed by the Treaty of *Berlin*, 1926.

H Helbig: Die Träger der Rapallo-Politik (1958).

Rat der Volksbeauftragten. The 'council of the people's delegates' was the transitional government which functioned from 10 November 1918 to 10 February 1919 in the aftermath of the *November Revolution* of 1918. The council consisted of 6 members, 3 belonging to the *SPD* (*Ebert, Scheidemann, Landsberg*) and three to the *USPD* (Barth, Dittmann, Haase). The council was responsible to the *Vollzugsrat* and later to the *Zentralrat*. Its decrees had legislative power. Since foreign policy was determined by the armistice (*Compiègne*), it concentrated on home affairs and gave priority to social policy. But it neglected the connection between social and economic policy, which led to a rapid fall in productivity. Its social legislation included the *eight-hour day* and unemployment benefits. The electoral system was reformed. The political attitude of the council was rooted in the pre-war discussion of the Social Democratic party programme. The dissensions within the Socialist movement paralysed the council, from which the Independents withdrew after the employment of troops against the *Volksmarinedivision*. They were replaced by *Noske* and *Wissel* of the right-wing of the *SPD*. The council was superseded by the first (provisional) government of the *Weimar Republic*, formed after the elections to the *National Assembly* (19 Jan 1919).

S Miller and H Potthof: Die Regierung der Volksbeauftragten (1969).

Rathenau, Walther (29 Sept 1867–24 June 1922); industrialist, writer and statesman. He was the son of the founder of the AEG trust, of which he became president in 1915, when he built up the raw materials department. His economic views envisaged a community with industrial self-government, co-operation of the employees, and state control. Interested in international reconciliation and an experienced economist, he took part in the *reparations* conference of Spa (1920) and London (1921). He was *Reichsminister* for Reconstruction in *Wirth*'s cabinet from May to Nov 1921 and led the German delegations at Wiesbaden and Cannes. On 1 Feb 1922 he became foreign minister and reluctantly signed the *Rapallo* treaty. He was shot by a member of the *Organisation Consul*. Rathenau combined democratic convictions and pacifist ideals with devotion to realistic ideas of European reconstruction. His assassination was a blow to the prospects of the stabilization of the *Weimar Republic*.

P Berglar: Walther Rathenau; Sein Leben, sein Werk, seine Persönlichkeit (1970).

121

Realpolitik. Political expression coined by L v Rochau in 1853, it was intended to admonish German Liberalism (which had been led too much by pure ideology in 1848–49) to adapt its programme to political reality. The expression has been particularly used to describe *Bismarck*'s foreign policy. *Realpolitik*, as a 'policy of the possible' is neither identical with ruthless power politics nor with a pure politics of self-interest; its end is rather the limitation of political aims according to the existing realities. It is often criticized by its opponents as opportunism without principles.

H U Wehler (ed): Ludwig August von Rochau: Grundsätze der Realpolitik (1972).

Reformverein. Association founded in Oct 1862 in Frankfurt by *grossdeutsch*, particularist minded Liberals and Conservatives as a body antagonistic to the *Nationalverein*. It was mainly influential among civil servants and intellectuals in south and central Germany. It was dissolved in 1866.

W Real: Der deutsche Reformverein (1966).

Registry Offices (Standesämter). Registry offices established in 1875 (in Prussia in 1874) to take over from the Church the documentation of births, marriages and deaths. Simultaneously civil marriage was made obligatory. The establishment of the registry offices was aimed at reducing the influence of the Church during the *Kulturkampf*.

Reichsämter. From 1871 to 1918 the supreme offices of the German empire, corresponding to ministries. They were directly subordinated to the *Reichskanzler* and were each headed by a secretary of state. They were: the *Auswärtiges Amt*, the 'Reichsamt des Innern' (created in 1879 from the *Reichskanzleramt*), and offices for railways (1873), colonies (1907), food (1916, *War Food Office*), economy (1917) and labour exchange (1918). Their growing importance was due to the increase in national activity as a consequence of the transition from economic laissez faire to state intervention and the acceptance of former Prussian ministerial functions. This development led to the formation of a virtual central government polarizing with the *Reichstag*. In 1919 the offices were replaced by ministries (*Reichsminister*).

Reichsarbeitsdienst. Obligatory labour in National Socialist Germany by the law of 26 June 1935. It applied to all young people of both sexes between 18 and 25 years. The duration of the service was 6 months. It was conceived as a union of the army, the 'workers' state', and youth. It propagated the nobility of manual work as a service for the people, and was used for ideological education and pre-military training. It helped to ease unemployment.

H Köhler: Arbeitsdienst in Deutschland (1967).

Reichsbahn. German national railways. Early construction of railways had been primarily financed by private investors. The first line was opened in 1835 (Nuremberg-Fürth). The concept of a national system as proposed by F *List* in the 1830s was premature. Only after the establishment of a *Customs Union* and the foundation of the Reich (1871) were there new initiatives to create a centralized railway system. But since the federal states had preserved most of their traffic sovereignty (*reserved rights*), the Reichsbahn project of 1876 fell through. In 1878–79 Prussia began to nationalize the railways and the process was concluded by 1884. Other states followed suit and carried it out by 1900. In 1895 a Prussian-Hessian Railway Community comprising about two thirds of the existing German railway network had been founded. In World War I the railways were placed under a common war direction. In 1920–24 the Reichsbahn was finally established as an autonomous enterprise.

Reichsbank. National issuing bank situated in Berlin. Replacing the Prussian Bank by the bank law of 14 Mar 1875, it soon grew into a powerful monetary institution for the national credit circulation under the supervision of the government. It received autonomy by the law of 26 May 1922, becoming completely independent of the government on 30 Aug 1924 in accordance with the *Dawes Plan*. From 10 Feb 1937 the Reichsbank again came under state influence; on 15 June 1939 it was directly subordinated to the *Reichskanzler*. It was discontinued in 1945.

Reichsbanner Schwarz-Rot-Gold. Para-military union founded by the Social Democrats in 1924. Its name was chosen as a reaction to the national unions marching under pre-republican colours (black-white-red), eg the *Stahlhelm*. The *Reichsbanner* at first also comprised the *Zentrum* and the Democrats, after whose withdrawal it became an auxiliary organization of the *SPD*. In 1931 the *Reichsbanner* united with the *Freie Gewerkschaften*, the workers' sports clubs and other left-wing republican unions under the name of the 'Iron Front'.
K Rohe: Das Reichsbanner Schwarz-Rot-Gold (1966).

Reichsdeputationshauptschluss. Final resolution of a committee of the Imperial Diet of the Holy Roman Empire, passed on 25 Feb 1803. Strongly influenced by France and Russia the resolution aimed at compensating the German princes for their cessions of territory to France on the left bank of the Rhine by the Treaty of Lunéville (1801). Almost all ecclesiastical principalities and imperial cities were mediatized and secularized. Thus the resolution led to an increase in territory of the south and west German middle states and of Prussia. The foundation of three new Protestant electorates (Baden, Württemberg, Hesse-Cassel) ended the supremacy of the Roman Catholic princes and dignitaries of the Imperial Diet ('Reichsstände').

Reichserbhofgesetz. Law of entail of 29 Sept 1933, which aimed at preserving the peasantry as the 'blood source' of the German people by maintaining old German hereditary customs. The entailed estate could only be bequeathed undivided and neither be sold nor debited. The hereditary farmer had to be a citizen of German blood who had proved his 'purity of blood' back to 1 Jan 1800. The law, which realized the blood and soil ideology of *National Socialism*, signified the application of the *Aryan racial doctrine* to German agriculture.

123

Reichsexekution. Constitutional clause of the *Reich Constitution* of 1919 (arts. 13 and 14) in the *Weimar Republic*. According to the Reichsexekution the right of the central state (Reich) overruled that of the provincial states (Länder). The Reichsexekution was applied only once on 28 Oct 1923 against the Socialist-Communist government in Saxony and Thuringia. After Minister-President Zeigner had refused to exclude Communists from his cabinet, *Stresemann* ordered the Reichsexekution. A government of the right instead of the popular front was then forestalled by the *Landtag*, which elected the Socialist Fellisch as new minister-president.

K Hohlfeld: Die Reichsexekution gegen Sachsen im Jahre 1923 (1964).

Reichskanzlei. Office of the *Reichskanzler* established in 1878–79. Its duty was to keep the Chancellor informed on affairs of the empire and to help him shape his decisions. From 1919 it also took care of the daily business of the government and developed into an organ of growing political influence. Its head from 1919 was a secretary of state, from 1937 a *Reichsminister*.

Reichskanzler. (1) From 1871 the highest government official of the German empire, appointed by the Kaiser. President of the *Bundesrat* and the only minister, the Reichskanzler headed the entire administration of the Reich. Subordinated to him were the secretaries of state of the *Reichsämter*. All orders of the Kaiser (except for military commando acts) needed the counter-signature of the Reichskanzler in order to become valid (from 1878 this could also be done by a secretary of state): thus he took parliamentary responsibility for them. The Reichskanzler was not responsible to the *Reichstag*. It was not until 30 Oct 1918 that he was declared responsible to parliament. (2) Head of the German government from 1919 to 1934. From 1919 the Reichskanzler was appointed and dismissed by the *Reichspräsident*. The Reichskanzler nominated the *Reichsminister*, who needed the endorsement of the President. The Reichskanzler determined the course of German policy.

Reichskanzleramt. From 1871 the supreme office for the administration of all internal affairs of the German empire. After the separation of a number of departments as *Reichsämter* in 1879, the remainder of the Reichskanzleramt continued as the 'Reichsamt des Innern' (imperial office of the interior).

Reichskommissariate. Administrative units in German-occupied Europe during World War II. In northern and western Europe (Norway under J Terboven as 'Reichskommissar', the Netherlands under *Seyss-Inquart*) they were intended to become parts of a 'Germanic Empire of the German Nation', while eastern Europe was to be an area for German colonization, where the population was to be subjected within four Reichskommissariate: Ukraine, Ostland (Lithuania, Latvia, Estonia, Belorussia), Muscovy and Caucasia. Because of the failure of the Russian campaign, only the first two of these could be established under the commissioners E Koch and H Lohse. Formally the Reichskommissariate were subordinated to the Minister for the Occupied Territories (*Rosenberg*), but the

Reichskommissariate had far-reaching powers of their own. In all Reichskommissariate resistance movements formed to counteract the ruthless Nazi occupation policy (*Einsatzgruppen*).

Reichskonkordat. Treaty between Germany and the Vatican concluded on 20 July 1933. It guaranteed the freedom of the Roman Catholic Church to regulate its own affairs. The concordat raised the international prestige of *National Socialism*, which had been weakened by its terrorist policy at home (*Schutzhaftbefehle*).

Reichskulturkammer. Institution established on 22 Sept 1933, consisting of 7 chambers for fine arts, music, theatre, literature, press, broadcasting and film under the directorship of Goebbels. It comprised those active in cultural work, who undertook to join their respective chambers and to obey its instructions. It was generally closed to politically unreliable artists, who were thus prevented from practising their profession. It cemented the *Gleichschaltung* of Germany's cultural scene.

Reichslandbund. Agrarian league which succeeded the *Bund der Landwirte* in 1921. It included farmers of all ranks. Politically it was connected with the *DNVP*. Under the impact of Reichslandbund pressure the *Reichstag* passed an agricultural aid programme in 1928. In 1929 the Reichslandbund became an organization within the *Green Front*. In 1933 it was merged in the *Reichsnährstand*.

D Gessner: Agrarverbände in der Weimarer Republik (1976).

Reichsmark. Monetary unit of Germany from 1924, replacing the *Rentenmark*. The Reichsmark was convertible in gold or foreign currencies. According to the bank law of 1924, one Reichsmark equalled 1/2790 kg of fine gold. This standard remained valid until July 1931. The devaluation of the Reichsmark began with the world economic crisis when the circulation of money increased rapidly in Nazi Germany. During World War II the Reichsmark was almost completely devalued.

Reichsminister. Members of the central government from 1919. They were appointed by the *Reichspräsident* after being nominated by the *Reichskanzler*. Every Reichsminister was responsible to the *Reichstag*, a fact which increased the instability of the many cabinets during the *Weimar Republic*. From 1933 they were appointed by the Chancellor (*Hitler*).

Reichsnährstand. Agricultural organization created by the law of 13 Sept 1933. It was subordinated to the minister of agriculture, Darré (national peasants' leader from 1934), who could authorize it to regulate the production, sale and prices of agricultural goods, if this seemed suitable to the economy as a whole. Together with the *Reichserbhofgesetz*, it set an end to a free market economy in the agricultural sector without solving the structural crisis.

J E Farquharson: The Plough and the Swastika. The NSDAP and Agriculture in Germany, 1928–45 (1976).

Reichspost. A German national postal system had been organized by the Taxis family in the late 16th century, only to be replaced by state posts in the early 19th century. The first stamps were issued in Bavaria in 1849. Under H v Stephan (1831–97), from 1870 General Postmaster of the *North German Confederation*, the postal system developed into a model communication institution. From 1876 it was administered by the Reichspost including the telegraphic service: from 1880 there existed a central Reichspost office. However, the separate postal offices of Bavaria and Württemberg remained autonomous. It was not until 1921 that an all-comprising Reichspost was founded, which became an independent institution in 1924.

Reichspräsident. German head of state from 1919 to 1934. According to § 43 of the Reich *constitution*, he was to be elected directly by the people for seven years. He was eligible for re-election. In the first vote the candidate needed an absolute majority. The Reichspräsident appointed and dismissed the *Reichskanzler*, appointed the civil servants of the central administration, and issued and proclaimed the laws for the Reich. He exercised supreme command over the *Reichswehr* and represented the nation internationally; he could conduct the *Reichsexekution* and exercise emergency powers. Because of the need for the Chancellor's counter-signature, the Reichspräsident was dependent upon co-operation with a government responsible to parliament until 1932, when the inefficacy of the *Reichstag* diminished this dependence. The first Reichspräsident, F *Ebert*, was still elected by the *Weimar National Assembly* on 11 Feb 1919 and remained in office until his death in 1925. On 26 Apr 1925 *Hindenburg* was elected to succeed him. He was re-elected on 10 Apr 1932. After his death in 1934 the National Socialists merged the offices of Reichspräsident and Chancellor in that of *Führer*.

Reichsrat. Representative organ of the German states in the *Weimar Republic*. It was the successor institution to the *Bundesrat*, but in contrast to the latter the Reichsrat could only influence and not determine decisions. Its objections could be overruled by the *Reichstag*. The Reichsrat could not initiate any bills itself. It had no influence upon the central government, which was not dependent upon it. It comprised 67 seats in 1926 and 66 in 1928, of which 26 were Prussian. The Reichsrat was abolished by the National Socialists on 14 Feb 1934 (*Gleichschaltung*).

Reichssicherheitshauptamt. Office of the *SS* established on 27 Sept 1939 to unite all security services of the party and the state, ie the security police (*Gestapo* and criminal investigation) and the *SD*. The Reichssicherheitshauptamt was headed by *Heydrich*. Its establishment completed the seizure of power by the SS in all fields of security. The Reichssicherheitshauptamt was responsible for organizing atrocities at home and in the occupied territories, for which it was classified as a criminal organization by the *Nuremberg Tribunal*.

Reichstag (1). German parliament according to the constitution of the *North*

German Confederation of 17 Apr 1867. From 1871 the Reichstag, together with the emperor (*Deutscher Kaiser*), embodied the unity of the German empire. Assisted by the *Bundesrat*, the Reichstag was responsible for the legislation of the empire and played an important role in decisions relating to the annual budget, but the *Reichskanzler* was not responsible to it. The Reichstag was elected in direct general elections by secret ballot on the basis of universal suffrage and consisted of 397 members. It was convened annually by the Kaiser, who alone had the right to adjourn and close it. Elections were first held at intervals of three years. After 1885 the period was extended to five years. The Reichstag could only be dissolved by a decision of the Bundesrat with the consent of the Kaiser.

E Deuerlein: Der Reichstag (1963).

Reichstag (2). German parliament from 1919. From 1919 the Reichstag was the body representing the sovereign people and embodying the supreme power of the Reich. It was then elected according to a system of proportional representation on the basis of universal adult suffrage. The Reichstag was the legislative organ of the *Weimar Republic* endorsing the budget, international treaties and other important federal laws. It could be dissolved but not prorogued or closed by the *Reichspräsident*. Since the central government needed the confidence of the Reichstag, the latter had a decisive influence upon the formation of the cabinet. The constitutional possibility to withdraw the confidence without determining a successor repeatedly led to falls of governments. During the final crisis of the republic in 1930–32 the Reichstag, dominated by the growing parliamentary parties of the extreme right and left, was prevented from expressing a homogenous political will. After the *Nazi seizure of power* the Reichstag remained formally in existence, but only served to acclaim the declarations of the National Socialist government.

Reichstag Fire. Burning of the *Reichstag* building in Berlin on the evening of 27 Feb 1933. The fire was exploited by the Nazis as a pretext for the first wave of arrests and the prohibition of the *KPD*. From Sept to Dec 1933 the trial in connection with the fire took place in Leipzig. The Dutch Communist van der Lubbe was sentenced to death, but other prominent Communists (Torgler, Dimitroff) were acquitted. It is likely that the fire was organized by the Nazis themselves, probably on *Göring*'s order.

W Hofer and E Calic (eds): Der Reichstagsbrand (1972).

Reichsstatthalter. Eighteen governors appointed by *Hitler* in 1933 to abolish the federal structure of Germany. The Reichsstatthalter, mostly the *Gauleiter* of the corresponding regions, were all National Socialists who were called upon to put into practice the principles laid down by the *Reichskanzler*. By the law of 30 Jan 1934 they were subordinated to the minister of the interior, but they became relatively independent because their areas of responsibility did not directly overlap with those of the minister.

Reichsverband der Deutschen Industrie (RVDI). Industrial association founded in 1919 as the successor to the *Bund der Industriellen* and the *Centralverband Deutscher Industrieller*. The RVDI united the representatives of the leading heavy, electrical engineering and chemical industries. Under its chairman (1925–1931) E *Duisberg*, the RDVI tried to preserve the 'autonomy of the economy' against the *Sozialpolitik* of the *Weimar Republic*, but in the legal sanctioning of the *eight-hour-day* (1927) and the introduction of *unemployment insurance* it made its limited power evident. From 1926 the RDVI demanded a radical reform of economic policy and favoured a corporative structure of the state. In 1934 it was re-organized as the 'Reichsgruppe Industrie'.

Reichsverweser. Title of Archduke Johann of Austria, who was elected regent by the *Frankfurt National Assembly* on 29 June 1848. The appointment of a regent had been enforced on 27 June by the moderate liberal majority of the national assembly (*Erbkaiserliche*). It was to solve the problem of a vacancy at the top executive level of the state. The Reichsverweser, who was aquitted of any responsibility to the national assembly, formed his cabinet, which, however, remained dependent on the goodwill of the states' executives because it had no army, police or civil service of its own.

Reichswehr. German armed forces from 1919 to 1935. Its structure was prescribed by the Treaty of *Versailles* and implemented by the defence regulations of 23 Mar 1921, according to which it was not to exceed 100,000 men with 4,000 officers (= 7 divisions); the navy ('Reichsmarine') was limited to 15,000 men and 1,500 officers (= 3 divisions). An air force was prohibited. Illegal preparations for a strengthening of the Reichswehr were made by the 'black Reichswehr' (units of temporary volunteers and labour commandos) and by secret technical co-operation with Soviet Russia. The supreme commander of the Reichswehr was the *Reichspräsident*, controlled by the Reichswehr minister (*Noske, Groener*). Its true head was the chief of the army command, General v *Seeckt*, who kept it aloof from the politics of the *Weimar Republic* (*Kapp-Putsch*), thereby creating for it the image of a state within the state. Only in 1932 did the Reichswehr interfere in the formation of a cabinet (*Schleicher*). After 30 Jan 1933 the Reichswehr became the forerunner of the *Wehrmacht*.
F L Carsten: The Reichswehr and Politics, 1918–33 (1966).

Reichswerke. Companies founded by the central government between 1937 and 1941. The most important were the Reichswerke 'Hermann *Göring*', the iron and ore shops with their headquarters at Salzgitter. They increased in size as a result of the confiscation of plants in the occupied territories. They were used by National Socialist officials to exert influence on the economy. Most of them were dismantled after World War II.

Reichswirtschaftskammer. Organization founded in 1933 to unite all industrial and commerical unions as a means for the *Gleichschaltung* of the economy. Its president was appointed by the government. The organization was intended to increase state influence upon the privately organized economy, but its complicated structure prevented the implementation of this task.

Reichswirtschaftsrat. Economic council provided by § 165 of the *constitution* of 1919. It was an extension of the previous 'workers' council' by the representation of entrepreneurs and other economists. In May 1920 a preliminary Reichswirtschaftsrat was constituted, but it never accomplished the tasks intended for it, ie to assist in the execution of nationalization laws. It was abolished on 23 Mar 1934. Its duties were partly taken over by the *Reichswirtschaftskammer.*

Reinsurance Treaty. Secret treaty concluded by *Bismarck* with Russia on 18 June 1887, according to which both powers mutually pledged benevolent neutrality for a period of three years in the event of war. The treaty did not apply to a German attack on France and a Russian offensive on Austria. By the treaty Germany recognized Russia's influence in Bulgaria and, in a top secret minute, the Russian interest in Constantinople and the straits. Although the Russian government was prepared to drop this clause, *Caprivi* and *Holstein* refused to prolong the treaty because it violated the essence of the *Triple Alliance.* By supporting Russia's oriental aims against Britain and Austria, the Reinsurance Treaty was designed to prevent a Franco-Russian alliance. But *Bismarck's* economic policy (*Sammlungspolitik*) helped to defeat his diplomacy: rising tariffs on Russian grain estranged the Russian landowners and the closing of German markets to Russian bonds in Nov 1887 drove them to Paris. The Reinsurance was a temporary phase of Bismarckian diplomacy, which could not bridge the gap between Pan-Slavism and *Pan-Germanism.*

R Wittram: 'Bismarcks Russlandpolitik nach der Reichsgründung', in Historische Zeitschrift 186 (1958).

Reitzenstein, Sigismund v (3 Feb 1766–5 Mar 1847); South German statesman. As minister of Baden in Paris (1796–1803) he obtained French support for the acquisitions that enlarged the margraviate to almost five times its previous size (*Reichsdeputationshauptschluss*). Under Karl Friedrich I (1728–1811) Baden became a grand duchy in 1806 and entered the Confederation of the *Rhine.* In 1809, as chief minister, Reitzenstein introduced a centralist system of government modelled on the Napoleonic pattern. In 1818 the granting of a constitution made Baden one of the first German states to introduce the parliamentary system. The deliberations of its *Landtag* echoed through Germany during the period of the Reaction. In Baden even further reforms of Reitzenstein's new ministry from 1832 to 1843 were unable to check radicalism in the duchy (*Baden, uprisings in*).

Rentenmark. New currency introduced on 20 Nov 1923 by *Stresemann's* government. Issued in strictly limited quantities, the Rentenmark successfully stabilized the monetary system after the inflation had reached its peak during the *Ruhrkampf.* Cover was provided by a mortgage on Germany's entire industrial and agricultural resources. In 1924 the Rentenmark was replaced by the *Reichsmark*.

Reparations. Payments for indemnification demanded by the victors of World War I in the Treaty of *Versailles*. The exact amount of reparations was regulated by a commission and by reparations conferences. In 1921 the Allies fixed the complete debt at 226,000 million gold marks to be paid in 42 annual instalments. Germany's refusal to pay (*Ruhrkampf*) led to the *London Ultimatum* (5 May 1921), which reduced the sum to 132,000 million. After Germany's economic collapse (inflation of 1923) new regulations became necessary. The *Dawes Plan* (1924), modified by the *Young Plan* (1929), took into account Germany's insolvency by granting foreign loans. On 1 July 1931 a year's moratorium was granted. The Lausanne agreement of 9 July 1932 envisaged a final payment of 3000 million, which was never made. By then Germany had paid $^1/_8$ of the sum originally demanded (and received loans equivalent to $^1/_5$). The question of reparations determined German financial policy in the 1920s and undermined her economic recovery and stabilization.

P Krüger: Deutschland und die Reparationen, 1918–19 (1973).

Reptilienfonds. Secret political fund financed from the interests of the *Welfenfonds*, originally devised by *Bismarck* to attack the supporters of the Welf dynasty, whom he had called 'reptiles' on 30 Jan 1869. Conversely, his opponents named the journalists working in the service of the government 'reptile press'.

R Nöll v d Nahmer: Bismarcks Reptilienfonds (1968).

Republikschutzgesetz. Law for the protection of the *Weimar Republic*, proclaimed after the assassination of W Rathenau (24 June 1922) on 21 July 1922. It was at first limited to five years; on 17 May 1927 it was extended for another two years. The law provided for the suppression of anti-republican elements. It was opposed in parliament by the *DNVP*, *KPD* and *Bayrische Volkspartei*. On 20 Mar 1930 the second Republikschutzgesetz was passed in a milder version. It was abrogated on 19 Dec 1932.

Reserved Rights. Prerogatives for the South German states Bavaria, Baden and Württemberg and the Hanse cities (Hamburg, Bremen, Lübeck) in the Reich, 1871–1918. They were conceded in the *November Treaties* and could not be changed without the consent of the states concerned. They related to the administration of the postal and telegraphic system. In the case of Bavaria they related to an army of her own, which had to be placed under the Kaiser's command in the event of war. The scope of the reserved rights is debatable, because the expression does not appear in the Reich *Constitution* of 1871 (art. 78).

Resettlement (Umsiedlung). Resettlement project for the attempted new order of Europe on ethnological lines, as announced by *Hitler* in the *Reichstag* speech on 6 Oct 1939. The isolated German population in the Baltic states and South Tyrol and the Balkans was to be transferred to Germany under the slogan 'Heim ins Reich'. Corresponding treaties were concluded with the countries concerned. To direct the Umsiedlung, *Himmler* was appointed Commissioner for the Consolidation of German Nationality. For the future, Nazi leadership also envisaged the Umsiedlung of Germans and other German peoples in the conquered territories of the east (eg Ukraine, Crimea). In practice most of the people were resettled in the annexed Polish territories with the aim of raising the proportion of the German nationals there, while Poles were driven out to the *Generalgouvernement* or liquidated. In 1944 the Umsiedlung took the shape of evacuation before the advancing Red Army; in 1945 the remainder of those resettled in the eastern provinces fell victim to the *Vertreibung*.

R L Köhl: RKFDV, German Resettlement and Population Policy, 1939–45 (1957).

Resistance. See July Plot.

Revisionspolitik. Policy aiming at a revision of the Treaty of *Versailles*, ie the territorial losses of Germany and the demands for *reparations*. It was mainly supported by the parties of the right (*DNVP*, *NSDAP*) and nationalist organizations (*Stahlhelm*). They demanded equality for Germany in armaments and denounced all attempts at détente (policy of *fulfilment*). The major territorial objects of the policy (*Anschluss, Sudetenland, Danzig*) were part of the Nazi programme and were successively achieved by blackmail or force after the *Nazi seizure of power*.

N Krekeler: Revisionspruch und geheime Ostpolitik der Weimarer Republik (1973); K Megerle: Deutsche Aussenpolitik 1925. Ansatz zu aktivem Revisionismus (1974).

Revolution of 1848 (Märzrevolution). German revolution which started in Mar 1848 in the states of the *Deutscher Bund*. While Metternich was forced to escape from Vienna (13–15 Mar), the days of unrest culminated in the uprising of 18 Mar in Berlin. After bitter street-fighting, causing 300 deaths (mainly journeymen, students and wage labourers), King *Friedrich Wilhelm IV* was forced to withdraw the army from Berlin and be present at the lying-in-state of the victims. A preliminary government under v Arnim was succeeded on 29 Mar by the Liberal ministry of *Camphausen/Hansemann*. The Prussian *Landtag*, convened on 2 Apr, passed an electoral law for the *Berlin National Assembly*. The revolution spread from the reactionary centres of Vienna and Berlin to several small German states, where it led to the appointment of Liberal cabinets. The uprising in *Schleswig-Holstein* was linked with the nationality conflict, one of the major questions to be dealt with by the *Frankfurt National Assembly* which met from 18 May 1848 to 21 Apr 1849 to discuss the two key issues of the revolution, ie the creation of German unity and representative government. The impotence of the assembly became apparent in Sept–Oct when riots in Frankfurt and southwest Germany by radical republicans had to be suppressed by Austrian and Prussian troops. While the assembly was entangled in constitutional debates, the counterrevolution triumphed and many of the achievements of the revolution were revoked by the end of the year 1848. The last flickerings of the revolution in 1849 (*constitutional campaign*) were liquidated in May–June, when the revolution was over. Inspired by the French February revolution (1848), it had been caused by the exclusion of the rising bourgeoisie from political power and by social grievances from the effects of the first phase of the industrial revolution. The failure of the revolution was due to dissensions within the revolutionary movement, which prevented the formation of a broad mass movement to confront reactionary forces.

V Valentin: Geschichte der deutschen Revolution 1848–1849 (repr 1970); R Stadelmann: Soziale und politische Geschichte der Revolution von 1848 (repr 1973); F Eyck: The Revolutions of 1848–49 (1973); P N Stearns: The Revolutions of 1848 (1974).

Rheinische Autonome. Group of Rhenish noblemen led by M v Loe as their spokesman. In the 1840s the Rheinische Autonome adhered to the corporative-reactionary doctrine of K L v Haller, defending feudal interests. The Rheinische Autonome were opposed to representative constitutionalism.

Rhine, Confederation of the. Confederation of initially 16 south and west German states, founded on 12 July 1806 at Napoleon's instigation and under his protectorate. It aimed at the domination of west Germany by France on the dissolution of the Holy Roman Empire. The constitution of the confederation (Rhine Act) committed the imperial princes to provide army contingents for the 'Grande Armée' of their French ally. In return the small states were raised in rank and increased in size at the cost of the small Imperial Estates. In consequence of the Prussian defeat of 1806 (Peace of *Tilsit*) the confederation was enlarged by the inclusion of Würzburg, Saxony and other central and north German small states until 1808; from 1807 it included the new kingdom of *Westphalia*. In 1808 the confederation comprised 325,800 sq km with 14.61 million inhabitants: by 1811 its territory totalled 283,100 sq km spanning four kingdoms, five grand duchies, 11 duchies and 16 principalities. At that time only electoral Hesse and Brunswick (apart from Prussia and Austria) did not belong to the confederation. The first prince of the confederation was Baron K T v Dalberg (1744–1817), who was appointed by Napoleon in 1806, and promoted to Grand Duke of Frankfurt in 1810. He lost his power with the overthrow of Napoleonic domination, while most of the member states of the confederation avoided their dissolution by joining the Prussian-Russian coalition at the beginning of the *wars of liberation*, during the course of which the confederation was dissolved (1814).

Rhineland. Prussian province from 1815. The Treaty of *Versailles* laid down that the Rhineland was to be occupied by Allied troops for 15 years and that a 30-mile-wide demilitarized zone was to be created on the right bank of the Rhine. The Rhineland was divided into French, Belgian, British and American occupation zones, administered by a commission at Koblenz. German interests were represented by a Rhineland commissioner, appointed by the central government. In 1921 a part of the industrial centre, and in 1923 most of it, was occupied by the French (*Ruhrkampf*); the right bank territory was cut off from the Reich by customs and passport frontiers. The separatist movement, active from 1918–19 and encouraged by the French, reached a climax with the proclamation of a Rhenish Republic (21 Oct 1923) and an autonomous Palatinate (12 Nov 1923). But the separatists received little support from the population and collapsed in the winter of 1923–24. The *Locarno* treaties confirmed the permanence of the demilitarized zone, but *Stresemann* secured the gradual evacuation of the Rhineland by the British (Nov 1926) and the French (June 1930). After the *Nazi seizure of power* the Rhineland became the first object of *Hitler*'s *Revisionspolitik*. On 7 Mar 1936 German troops moved into the demilitarized zone. A mere condemnation of this violation of international agreements was the only reaction of the League of Nations.

J T Emmerson: The Rhineland Crisis: 7 Mar 1936 (1976).

Ribbentrop, Joachim v (30 Apr 1893–16 Oct 1946); National Socialist diplomat. In 1933 he became *Hitler*'s adviser on foreign policy. In 1934 he was special delegate for disarmament questions, and on 18 June 1935 he signed the *London Naval Agreement*. In 1936 he became ambassador in London, where he was disappointed at the failure to achieve an understanding with Britain. His tenure of office as minister for foreign affairs (from 4 Feb 1938) was marked by an aggressive policy. He signed the *Ribbentrop-Molotov Pact* and the *Three Powers' Pact* (Sept 1939, 1940). Under him the *Auswärtiges Amt* was largely concerned with the reshaping of Europe. The *Nuremberg Tribunal* sentenced him to death and he was hanged.

W Michalka: Joachim von Ribbentrop und die deutsche Englandpolitik 1933–1940 (1977).

Ribbentrop-Molotov Pact. Non-aggression treaty concluded on 23 Sept 1939 between Soviet Russia and National Socialist Germany. It was to have been in force for 10 years. An additional minute delineated the mutual spheres of interest by a line following the northern frontier of Lithuania and the Curzon line for Poland, which was practically partitioned by the treaty. *Hitler*'s motive in making a pact with his arch-friend was to keep the back free for the *Blitzkriege* against Poland and in the west. The pact was succeeded by several economic agreements in 1940–41. Germany broke the pact by Operation *Barbarossa*.

Ph W Fabry: Der Hitler-Stalin-Pact (1962).

Richter, Eugen (30 July 1838– 10 Mar 1906); Liberal parliamentarian. He was the spokesman of the *Fortschrittspartei*, a member of the Reichstag from 1867 and also the *Abgeordnetenhaus* from 1869. After the formation of the *Freisinnige Partei* he was elected chairman of its executive board. Representing petty-bourgeois interests he tried to use the limited possibilities in the Reichstag to oppose the issues of protective tariff, the *Septennat*, and the *social insurance*. When his party split over *Caprivi*'s army bill of 1893, the majority followed Richter into the new *Freisinnige Volkspartei*, which could not win parliamentary importance, for by then Richter had failed to present an alternative to *Bismarck*. He thus contributed to the failure of left-wing Liberalism in Germany.

Röhm Putsch (Night of the Long Knives). Erroneous Nazi term for the purge of 30 June–2 July 1934 which resulted in the murder of the *SA* leader Röhm (1887–1934), who had been a close companion of *Hitler* since the 1920s (participant in the *Munich Putsch*). The Röhm Putsch was the reaction to Röhm's demands for revolutionary social change (eg by an absorption of the SA into the *Wehrmacht*) and to an alleged impending coup d'état by the SA. Hitler, supported by *Göring* and *Himmler*, regarded big business and the army as fundamental to his power. He invited the SA leaders to a conference at Bad Wiessee (Bavaria) and had them shot by *SS* men. He further exploited the situation to liquidate old opponents and rivals (eg *Kahr*, *Schleicher*, G *Strasser*). The Röhm Putsch was indirectly assisted by the Wehrmacht and tolerated by bourgeois public opinion, after being justified by *Goebbels* and Hitler, who denounced the SA leadership as a treacherous band of homosexuals. The putsch was given the semblance of justice by the cabinet's law of 3 July, declaring it as self-defence of the state. The putsch was an open violation of law by the state's executive.

M Gallo: Der schwarze Freitag der SA (1972).

Romanticism, political. Constitutional concept developed at the turn of the 18th century by Novalis (1772–1801), F Schlegel (1772–1829) and A Müller (1779–1829). It was directed against the absolutist state. Its exponents sought to revive the idea of a corporate Christian state, resuming medieval traditions. It was opposed to the Enlightenment and the ideas of equality and progress as propagated by the French Revolution of 1789.

Rome-Berlin Axis (Achse Berlin-Rom). Term for the relationship between Nazi Germany and Fascist Italy, coined by Mussolini on 1 Nov 1936 in reference to the agreement concluded on 25 Oct 1936. *Hitler*'s first meeting with Mussolini after the *Nazi seizure of power* in 1934 had been chilly, because the Duce resented German designs on Austria (*Anschluss*), which was regarded as a bulwark for Italy's German-speaking province South Tyrol. But Italian expansionist policy in Abyssinia (1935–36) necessitated an approach to Germany, which was expressed by common intervention in the Spanish Civil War and Italy's signing of the *Anti-Comintern Pact* in 1937. The Rome-Berlin Axis was intensified and formalized by the conclusion of the *Steel Pact* (22 May 1939) and an accord on the *resettlement* of the South Tyrolese (23 June 1939), removing Mussolini's hesitations in entering the war on Germany's side (10 June 1940). The Rome-Berlin Axis was a prerequisite for Nazi foreign policy, but, ill-prepared for waging a world-wide war, Italy soon became a liability for Germany, a fact which led to the operation *Axis*.

E Wiskemann: The Rome-Berlin Axis (1949); F W Deakin: The Brutal Friendship (1962).

Rommel, Erwin (15 Nov 1891–14 Oct 1944); field marshal. As the *Wehrmacht*'s liaison officer to *Schirach*, he had considerable influence upon the militarist education of the youth (*Hitler Youth*). At the outbreak of war he was commissioned with the protection of the Führer's headquarters. This brought him into close contact with Nazi leaders, which explains his rapid rise in the army. In 1941 he became supreme commander of the *Afrika Korps* and fought with great skill against the British. After his subsequent defeat he was evacuated, because the Nazis wanted to make propagandist use of his popularity. He was given commands in Italy and France but recognized the inevitability of Germany's defeat and came into contact with the organizers of the *July Plot* (1944). Badly wounded during the Allied invasion, Rommel was unable to take part in the plot but was denounced and forced to commit suicide.

D Young: Rommel (1950); R Lewin: Rommel as Military Commander (1968).

Roon, Albrecht Graf v (13 Apr 1803–23 Feb 1879); Prussian soldier and minister. He took part in the suppression of the second *Baden Uprising* (1849) under the supreme command of the future *Wilhelm I*, on whose orders he drew up a memorandum on the reorganization of the army. When Wilhelm took over the regency in 1858, Roon became major general and on 5 Dec 1859 he was appointed minister of war. Roon's reformist plans were brought before the *Landtag* in Feb 1860 and carried out in 1860–61 despite opposition by the *Abgeordnetenhaus*, which led to the *constitutional conflict*. His reform, which aimed at an increase of the numerical and combative strength of the army, stood the test in 1866 (*Seven Weeks' War*) and 1870 (*Franco-Prussian War*). Roon, who was minister for the navy as well, also acted as minister-president in 1873. He was forced to resign by ill-health. A staunch Conservative Old Prussian, he had helped to appoint *Bismarck* as Chancellor in 1862. His work provided the conditions for the war plans of the elder *Moltke*. Thus Roon was among those who helped to found the German Empire by military means.

Rosenberg, Alfred (12 Jan 1893–16 Oct 1946); National Socialist ideologist. A native of the Baltic, Rosenberg became editor of the *Völkischer Beobachter* in 1921. In 1930 he entered the *Reichstag* for the *NSDAP* and became the spokesman of its parliamentary party on questions of foreign policy. He was also head of the foreign policy office of the party, but exerted little influence on Nazi policy after the *Nazi seizure of power*. In 1941 he was appointed minister for the occupied territories, in which capacity he was largely responsible for outrages in the east. A diehard racist, he had always tried to provide an ideological basis for *National Socialism*, as in his pseudo-scientific 'The Myth of the Twentieth Century' (1930), which glorified the *Aryan racial doctrine*. The *Nuremberg Tribunal* sentenced him to death and he was executed.

R Cecil: The Myth of the Master Race. Alfred Rosenberg and Nazi Ideology (1972).

Roter Frontkämpferbund. Defence organization of the *KPD* in the *Weimar Republic*, founded in 1924. It came under the leadership of Thählmann in

1925. In 1928 it had about 120,000 members. In 1929 it was prohibited in Prussia, and soon afterwards in other German states as well.

Ruhrkampf. Strife in the Ruhr region, Germany's leading mining and manufacturing area. The French wanted to enforce the punctual payment of *reparations* and occupied Düsseldorf and Duisburg in 1921. The threat of complete occupation led to the German acceptance of the *London Ultimatum*. When Germany lagged behind with deliveries for 1922–23, French and Belgian troops moved into the Ruhr basin on 11 Jan 1923. The population obeyed a call for passive resistance by the *Cuno* government. French attempts to take over the administration failed. In Germany the Ruhrkampf caused inflation. Passive resistance was called off by *Stresemann* on 26 Sept 1923. The occupation, which had been condemned by the British and the Americans, was suspended by the *Dawes Plan* by Aug 1925.

Ruhr Strike. Miners' strike of 1889 in the Ruhr area, centring on Gelsenkirchen. In May 1889 90,000 out of 120,000 Ruhr miners were on strike. The army was used against them, causing six deaths. The strike was supported by public opinion and a miners' delegation was received by *Wilhelm II*. Though little was achieved in real terms, the strike demonstrated the failure of *Bismarck's* concept of solving the social question by social legislation (*Sozialpolitik*). The Ruhr strike of 1889 was the starting-point for the formation of the miners' movement which organized the strike of 1905.

D Fricke: Der Ruhrbergarbeiterstreik von 1905 (1955).

Rundstedt, Gerd v (12 Dec 1875–24 Feb 1953); field marshal. Leader of Gruppenkommando, Rundstedt favoured the eclipse of the Prussian government of *Braun-Severing*. He was reactivated in 1939 for the *Blitzkriege* against Poland, France, and Russia, but made a scapegoat for the latter's failure and dismissed by *Hitler* on 3 Dec 1941. From Mar 1942 he was supreme commander in the west (interrupted by the invasion in 1944) and chairman of the *Wehrmacht's* court of honour that extradited the officers involved in the *July Plot* (1944) to the *Volksgerichtshof*. He was arrested at the end of World War II but released by the Allies in 1949.

G Blumentritt: Von Rundstedt: The Soldier and the Man (1962).

SA (Sturmabteilung). Storm troops of the *NSDAP*, founded in 1921. Up to 1933 the SA's main function was the protection of party assemblies and the initiation of street fighting with political rivals. After the *Nazi seizure of power* the leadership of the SA, headed by E Röhm, wanted to merge the SA with the *Wehrmacht* to create a people's army. Since they also demanded a social revolution undesirable to *Hitler*, the latter had them liquidated in 1934 (*Röhm Putsch*). Thereafter the SA declined. Membership, which had risen by the absorption of other para-military unions (eg *Stahlhelm*) in 1933, fell from 4.5 million (1934) to 1.5 million (1939). As main organizer of *Anti-Semitism (Jews, boycott of)*, the SA tried in vain to regain prominence in the *Crystal Night*. In last years of the National Socialist regime the vulgarity of the SA was replaced more and more by the bureaucratic terror of *SS* and *SD*. The SA lost all influence and was not classified as a criminal organization by the *Nuremberg Tribunal*.

H Bennecke: Hitler und die Sturmabteilung (1962).

Saar District. Political entity created in 1920 by the Treaty of *Versailles* out of the southern parts of the Rhenish province and the western parts of the Bavarian palatinate. On 10 Jan 1920 the Saar district was placed under a League of Nations government for 15 years. France was given the right to exploit the coal mines. In 1935 a plebiscite decided in favour (90.5 per cent votes) of its return to Germany. The mines were bought back for 900 million francs.

Sammlungspolitik. Policy uniting the interest of industry and agriculture for the introduction of a protective tariff in 1879 (*Protective Tariff*). In 1887 it was resumed by *Bismarck* with the formation of the 'cartel', an agreement of National Liberals and Conservatives to spare each other in the election campaign. The policy was intensified in the 1890s by *Miquel* who proclaimed a revision of *Caprivi*'s trade policy and aimed at a union of all elements interested in preserving the social order, ie from the Junkers to the middle classes. The increase of grain tariffs in 1902 was one of the most debated legislative measures of the Wilhelmine era. The alliance of 'rye and iron' caused a sharp rise in consumers' costs and led a third of the electorate into the camp of the *SPD*. Thus it increased the antagonism between the ruling classes and the working-class in imperial Germany.

D Stegmann: Die Erben Bismarcks. ... Sammlungspolitik 1897–1918 (1970).

Samoa. Centre of the South Sea trade of the German company Goddefroy in the 1870s, which stimulated the Samoa bill in the Reichstag on 14 Apr 1880 by colonial enthusiasts, who were defeated by 128 to 112 votes with their proposal that the Reich should guarantee the financing of a plantation company for Samoa. In 1889 the Samoa conference in Berlin regulated the rights of the powers interested (Germany, Britain, USA) by declaring the neutrality of Samoa, which amounted to a de facto tripartite protectorate, which did not operate successfully. On 2 Dec 1899, after diplomatic rivalries and indigenous turmoil, the Samoa convention divided the islands between Germany and the USA, while Britain withdrew for the consideration of her claims to Tonga and the southern Solomons. Germany controlled Western Samoa (Upolu and Savaii) until 30 Aug 1914, when it was occupied by New Zealand, which acted as the mandatory power from 1919 until its independence in 1962.

P M Kennedy: The Samoan Tangle – The Partition of the Samoan Islands, 1898–1899 (1975).

Sand, Karl Ludwig (5 Oct 1795–20 May 1820); nationalist student. He founded the first of the patriotic student corporations (*Burschenschaften*) in 1816. In 1817 he took part in the *Wartburg Festival*. He became convinced that only individual terror could bring progress against reactionary forces in Germany.

He, therefore, stabbed the polemical writer Kotzebue at Mannheim on 23 Mar 1819. Sand was publicly executed in Munich. His conduct led to the *Carlsbad Decrees* and the persecution of the *demagogues*.

Schacht, Hjalmar (22 Jan 1877–3 June 1970); banker. He was commissioner for monetary matters in 1923 and president of the *Reichsbank*, 1924–1929. Until 1926 he was a member of the *DDP* (which he had helped to found), but then turned towards the right (*Harzburg Front*) and interceded for *Hitler's* appointment, under whom Schacht was again president of the Reichsbank (until 1939) and also minister of economics (1934–37). Schacht's monetary policy helped to finance rearmament, of which he approved, although he knew the economic situation and Hitler's aims. Schacht resigned after the *Fritsch Plot* (1938) and sided with the resistance, for which he was imprisoned in a *concentration camp* after the *July Plot* (1944). Schacht was acquitted by the *Nuremberg Tribunal* but detained by the Germans until 1948.

E Beck: Verdict on Schacht (1955).

Scharnhorst, Gerhard v (12 Nov 1755–28 June 1813); Prussian general and reformer. In 1806, after Prussia's surrender to Napoleon (*Jena – Auerstedt*), Scharnhorst was commissioned with the reorganization of Prussia's army. He took over the war department without ranking as minister, introduced the 'allgemeine *Wehrpflicht*' (general conscription) and tried to link the army with the people by forging a new relationship between officers and privates. To circumvent the limitations of the *Paris Convention*, Scharnhorst invented the *Krümper-System* for short-term enlistment. He also created the *Landwehr* (militia), for which the noble privileges were abolished. In 1810 Scharnhorst lost his cabinet office on Napoleon's behest, but he remained chief-of-staff. In 1813 he prepared the war for liberation. During negotiations for a coalition with Austria he died of wounds received in the battle of Gross Görschen.

R Höhn: Scharnhorsts Vermächtnis (2nd ed. 1972).

Scheidemann, Philipp (26 July 1865–29 Nov 1939); Social Democratic parliamentarian and statesman. He was a member of the *Reichstag* from 1903 and its vice-president in 1912 and 1918. In 1914 he became joint president (with *Ebert*) of the *SPD*. During World War I he was spokesman of the party's moderate wing. In 1918 he became secretary of state without portfolio in *Max von Baden's* cabinet. In order to prevent the formation of a Soviet republic he promulgated the republic from the balcony of the Reichstag building on 9 Nov 1918 without Ebert's consent. He then became a member of the *Rat der Volksbeauftragten*. After the failure of the *November Revolution* he was elected to the National Assembly and on 13 Feb 1919 formed the first cabinet of the *Weimar Republic*. However, his tenure lasted only until 20 July 1919, when he resigned, because he disapproved of the Treaty of *Versailles*. On 1920 Scheidemann was responsible for *Noske's* dismissal. He continued to fight against the right as a deputy until 1933, when he emigrated to Copenhagen.

138

Schirach, Baldur v (9 May 1907–8 Aug 1974); National Socialist. He joined the National Socialist students' movement in 1927. From 1931 he led all youth organizations (*Hitler Youth*) of the *NSDAP*. On 17 June 1933 Hitler appointed him 'national youth leader' in which capacity he directed the *Gleichschaltung* of the bourgeois youth organizations. He greatly influenced the preparation of the young Germans for war. In 1940 he became *Gauleiter, Reichsstatthalter*, and defence commissioner for Vienna. The *Nuremberg Tribunal* sentenced him to 20 years' imprisonment, which he served until 1966.

Schleicher, Kurt v (7 Apr 1882–30 June 1934); general. He held leading posts in the *Reichswehr* as a collaborator of *Groener* and *Seeckt*. As a confidant of *Hindenburg* he influenced the appointments of *Brüning* and *Papen* as well as the dismissal of Groener, whom he prevented from using the army against the *SA*. Schleicher was Reichswehr minister in the *Cabinet of Barons* and led a government himself from Dec 1932 to Jan 1933. He failed to split the *NSDAP* (G *Strasser*) to integrate the Nazis into the state and tried in vain to win the support of the trade unions. He wanted to make the Reichswehr the centre of power to keep the Nazis under control and would have served under *Hitler* if he had been left in charge of the army and thus able to prevent any violation of law and constitution. He was therefore regarded as a dangerous rival by Hitler, who had him murdered during the *Röhm Putsch*.

T Vogelsang: Kurt von Schleicher (1965).

Schleswig-Holstein. Two duchies linking Denmark with Prussia. From 1815 Holstein belonged to the *Deutscher Bund*. In 1846 the Danish Crown, which ruled over Schleswig-Holstein in personal union, tried to separate Schleswig from Schleswig-Holstein by extending its female hereditary law to Schleswig. These endeavours were supported by the *Eiderdänen*. In Mar 1848 the predominantly German population of Schleswig-Holstein reacted with an uprising, established its own government and declared union with Germany. In harmony with German public opinion, the *Bundestag* commissioned Prussia and Hanover to intervene in favour of the population of Schleswig-Holstein. The war of 1848–50, though initially successful, was interrupted by the armistices of 26 Aug 1848 and 10 July 1849. The peace of Berlin (2 July 1850) separated Schleswig from Holstein. The London Protocol of 8 May 1852 guaranteed the legality of the Danish succession regulations in the whole monarchy but the constitutional status of Schleswig remained open. In the patent of 30 Mar 1863 the Danish King Frederick VII revised the constitution of 1854–55 (which had been suspended for Holstein in Nov 1858) by proclaiming a constitutional unity for his monarchy. After the king's death in Nov 1863, Christian IX of the House of Glücksburg inherited the Danish Crown; the claims of the Duke of Augustenburg to Schleswig-Holstein remained unheeded. Thereupon Prussia and Austria intervened jointly against Denmark in Jan 1864. On 18 Apr they stormed the fortress of Düppel and conquered the whole of Jutland. The peace of Vienna of 30 Oct enforced the cession of Schleswig-Holstein. Tension among the victorious countries was not eased by the *Gastein Convention* (1865). Complaints of anti-Prussian agitation served as a pretext for *Bismarck* to wage the war with Austria in 1866 (*Seven Weeks' War*), after which Schleswig-Holstein became a Prussian *Provinz* (1867). The retrocession of North Schleswig (intended in 1878) was not carried out before the plebiscite in 1920 (*plebiscite districts*).

Schlieffen Plan. Strategic concept devised in 1902 by Count Alfred Schlieffen, chief of the general staff, 1891–1905. The plan was to be the answer to the eventuality of Germany facing a two-front war against France and Russia. Accordingly maximum strength was to be employed in the west to win a quick decisive victory over France, while Russia was to be contained by a weaker force. Since a frontal attack upon France was unlikely to bring immediate success, the plan provided for an advance through Belgium and north-east France with an overwhelmingly strong right wing that would encircle the French armies. Schlieffen's advice 'to keep the right wing strong' was disregarded in 1914 by his successor H J L *Moltke* (the younger). But the Schlieffen Plan contained inherent flaws: overestimating the speed of advance in face of Belgian opposition and the demolition of rail and road connections. The plan also ignored the political consequences of violating Belgian neutrality, which gave Britain reason to interfere instead of discouraging her by a *Blitzkrieg*. The application of the plan is proof that by 1914 German policy was determined by military needs.

G Ritter: Schlieffen Plan – Critique of a Myth (1958).

Schmitt, Carl (11 July 1888–   ); constitutional lawyer. Authoritarian critic of Liberalism and parliamentary democracy between World Wars I and II. From 1933 to 1945 Schmitt taught at *Berlin University* and helped to formulate and justify the constitutional law in the first years of National Socialist rule.

Scholl, Hans (22 Sept 1918–22 Feb 1943) and Sophia (9 May 1921–22 Feb 1943), brother and sister who founded the resistance group 'The White Rose' at Munich University. After *Stalingrad* they distributed a leaflet appealing to their fellow students to resist the National Socialist regime. They were betrayed, arrested and sentenced to death by the *Volksgerichtshof*, and executed.

School Supervision Law (Schulaufsichtsgesetz). Law of 11 Mar 1872 made at the beginning of the *Kulturkampf* to effect the separation of state and church in education. The law abolished the ecclesiastical inspection of local and district schools in Prussia by placing all municipal and private schools under state supervision. Since it also affected the Protestants, the law met with the opposition of the Old Conservatives, who broke with *Bismarck*. The law also aimed at reducing Polish influence in the eastern provinces.

Schulze-Delitzsch, Franz H (29 Aug 1808–29 Apr 1883); founder of the urban co-operative banks. He aimed at securing the material existence of craftsmen, artisans and tradesmen. He considered that credit, provided by the accumulated savings of small investors, would enable them to improve their efficiency and increase their business. By 1859 there were 80 such 'Volksbanken', whose credit was only available to members. Rural needs were differently catered for by *Raiffeisen*. Schulze-Delitzsch, who refused state intervention, also initiated co-operative production and retail stores (*Konsumvereine*).

Schutzgebiete. Term used to denote the German overseas protectorates: *German South-West Africa, German East Africa*, the *Cameroons, Togo, German New Guinea, Samoa*, and *Kiachow*. At the beginning of the German *Kolonialpolitik* the term Schutzgebiete was interpreted in the restricted sense of protecting the German colonialists against foreign powers and African resistance and only gradually did the Germans come to think of protecting the Africans as well. The Schutzgebiete were administered by the colonial office (*Reichsämter*) and colonial legislation was in the hands of the *Bundesrat* and the *Reichstag*. The Kaiser and the *Reichskanzler* had the right of issuing decrees, the latter also exercised command over the *Schutztruppe*. A governor appointed by the Kaiser was in charge of each territory. In 1914 the Schutzgebiete extended over 2,963,000 sq km with 29,000 whites out of a total of 12 million inhabitants. After the outbreak of World War I all the Schutzgebiete were invaded by the Allies, who administered them as mandates after 1919 (*Versailles*).

P Gifford and W M R Louis (eds): Britain and Germany in Africa (1967).

Schutzhaftbefehle. Orders to arrest political opponents of *National Socialism*, issued on the basis of a *Notverordnung* of 4 Feb 1933 and a decree of the minister of the interior (*Frick*). Instead of protecting the prisoners from personal dangers, as they claimed, the orders only served to legalize their arrests in the *concentration camps*.

Schutztruppe. From 1891 German colonial troops stationed in the *Schutzgebiete* for keeping public order and preventing the establishment of a slave trade. Their numbers were increased for the quelling of native uprisings between 1904 and 1907 in *German South-West* and *German East Africa*. In World War I they fought with bravery in East Africa in a guerrilla war organized by Gen P v Lettow-Vorbeck (1870–1964) with loyal native soldiers, the 'Askari'.

L Bode: Die Operationen in Ostafrika (1951).

SD (Sicherheitsdienst). Security service of the *SS*, founded in 1932 by *Heydrich* on behalf of *Himmler*. The SD became the security service of the entire *NSDAP*, spying upon the party leadership and carrying out purges (*Röhm Putsch*). In 1939 the SD was integrated into the *Reichssicherheitshauptamt*. Its activities were divided into three offices, for interior, foreign and ideological affairs. With its strict organizational structure and highly qualified staff, the SD was the backbone of the National Socialist security organs.

A Ramme: Der SD der SS (1969).

Sea Lion (Seelöwe). Code word for the landing operation in England, which *Hitler* ordered to prepare for in his directive no 16 of 16 July 1940. In spite of it

Hitler still hoped to induce Britain to conclude peace (*Reichstag* speech of 19 July), but Halifax's negative reply (22 July) made such plans illusory. Operation Sea Lion envisaged a speedy invasion of southern England, but on 14 Sept it had to be postponed until the destruction of the Royal Air Force (*Battle of Britain*), which, together with warding off the Royal Navy, was absolutely necessary for the success of the operation. But both proved to be beyond Germany's capacity.

R Wheatley: Operation Sea Lion (1958).

Sedan, Battle of. (1) On 1 Sept 1870 in the *Franco-Prussian War*: The German armies succeeded in encircling the French troops. Napolean III surrendered with nearly 82,000 officers and men; 17,000 French troops were killed or wounded while the Germans lost less than 9,000. Owing to French miscalculations of German strength, Sedan led to the collapse of French military power. The victory of Sedan was celebrated annually in imperial Germany as public manifestation of *Pan-Germanism*.
(2) On 13 May 1940 in World War II: German advance headed by Guderian's panzer division which routed the French forces at the beginning of Germany's invasion of France during the campaign in the west (*Blitzkriege*).

Seeckt, Hans v (22 Apr 1866–27 Dec 1936); general. In Mar 1920 he took over the army leadership of the *Reichswehr*. He maintained a neutral attitude during the *Kapp-Putsch* and in Nov 1923 he was given the executive power, which he did not use for political influence. The participation of a Hohenzollern prince in a manoeuvre forced his resignation in 1926. He had built up an army disregarding restrictions placed by *Versailles* on rearmament. He co-operated with Soviet Russia, in anticipation of a future war against France and Poland. His maxim of an unpolitical army influenced the officers' corps and indirectly prepared an instrument for carrying out the designs of *National Socialism* (*Wehrmacht*).

H Meier-Welker: Seeckt (1967); C Guske: Das politische Denken des Generals von Seeckt (1971).

Seehandlung. Overseas trading corporation founded in 1772 by Frederick the Great. It was originally intended to stimulate trade in the Vistula valley. In the 1820s it was reorganized by Chr v Rother, also head of the Royal Bank in Berlin. The Seehandlung enabled linen to be imported from Silesia (where it owned several factories), thereby giving new employment for declining crafts. A regular service of Seehandlung ships between Hamburg and overseas markets was established, including trade in wool, flour and alum. The Seehandlung fostered internal communications by building highways and financing railway constructions. It turned more and more into a financial institution for raising government loans, changing its name to Prussian State Bank.

September Programme. First German war aims programme communicated by *Bethmann Hollweg* to his secretary of the interior, C v Delbrück, on 9 Sept

142

1914. The programme demanded the 'securing of the German empire to the west and east for the foreseeable future'. France was to be weakened (annexation of its north-eastern iron ore basin) so as to make it cease to be a great power; Russia was to be averted from the German frontiers by the 'liberation' of its non-Russian subject nationalities (*Insurrektionspolitik*). The Chancellor envisaged a German-dominated *Mitteleuropa* (Belgium a vassal state, hegemony over east-central Europe) and a *Mittelafrika* colonial empire. The programme was drafted at the climax of the battle of the *Marne* in the hope of victory, but its gist remained unchanged in 1916–17 and it was partly realized in the east by the Treaty of *Brest-Litovsk*. The programme was inspired by industrialists like *Rathenau* and Gwinner of the *Deutsche Bank* and its main ideas had been propagated in the memorandum of 28 Aug 1914 of the *Alldeutscher Verband* (seconded by *Krupp* and *Stinnes*) and in an even more extreme form by *Thyssen*'s note of 9 Sept, all desiring the domination of *Pan-Germanism*.

F Fischer: Germany's Aims in the First World War (1967).

Septennat. Seven-year term for the military budget in the Bismarckian era. It was proposed by the government and carried by the *Reichstag* majority in 1874, 1880 and 1887. In 1893 the Septennat was replaced by the 'Quinquennat' (five year term).

Seven Weeks' (Austro-Prussian) War. Decisive war between Prussia and Austria for hegemony over Germany in summer 1886. *Bismarck* prepared for the war by an alliance with Italy (8 Apr 1866) and secured Russian and French neutrality. He then provoked war with a move for federal reform (on 9 Apr 1866) and the invasion of Holstein by Prussian troops (contrary to the *Gastein Convention*). Thereupon the *Bundestag* resolved to mobilize the federal troops against Prussia on 14 June at the initiative of Austria. This was regarded as a declaration of war by Prussia. The south German states and Saxony and Hanover stood on Austria's side, whereas Prussia was supported by Saxe-Coburg and Lippe. Under the elder *Moltke*'s plan, the Prussian army advanced into Bohemia, where it defeated the Austrians at *Königgrätz* on 3 July. A day later Prussian troops stood before Vienna. Meanwhile the Prussians occupied the Electorate of Hesse, Saxony and Hanover (capitulation at *Langensalza* on 29 June). A Prussian army also fought victoriously against south German troops in Hesse and Franconia. Then Bismarck urged a quick termination of the war in order to prevent the intervention of France. The preliminary peace of Nikolsburg on 26 July 1866 was followed by the peace of Prague on 23 Aug 1866. On payment of a war contribution Austria kept all her territories but had to consent to the dissolution of the *Deutscher Bund* and the foundation of the *North German Confederation*. Peace with the south German states, with whom alliances against France had already been concluded, was made in Aug–Sept 1866 in Berlin. Prussia annexed Hanover, Hessen-Kassel, Nassau, Frankfurt and *Schleswig-Holstein*. Besides the exclusion of Austria from Germany and the preparation of the *kleindeutsch* solution of German unification, the Seven

Weeks' War resulted in a diplomatic defeat for France, thus paving the way for the *Franco-Prussian War* of 1870–71.

W v Groote and U v Gersdorff (eds); Entscheidung 1866 (1966); A Wandruszka: Schicksalsjahr 1866 (1966).

Severing, Carl (1 June 1875–23 July 1952); Social Democratic politician. He represented the *SPD* in the *Reichstag* from 1907 to 1911 and again from 1920 to 1933. From 1920 to 1926 and from 1930 to 1933 he was Prussian minister of the interior in O *Braun*'s governments and from June 1928 to Mar 1930 *Reichsminister* of the interior. During his tenure of office he defended the *Weimar Republic* against extremists of the left (suppressing the Communist rising of 1920) and the right (eg by imposing restrictions on *Hitler* in 1923). But he remained passive towards *Papen*'s coup d'état in 1932. In 1933 he was forced to quit his office.

Seyss-Inquart, Arthur (22 July 1892–16 Oct 1946); Austrian National Socialist. Due to *Hitler*'s demands he was appointed Austrian minister of the interior and of security on 18 Feb 1938. On 11 Mar Seyss-Inquart organized the *Anschluss*, on 15 Mar he became *Reichsstatthalter* of Austria. In Mar 1939 he prepared the annexation of *Bohemia-Moravia*. In Sept 1939 he became head of the civil administration in southern Poland, in Oct deputy to Governor General *Frank*. On 18 May he became commissioner for the Dutch *Reichskommissariat*. He shared responsibility for the persecution and murder of thousands of resistance fighters and Jews, particularly in the Netherlands, for which the *Nuremberg Tribunal* sentenced him to death.

W Rosar: Deutsche Gemeinschaft. Seyss-Inquart und der Anschluss (1971).

Sickness Insurance Act (Krankenversicherungsgesetz). First Act of Bismarck's social legislation (*social insurance*), passed in 1883 to introduce compulsory insurance against sickness. It covered the great majority of the workers, who had to pay two-thirds (the entrepreneurs had to pay the remaining third) of the contributions to the health-insurance offices, which were established in 1884 and on whose committees the workers also had a two-thirds share. The state prescribed minimum payments of sickness costs and benefits. In 1913 the act was extended to cover agricultural labourers and household employees by the Reichsversicherungsordnung.

Siegfried Line. Fortified line at the western front in World War I running from Arras via St Quentin to Laffeux. After the failure at *Verdun* the *Oberste Heeresleitung* decided to give up the salient between Arras and Soissons and in autumn 1916 rapidly constructed the Siegfried Line or '*Hindenburg* Line' (because of the field marshal's visit to the western front which made him conscious of the danger there). The Siegfried Line spared the German troops and facilitated reconnaissance of Allied dispositions at the Somme. *Ludendorff* made this strategic retreat more effective by planned demolitions in the area from 4 Feb 1917, and from 15 to 20 Mar the withdrawal was made under the code-word 'Alberich'. The Siegfried Line enabled the Germans to hold out against all Allied attacks in 1917 without too many losses.

J Terraine: The Western Front, 1914–1917 (1965).

Siemens, Werner v (13 Dec 1816–6 Dec 1892); inventor-enterpreneur. In 1847 Siemens, together with J G Halske, founded a telegraphic factory, which built the first underground telegraphic line in 1848–49. In 1866 he invented the dynamo machine and in 1879 he built the first electrical locomotive and weaver's loom. He expanded his firm to all fields of electrical engineering and gained orders from all countries, notably Russia and Britain, where his brother Karl was in charge of a branch. After his retirement (1890) his firm continued to be Germany's leading enterprise in all fields of electrical engineering. His success was typical of German achievement during the 'second' industrial revolution.

J Kocka: Unternehmensverwaltung und Angestelltenschaft am Beispiel Siemens, 1847 bis 1914 (1969).

Silesian Weavers' Uprising. Uprising of the Silesian handloom weavers in 1844, largely caused by the inability of the German linen industry to adapt itself to machinery and steam. They protested against the sinking of the living standard below living wage. The uprising was directed against the manufacturers. The authorities quelled it by military force; many weavers were arrested. In spite of its failure the uprising strengthened the proletarian movement in Germany in its development into a mass movement. Its repercussions lasted until the *Revolution of 1848*.

B Gloger: Als Rübezahl schlief. Vom Aufstand der schlesischen Weber (1961).

Six Articles. Reactionary measure against the repercussions of the French July revolution of 1830 (*Hambach Festival*, 1832), which Metternich persuaded the *Bundestag* to pass on 28 June 1832, thereby stiffening the decisions taken in 1819–20 (*Carlsbad Decrees*). The Six Articles created a federal commission to supervise local assemblies and served as a pretext for ushering in a wave of prohibitions in the German states. An unsuccessful putsch against the Frankfurt guard on 3 Apr 1833 aggravated the situation. After the Vienna ministerial conferences of June 1834 a commission of inquiry was established, which strengthened the measures against the press and the universities with further persecutions of *demagogues*. This was the climax of the policy of restoration aimed at suppressing bourgeois liberal forces. It was in marked contrast to the tendencies of the industrial age.

Social insurance Collective system based on organized self-help, introduced in the 1880s as a measure of *Sozialpolitik*. *Bismarck*'s plan to have it financed by the state failed in 1881, when the *Reichstag* refused to grant a tobacco monopoly. In 1883 the *Sickness Insurance Act* introduced compulsory insurance for a large population of the workers, in 1884 the *Industrial Accident Act* followed and in 1889 the *Old-Age Insurance Act* was proclaimed. These insurance laws

145

were intended to secure a minimum means of livelihood to the workers in case of illness or retirement by the payment of pensions. Some deficiencies of the social insurance legislation were amended between 1892 and 1903. In 1911 the social insurance was extended and co-ordinated by the Reichs-versicherungsordnung. In 1927 the *Unemployment Insurance Act* was introduced. Though the social insurance was a pioneer work of social legislation, the working class was gradually integrated into the state by its growing social security and had no incentive to fight for civil rights.

G Erdmann: Die Entwicklung der Sozialgesetzgebung (2nd ed., 1957).

Solf, Wilhelm (5 Oct 1862–6 Feb 1936); diplomat. In 1900 he became governor of *Samoa* and in 1911 secretary of state of the 'Reichskolonialamt'. From Oct to Dec 1918 he was secretary of state of the *Auswärtiges Amt*, and from 1920 to 1928 ambassador in Tokyo. After 1933 the 'Solf circle', a loose group of resistance against *Hitler*, assembled around him and his wife.

E v Vietsch: Wilhelm Solf. Botschafter zwischen den Zeiten (1961).

Sozialistengesetz. Anti-Socialist law tabled by *Bismarck*, who used two attempts at assassination on *Wilhelm I* by anarchists (11 May and 2 June 1878) as a pretext for an 'exceptional law' that would bar the Social Democrats from all political activity. The first bill, a clumsy copy of a British law against the Irish Fenians, was drafted too crudely to find Liberal approval and was rejected on 24 May. But when Bismarck had the *Reichstag* dissolved, the new elections resulted in Conservative gains and forced the National Liberals, whose power Bismarck also wanted to break, to abandon their principle by consenting to the Sozialistengesetz. (They only insisted on its restriction for $2^1/_2$ years, forcing Bismarck to apply 4 times for the renewal of the statute.) On 18 Oct 1878 the 'law against dangerous aspirations of Social Democracy' was passed with 221 votes. The Sozialistengesetz prohibited all Social Democratic, Socialist, or Communist societies, assemblies and pamphlets. Socialist agitators could be expelled from certain 'endangered' districts. Thus the law destroyed the whole Social-Democratic party organization and in 1880 its congress in exile at Wyden (Switzerland) adapted itself to this repression with a resolution to achieve Social-Democratic aims 'by all means'. The law had placed the Social-Democrats under a special penal law not for crimes committed but for their convictions, thereby violating the contemporary sense of justice and increasing workers' opposition against the state and its ruling classes. But the law failed to curb the success of the *SPD*: after a slight decline in 1881 its vote rose from 550,000 in 1884 to 1.4 million in 1890, when the Sozialistengesetz was abolished.

W Pack: Das parlamentarische Ringen um das Sozialistengesetz Bismarcks (1961); V Lidtke: The Outlawed Party. Social Democracy in Germany, 1878–90 (1966).

Sozialpolitik. Expression first used by H Riehl in 1840 for a policy of state intervention against the excesses of Manchester Liberalism with the aim of removing the causes of social unrest. In 1872 the 'Verein für Sozialpolitik', inspired by the *Kathedersozialisten*, demanded an improvement of the working and living conditions of the working class as a prerequisite for its integration into the state. After his *Sozialistengesetz* had proved unavailing, *Bismarck* tried to reconcile the workers (from 1881) with social legislation (*social insurance*), which was resumed under *Wilhelm II* with the February decrees of 1890, which announced the extension of the Bismarckian acts. But Sozialpolitik did not win over the working class from the Socialist movement, because the workers, who remained mere objects of social institutions, were denied full political rights (*three-class suffrage*). Sozialpolitik thus made provision for material improvements but did not lead to social emancipation.

K E Born: Staat und Sozialpolitik seit Bismarcks Sturz (1957).

Spartacist Uprising. Strike and unrest in Berlin from 5 to 12 Jan 1919, caused by the dismissal of the president of the police (Eichhorn), an independent Socialist. Thereupon the *USPD* and the *Spartakusbund* called for the demonstrations on 5–6 Jan, which developed into a violent clash with government troops led by *Noske*. The uprising was suppressed on 12 Jan and in connection with it R *Luxemburg* and K *Liebknecht* were arrested and murdered. The uprising was an open confrontation between the revolutionary radical Socialists and the Social Democrats, who only got the upper hand with the assistance of the old forces. The failure of the uprising meant a decisive turn in the development after the *November Revolution*.

E Waldmann: The Spartacist Uprising (1958).

Spartakusbund. Left-wing radical-revolutionary organization founded in 1916 out of ex-members of the *SPD*. Its founders and leaders were R *Luxemburg* and K *Liebknecht*. The name was derived from the latter's 'Spartakus letters' issued from 1916. In 1917 the Spartakusbund joined the *USPD*; in 1918 it withdrew from the SPD and constituted itself as the *KPD*. After the Russian Revolution the Spartakusbund represented the Bolshevik course. During the *November Revolution* it demanded a Soviet system and opposed the policy of the Social Democrats (*Spartacist Uprising*, 1919).

G Badia: Les Spartakistes 1918 (1966).

SPD (Sozialdemokratische Partei Deutschlands). Social Democratic party founded in 1875 as 'Sozialistische Arbeiterpartei Deutschlands' by a merger of the Lasallean *ADAV* with the 'Sozialdemokratische Arbeiterpartei' (SAP) of W *Liebknecht* and A *Bebel* on the basis of the Gotha programme, which was indebted to Marxism and international socialism. In 1878 the party was forbidden by the *Sozialistengesetz* but could still participate successfully in the *Reichstag* elections (1884: 9.7 per cent). In 1890 the Social Democrats became the strongest party with 19.7 per cent of the votes. In that year it was re-founded under the name of *SPD*. Its new Erfurt programme by K *Kautsky* was still Marxist, but throughout its history the SPD remained faithful to parliamentary constitutionalism. From 1898 it also took part in the Prussian

147

Landtag elections with good results in spite of the discriminatory *three-class suffrage*. Prior to World War I, when the SPD improved its federal percentage to 34.8 in 1912, it was shaken by an ideological dispute between the revolutionary Marxists and reformist revisionists (E *Bernstein*), who were dominant after 1907 with the support of the Freie *Gewerkschaften*. By 1914 the SPD was the best organized party in the country. Its approval of the war budget (*Burgfriede*) led to the splitting off of the *USPD*, while the majority of socialists from 1917 co-operated with the *Zentrum* and the *Fortschrittspartei*. In the *November Revolution* (1918) the Social Democrats (*Ebert*) were determined to preserve the parliamentary system of the new *Weimar Republic*. After the first elections they formed the *Weimar Coalition*. The first *Reichspräsident*, the chancellors G *Bauer* and H *Müller* and other leading ministers (*Noske*) came from SPD ranks. The party programmes (Görlitz 1921, Heidelberg 1925) became increasingly reformist. The SPD share in the Reichstag elections fluctuated from 21.6 per cent (1920) to 29.8 per cent (1928) to 18.3 per cent (Mar 1933). The SPD was too indecisive to share responsibility after the world economic crisis. SPD opposition to Nazi totalitarianism, manifested in its vote against the *Enabling Act*, came too late to save the republic. On 7 July 1933 the SPD was excluded from all parliaments. Persecution forced many leading Social Democrats into exile (Prague, Paris, London, USA), from where they declined co-operation with the Communists. Resistance within Germany was confined to small circles (*Leber, Leuschner*, Mierendorff). The SPD leadership in London (E Ollenhauer) became the nucleus of the post-war West German SPD.

C E Schorske: German Social Democracy 1905–1917 (1955); W Theimer: Von Bebel zu Ollenhauer. Der Weg der deutschen Sozialdemokratie (1957).

Speer, Albert (19 Mar 1905–   ); National Socialist architect and economist. He joined the *NSDSP* in 1931. After the *Nazi seizure of power* he was occupied with Nazi building schemes for a new chancery and the Nuremberg party rally ground. On 15 Feb 1942 he succeeded Todt as minister for armaments and munitions, in Sept 1943 he became minister for armaments and war production, thus directing the entire production of the German economy. He unleashed considerable resources of industry by rationalization and mass production. In 1945 Speer impeded the execution of the *Nero Order*. The *Nuremberg Tribunal* sentenced him to 20 years' imprisonment. He was released in 1967 and published his memoirs. He had shown great talent in mobilizing Germany's economy for total warfare.

G Janssen: Das Ministerium Speer (1968).

Spengler, Oswald (29 May 1880–8 May 1936); philosopher. His reputation rests entirely on his work 'The Decline of the West', published 1918–1922. This study in the philosophy of history compares Western civilization with the Greco-Roman world and claims that all civilizations pass through a cycle of growth and decay. He contended that his approach enabled him to predict the future stages of Western history, which, according to him, was already on the decline. Spengler's view, influenced by *Nietzsche*, was an expression of the ideology of cultural despair.

H Stuart Hughes: Oswald Spengler: A Critical Estimate (1952).

Sportpalast Speech. See *Goebbels*.

SS (Schutzstaffel). Special formation of the *NSDAP*, originally founded as the bodyguard for National Socialist leaders in 1925. In 1929 Himmler was appointed 'Reichsführer *SS*', but remained subordinated to the *SA* until 1934 (*Röhm Putsch*). The central organization of the SS consisted of 12 offices. The real basis for SS power was the *Reichssicherheitshauptamt*, which comprised the security service of the *SS* (*SD*). The economic and administrative head office controlled the *concentration camps* and was competent for the SS economic empires in the occupied territories. In 1939 the SS had 240,000 members. It had an elitist aura (*Aryan racial doctrine*) and embodied the totalitarianism of *National Socialism*. As a party within the party the SS permeated the entire structure of the National Socialist state, including army, education and science. It maintained research institutes for military science and biology ('Ahnenerbe') and provided the staff for the *Ordensburgen*. A special section of the SS were the 'death's head units', who provided the guards for the *concentration camps*. Most of them, together with the SS reserves, formed the pugnacious 'Waffen SS' which fought side by side with the *Wehrmacht* and comprised 40 divisions by the end of the war, including foreign volunteers. Owing to its powerful position, the SS had a large share in all war crimes and was thus declared a criminal organization by the *Nuremberg Tribunal*.

G Reitlinger: The SS. Alibi of a Nation (1956); H Höhne: Der Orden unter dem Totenkopf. Die Geschichte der SS, 2 vols (1967).

Staatsgerichtshof. Court established by the *Republikschutzgesetz* and opened on 1 Nov 1922. It also included lay judges. It had to decide cases of constitutional conflict between the central government (Reich) and the states (Länder), as for example between the Reich and Prussia in 1932 (*Braun-Papen*).

Staatsministerium. The supreme government office in Prussia. Originally it included only the heads of the Prussian government offices, but after 1871 more and more heads of the *Reichsämter* (secretaries of state) entered it as state ministers without portfolio and regularly participated in its deliberations and resolutions to influence it in favour of the opinion of the central government. By 1914 there were six imperial representatives in it, among them the minister of war and the *Reichskanzler*, almost equalling in number the Prussian departmental ministers. This development eased the dualism between Prussia and the Reich, caused by the different suffrage (*three-class suffrage*).

Staatsrat. Prussian privy council created by the decree of 20 Mar 1817 on *Hardenberg*'s initiative. The nominal head of the Staatsrat was the King, who never used his right, which passed to an appointed president (after

Hardenberg's death). Its members were the royal princes, the state ministers, field marshals, commanding generals, the *Oberpräsidenten*, and 34 persons nominated by the King. It was not an organ with constitutional rights in administration or legislation; it only had advisory competence for legislative and administrative regulations. But its judgment was appreciated by the King, and in practice no bill was passed without its consent.

Stab-in-the-Back Legend. A false version of Germany's collapse in World War I, spread by military and nationalist circles around *Hindenburg* and *Ludendorff*, after the latter's interview with the British general, Sir Neill Malcolm, who first used the phrase. According to the legend, Germany's defeat was not caused by the enemy's superiority but by the left-wing pacifists at home. In the *Weimar Republic* the legend became an argument of the parties of the right against the exponents of the policy of *fulfilment*.

J Petzold: Die Dolchstosslegende (1963).

Stahl, Friedrich Julius (16 Jan 1802–10 Aug 1861); Conservative theorist and politician. Professor for constitutional and ecclesiastical law in the *Berlin University* (from 1840), he was an active contributor to the *Kreuzzeitung*. As a member of the first Prussian chamber (from 1849) and the *Erfurt Parliament* (from 1850) he defended the monarchic principle. He viewed the state as the manifested will of God and concluded from this that nobody had the right to overthrow the ruling authority, which, represented by an independent king, could take counter-revolutionary measures. His doctrine, which can be traced in all Prussian constitutions from 5 Dec 1848, provided for a parliament that was strictly limited and ineffectual. He was the most important spokesman of reactionary elements.

D Grosser: Grundlagen und Struktur der Staatslehre Friedrich Julius Stahls (1963).

Stahlhelm. Association of ex-servicemen founded on 25 Dec 1918 by F Seldte (1882–1947). From 1918 to 1923 it fought beside the volunteer forces (*Freikorps*). In 1924 it was extended to an organization for veterans. In the mid-twenties it had 400,000 members. The Stahlhelm was anti-republican and from the late twenties it became militant in its demand for an authoritarian government. Originally linked with the *DNVP*, it sided with the national opposition of the *Harzburg Front* (from 1930). The entry of its leader into *Hitler*'s cabinet as minister of labour in Jan 1933 contributed to the *Nazi seizure of power*. In 1934 it was converted into a 'National Socialist front-line fighters' union', but dissensions with the new Nazi members led to its dissolution in 1935.

V Berghahn: Der Stahlhelm, Bund der Frontsoldaten 1918–1935 (1966).

Stalingrad, Battle of. After the failure of *Barbarossa*, Germany tried to obtain control of the economic resources in southern Russia as a step towards final victory. From June to Sept 1942 the attacking wings were successful and reached Mt Elbrus (21 Aug) and on 15 Oct 1942, Stalingrad, where the offensive stalled and the 6th army was encircled on 22 Nov. On 8 Nov *Hitler* had publicly insisted on holding Stalingrad. The *Luftwaffe* was ordered to bring support and reserves, but the ersatz operation failed 50 km in front of Stalingrad. On 31 Jan General Paulus was forced to surrender. Stalingrad was the decisive turning-point of World War II, which could not be reversed by operation 'Zitadelle' leading up to the battle near Kursk (8–15 July 1943). The Red Army commanded the initiative in the east and systematically continued its way to *Berlin*.

R Seth: Stalingrad; Point of Return (1959); W Craig; Enemy at the Gates – the Battle for Stalingrad (1973); J Piekalkiewicz: Stalingrad. Anatomie einer Schlacht (1977).

Stauffenberg, Claus Schenk v (15 Nov 1907–20 July 1944); officer. He became alienated from the National Socialist regime after the outbreak of World War II. After *Stalingrad* he recognized the necessity of liberating Germany from Nazi dictatorship. He gathered around himself patriotic officers and established links with the *Kreisau Circle* and with *Goerdeler*. His position as chief of the general staff of the reserve army enabled him to initiate the assault on *Hitler* in the *Wolfsschanze* and the ensuing *July Plot* (1944). Stauffenberg was shot the same day. He was courageous in his vain attempt to reestablish a democratic set-up in Germany.

C Müller: Oberst i G Stauffenberg (1970).

Steel Pact. German-Italian alliance concluded on 22 May 1939 in Berlin by *Ribbentrop* and Count Ciano. The two powers, hitherto loosely tied by the October Protocols of 1936 (*Rome-Berlin Axis*), assured each other of their mutual political and diplomatic support against 'threats from outside'. Article 3 of the pact stipulated that the respective partners were obliged to enter war as an ally, if one of the two signatories was involved in a belligerent struggle with a foreign power. Impressed by early German successes (*Blitzkriege*) and appeased by the German renunciation of claims on South Tyrol (23 June 1939), Italy entered World War II on 10 June 1940. Due to her military and economic weakness she could never satisfactorily implement the pact, eg the general staffs of the two powers never consulted each other. On 3 Sept 1943 the Italian chief-of-staff Badoglio concluded a separate armistice with the Allies, thereby violating article 5 of the pact.

Stegerwald, Adam (14 Dec 1874–7 Dec 1945); Christian trade unionist and politician. He organized the formation of the *Christliche Gewerkschaften*, of which he was general secretary in 1902. He became president of the general union (Gesamtverband) in 1903. From 1919 to 1929 he was president of the *DGB*. In 1919 he also embarked on a parliamentary career as representative of the *Zentrum*, whose deputy president he became in 1920. From 1919 to 1921 he was Prussian minister of social welfare, in 1921 also minister-president. Originally in the right wing of his party, he turned against the nationalist groupings and in 1929, after resigning from all trade union offices, entered H Müller's cabinet as *Reichsminister* of transport. Under *Brüning* he served as minister of labour. In Mar 1933 Stegerwald, together with *Kaas*, conducted negotiations, with *Hitler* about the acceptance of the *Enabling Act*. After the *Gleichschaltung* he withdrew from public life.

H J Schorr: Adam Stegerwald; Gewerkschafter und Politiker der ersten Deutschen Republik (1966).

Stein, Freiherr Karl vom und zum (26 Oct 1757–29 June 1831); statesman and reformer. A Prussian civil servant from 1780, he became an expert in administration. An opponent of absolutism, he was a cautious adherent of the Enlightenment but rejected the ideas of the French Revolution. In Oct 1804 he was appointed minister for economics and finance, but he was dismissed on 3 Jan 1807, because his proposed reforms would have replaced the existing cabinet council by responsible ministries. In his Nassau memorandum of June 1807 he published his programme of bourgois reforms. After the Peace of *Tilsit* Stein was reinstated as minister and given great powers on Napoleon's behest. During his short term in office Stein then paved the ground for the entire Prussian-German interior development in the 19th century. He decreed the edicts for the *peasants' liberation* (1807) and the municipal ordinance (1808) and introduced administrative reforms. His reforms led to the rise of bourgeois influence in municipal affairs and greater involvement of the citizens against Napoleonic domination. In 1808 a letter from Stein expressing the wish for a *war of liberation* came into Napoleon's hands and Stein was again dismissed on 24 Nov. Outlawed on 16 Dec, he fled to Prague. In 1812 he was called to Russia as an adviser to Czar Alexander I, whom he persuaded to continue the war against Napoleon outside Russia. In 1813 Stein, together with *Yorck*, directed the uprising in East Prussia and mediated the Russo-Prussian alliance. In 1813–14 he was head of the central administrative council for the liberated territories. Stein's desire for a strong united Germany was not fulfilled. At the Congress of *Vienna*, as Russian delegate, Stein stood in strong opposition to Metternich's policy of restoration. In 1816 Stein retired; in 1819 he founded the *Monumenta Germaniae Historica*.

D Schwab: Die 'Selbstverwaltungsidee' des Freiherrn vom Stein (1971).

Stinnes, Hugo (12 Feb 1870–10 Apr 1924); industrialist. Prior to World War I he transformed his inherited concern into one of the biggest enterprises in the coal, iron and electric industry in Germany; from 1919 he tried to achieve a dominating position in Europe. He then commanded over 1553 separate enterprises. He co-operated with *Thyssen* and *Kirdorf*. From 1920 to 1924 Stinnes was a member of the *Reichstag* for the *DNVP*. He also served in the German delegation at the Spa conference on *reparations*. He only opposed the *Weimar Coalition*. He is said to have been the main profiteer of the inflation of 1923.

Stoecker, Adolf (11 Dec 1835–7 Feb 1909); Protestant pastor. From 1874 to 1889 he was court chaplain in Berlin and was interested in *Sozialpolitik*. As a member of the *Abgeordnetenhaus* (1879–98) and the *Reichstag* (1881–93) he belonged to the ultra-Conservative wing of the *Kreuzzeitung* party. His foundation of the 'Christlich-Soziale Arbeiterpartei' was a failure. In 1890 he helped to found the *Evangelisch-Sozialer Kongress* which he left after differences with *Naumann*. Stoecker fought fervently against progressive Liberalism, which he saw represented by the 'modern Zionism' of the Berlin press (*Ullstein*). He tried in vain to exercise a Christian-national influence on the working class, but he shared responsibility for stirring up *anti-Semitism* among the lower middle classes in Berlin.

K Kupisch: Adolf Stoecker und Volkstribum (1970).

Strafgesetzbuch. Penal code passed on 31 May 1870, replacing the Prussian penal law of 1851. It was influenced by liberal legal principles.

Strasser, Gregor (31 May 1892–30 June 1934); National Socialist. He was an influential exponent of *National Socialism* from its beginning. He took part in The *Munich (Bierkeller) Putsch* and was sentenced to $1^1/_2$ years' imprisonment but prematurely released because of his election to the Bavarian *Landtag* in 1924. From 1925 he built up the *NSDAP* in north Germany. He represented an anti-capitalist state feudalism, which brought him into opposition to *Hitler*, who had just avoided a secession of the north German party organization in 1925–26. When Hitler opposed Strasser's entry into *Schleicher*'s cabinet, Strasser laid down all his party offices. During the *Röhm Putsch* he was shot by order of *Himmler* and *Göring* who were afraid of his political comeback.

Strasser, Otto (10 Sept 1897–27 Aug 1974); National Socialist. The brother of Gregor *Strasser*, he was a member of the *NSDAP* from 1925 to 1930. After his break with *Hitler*, he founded the 'Fighting Community of Revolutionary National Socialists' (Black Front), an organization of all anti-capitalist adherents of the National Socialist movement. In 1933 he emigrated, but he failed to form an anti-Hitler front abroad.

Streicher, Julius (12 Feb 1885–16 Oct 1946); National Socialist. In 1921 he joined his nationalist splinter group to the *NSDAP*. He took part in the *Munich (Bierkeller) Putsch* and became a vociferous propagandist of the party with his mouthpiece 'Der Stürmer' (from 1923). In 1925 he was appointed *Gauleiter* in Franconia; in 1932 he entered the *Reichstag*. After the *Nazi seizure of power* he increased his anti-Semitic agitation: he propagated the boycott of the *Jews*, prepared the *Nuremberg Laws*, and helped to organize the *Crystal Night* in 1938. His moral depravity caused his dismissal as Gauleiter in 1940, but because of his close connection with *Hitler*, he could continue his racist and militarist propaganda, for which the *Nuremberg Tribunal* sentenced him to death.

R Lenman: 'Julius Streicher and the Origins of the NSDAP in Nuremberg 1919–23', in A J Nicholls and E Matthias: German Democracy and the Triumph of Hitler (1971).

Stresemann, Gustav (10 May 1878–3 Oct 1929); statesman. National Liberal deputy in the *Reichstag* (1907–12, 1914–18). In 1917 he became leader of his parliamentary party, working for the downfall of *Bethmann Hollweg*. Stresemann approved of annexationist aims and voted against the *peace resolution*. In 1918 he founded the *DVP*. On 12 Aug 1923 he became *Reichskanzler* of the first grand coalition and was the first Liberal chancellor. During his 100 days in office he ended the *Ruhrkampf*, overcame inflation (*Rentenmark*), suppressed the separatists in the *Rhineland*, and put down the *Hamburg Uprising* and the *Munich (Bierkeller) Putsch* with the help of the *Reichswehr*. But the *SPD* resented his conduct against the popular front government in Saxony (*Reichsexekution*) and withdrew its support on 22 Nov. From then on Stresemann was *Reichsminister* for foreign affairs and was mainly concerned with the problem of the *reparations*, which he wanted to solve through a realistic policy of *fulfilment*. He started a policy of détente with France in negotiations with the French Prime Minister Briand, with whom he shared the Nobel Prize for Peace in 1926. His major decisions were the acceptance of the *Dawes Plan* (1924) and the *Young Plan* (1929), the conclusion of the *Locarno* treaties (1925), and Germany's entry into the League of Nations (1926). He also co-operated with Russia (*Berlin Treaty* of 1926). In his endeavours he was heavily attacked by the right, also within his own party (*Stinnes*). In his home policy as Chancellor he defended parliamentary democracy. His foreign policy, though designed as a peaceful *Revisionspolitik*, restored international recognition for Germany. He was one of the most controversial politicians of the *Weimar Republic*.

H A Turner: Stresemann and the Politics of the Weimar Republic (1963); F Hirsch: Gustav Stresemann (1964); J Walsdorff: Gustav Stresemann – Bibliographie (1973).

Stumm-Halberg, Karl Baron v (30 Mar 1836–8 Mar 1901); industrialist. Leading entrepreneur in the *Saar district*, he was a protagonist of a patriarchal system in the economy and a strong opponent of the *Freie Gewerkschaften*. He helped to found the *Freikonservative Partei*. He had been an advocate of *Bismarck's Sozialpolitik* and introduced welfare institutions in his own firm, but was opposed to any form of partnership with the workers and became the antagonist of *Berlepsch* and *Lohmann*. From 1896 he was greatly instrumental in turning *Wilhelm II* against the *SPD*. His name is linked with suggestions for tightening up regulations against labour organizations.

Sudeten Germans (Sudetendeutsche). German minority living in the northern mountain regions of Czechoslovakia. They numbered 3.2 million in 1938. They were maltreated by the Czechoslovak authorities and aspired inclusion in the German state. Their militant representative was the Sudetendeutsche party led by *Henlein*, which acted as a fifth column for Nazi Germany in the preparation of the destruction of Czechoslovakia. The aspirations of the Sudeten Germans were fulfilled by the *Munich Agreement* of 29 Sept 1938. In 1945 the Sudeten Germans were expelled from Czechoslovakia (*Vertreibung*).

R M Smelser: The Sudeten Problem, 1933–1938 (1975).

Swastika (Hakenkreuz). Interpreted as a sun wheel in Germany, the Swastika was accepted as their symbol by anti-Semitic organizations at the suggestion of the nationalist ideologist C v List in 1910. The *NSDAP* made it its party emblem and after the *Nazi seizure of power* it was inserted in most official insignia. On 15 Sept 1935 it became the national flag.

Tangier, landing in. *Wilhelm II* landed in the Moroccan port of Tangier on 31 Mar 1905. In front of the diplomatic corps the Kaiser assured the Sultan that he regarded him as an absolutely free sovereign and that he wanted to preserve an independent Morocco for peaceful competition of all nations. This dramatic gesture was a challenge to French attempts to secure semi-colonial influence in Morocco. The incident, which was conceived by the *Auswärtiges Amt* (*Holstein*), caused the first Moroccan crisis, which the German government deliberately engineered to test the entente cordiale, which provided for British support of special French interests in Morocco. Tension due to the provocation was relieved by the summoning of the conference at *Algeciras*.

Tannenberg. Battle in World War I, 26–30 Aug 1914. After the Russian invasion of East Prussia with 2 armies the Germans (under General v Prittwitz) retreated behind the Vistula. The new commanders, *Hindenburg* and *Ludendorff*, decided to make use of Major Max Hoffmann's plan to concentrate all but one division against Samsonov's army, which was surrounded and exterminated. The Germans captured 100,000 prisoners and large quantities of guns. Thereafter, strengthened by reinforcements from the west, they turned against Rennenkampf's army which had been largely responsible for the success of Tannenberg. From 6 to 15 Sept the Russians again suffered a devastating defeat in the 'battle of the Masurian lakes', where they lost another 125,000 men. Tannenberg saved Germany from further foreign invasion during World War I and fostered hopes for a decisive victory in the east. The military success of Tannenberg also prepared the advent to political power of the third *Oberste Heeresleitung*, because of the Hindenburg myth, which was incarnated in the national monument erected near Hohenstein in 1927. (It was blown up in 1945 before the advent of the Red Army.)

G Evans: Tannenberg 1410: 1914 (1971).

Tauroggen, Convention of. Agreement concluded at Tauroggen in Lithuania on 30 Dec 1812 by *Yorck von Wartenburg* (without authorization by his King) and the Russian General Diebitsch. As a result, the Prussian auxiliary corps, intended for Napoleon's Russian campaign, was neutralized, thereby allowing the Russians to occupy the Baltic coast between Königsberg and Memel. Tauroggen was a decisive impetus for the Prussian national uprising in the following year (*wars of liberation*).

H Bock: Rebell im Preussenrock. Tauroggen 1812 (1963).

Technische Hochschulen. Colleges for the training of technical management (engineers). The demand for professional training was first recognized by the

Prussian civil servant P Beuth (1781–1853), who initiated an Association for the Promotion of Technical Knowledge (1820) and the Berlin Technical Institute (established in 1821) to provide two-year training courses for boys over the age of twelve. Its students, unlike those of universities, were not recruited from the humanist *Gymnasium* but from the new type of 'Realschule', whose curricula included applied science. Similar colleges were founded in Karlsruhe, Munich and elsewhere. They co-operated with industry and were instrumental in bringing about Germany's industrial advance in the late 19th century.

Teplitz Punktation. Agreement between Austria and Prussia concluded by Metternich and *Hardenberg* on 1 Aug 1819. It determined a common federal policy towards the liberal forces and established the restoration system in Germany. It envisaged the surveillance of the universities, the press and the *Landtage*. The autonomy and inviolability of the German states, as guaranteed by § 2 of the Federal Act of the *Deutscher Bund*, were interpreted in a limited sense by the two main powers. Accordingly, no principles incompatible with the security of the Confederation were to be applied; otherwise a federal intervention would ensue. It formed the bases for the *Carlsbad Decrees*.

Thälmann, Ernst (16 Apr 1886–18 Aug 1944); Communist. From 1924 he was a *Reichstag* deputy for the *KPD* and in 1925, after Stalin had urged the succession of Ruth Fischer, he became president of the party. He was also leader of the *Roter Frontkämpferbund*. In 1925 and 1932 he stood as candidate for the office of *Reichspräsident*. In 1933 he was detained and imprisoned in *concentration camps* until his assassination in 1944. He was a faithful follower of the Moscow directorate of his party.
W Bredel: Ernst Thälmann (1961).

Thälmann-Bataillon. Contingent of German *anti-Fascists* who fought during the Spanish Civil War. It was the backbone of the international brigades which fought on the Republican side against the interventionists of the *Rome-Berlin Axis*.

Third Reich (Drittes Reich). Term used in medieval historiography for a future golden period in which the difference between ideas and reality will disappear. It was a catchword of conservative-romanticist nationalism after the publication of Mueller van den Bruck's 'Das Dritte Reich' in 1923. In 1933 *National Socialism* adopted the term for the era of the Fascist German state.
P H Silfen: The Völkisch Ideology and the Roots of Nazism (1976).

Thousand-Year Reich. In Christianity a term used to denote the kingdom of Christ after his Second Coming. The term was used blasphemously by the National Socialists for their rule in Germany. In view of its mere 12-year existence, the term has generally been used in an ironic sense since 1945.

Three-class suffrage. Electoral law for the *Abgeordnetenhaus* in Prussia from 1849 to 1918 (from 1896 also in Saxony), according to which every constituency was divided into three classes, each representing one third of the total amount of taxes levied. Thus the voting power was on average divided by 82:14:4; ie the few highest taxed had as many votes as the greater number of the middle class and the mass of the lowest taxed citizens. All attempts at a reform of the system, which favoured the Conservatives against the *SPD*, fell through until the *November Revolution* (1918), although the prospect of its abolition had been held out in the 'Easter message' of *Wilhelm II* on 7 Apr 1917.

R Patemann: Der Kampf um die preussische Wahlreform im ersten Weltkrieg (1964).

Three Emperors' Alliance. Agreement between Germany, Austria and Russia initiated by *Bismarck* and publicly announced in 1872, when the emperors of the three countries met in Berlin. It was inspired by Austro-Russian rivalry in the Balkans. In 1881 a treaty of neutrality pledged benevolent neutrality in the event of an attack by other powers on a partner and agreed to try to localize the conflicts arising, for example, from the Balkan question. But Bismarck failed to attain a definition of their spheres of interest by Russia and Austria. Despite a further meeting of the emperors at Skierniewice (1884) he could not prevent the break-up of the Three Emperors' Alliance during the Balkan crisis of 1886. It formally expired in 1887.

W N Medlicott: Bismarck and the Three Emperors Alliance 1881–1887, in Transactions of the Royal Historical Society 27 (1945).

Three Kings' Alliance. Treaty concluded on 26 May 1849 between Saxony, Hanover and Prussia, who all agreed with Prussia's *union plan*. The treaty contained a clause for giving notice in case a German state did not join the alliance. In fact, except for Württemberg and Bavaria, all the larger states joined it. The recovery of Austria and her rejection of federal reform led to the withdrawal of Saxony and Hanover from the alliance.

Three Powers' Pact. Treaty concluded on 27 Sept 1940 in Berlin between Germany, Italy and Japan with a view to re-arranging their spheres of interest in Europe and Asia. It left untouched the relations of each member with Soviet Russia. In 1940 Hungary, Rumania and Slovakia; in 1941 Bulgaria and Yugoslavia (revoked after two days) entered the pact. On 18 Jan 1942 the pact was supplemented by a military alliance; on 11 Dec 1942 the partners agreed that no member must conclude an armistice or peace without the consent of the others. After Germany's surrender, Japan regarded the pact as having been violated and cancelled it on 6 May 1945.

Thyssen, Fritz (9 Nov 1873–8 Feb 1951); industrialist. From 1926 he was chairman of the supervisory board of the biggest iron and ore trust; in 1928 he chaired the international crude steel community. He was among the most outspoken opponents of the *Weimar Republic* and an early supporter of the *Stahlhelm* and the *NSDAP*. In 1932 he signed a petition of bankers to

157

Hindenburg asking for the appointment of *Hitler*. After the *Nazi seizure of power* he differed with Hitler about the appropriateness of starting a war, which Thyssen regarded as precipitous. He emigrated to France and was extradited in 1940, put into a *concentration camp* and later detained by the Americans, who released him in 1948, classifying him as a fellow-traveller.

W Treue: Die Feuer verlöschen nie. August-Thyssen-Hütte 1819–1926 (1966).

Tilsit, Peace of. Franco-Prussian peace treaty of 9 July 1807, ending the war between the two powers lost by Prussia. Prussia was asked to accept the conditions as dictated by the victor within 48 hours without further negotiations. It was made to cede all Polish possessions and to evacuate all territories west of the River Elbe. Thus Prussian territory remained limited to the provinces of Brandenburg, Pommerania, (East) Prussia and Silesia. Prussia was made to join the continental blockade against Russia. An additional convention concluded at Königsberg regulated the retreat of the French troops, which was illusory because Prussia was unable to pay the pending contributions. So Prussia had to endure French occupation. The Peace of Tilsit ended the existence of the Prussian state as an independent European power.

Tirpitz, Alfred v (19 Mar 1849–6 Mar 1930); admiral and politician. He became state secretary of the naval office (*Reichsämter*) in 1897. He strove to build up a navy that was technologically advanced and militarily effective, holding that the best defence was a powerful battle fleet (*Flottenpolitik*). His views as a sailor were sound but his political ideas were naive. He made naval service popular with the help of the *Flottenverein*, persuaded *Wilhelm II* and the *Reichstag* to accept his plans. He saw international problems very narrowly, believing that the British would stifle German trade unless afraid of the risk of war. This basis of his strategic thought largely determined German foreign policy before 1914. His power in wartime was limited. The executive command of the navy was separate. The concentration on submarines (*U-Boat-Warfare*) was contrary to his stipulations and he resigned in 1916. His subsequent activities in party politics (foundation of the *Vaterlandspartei* with W *Kapp* in 1917; member of the *Reichstag* for the *DNVP* in 1924–25) are overshadowed by his pre-war position as creator of the German navy.

V Berghan: Der Tirpitz-Plan (1974).

Togo. German protectorate (*Schutzgebiete*) from 1884, German merchants and missionaries having been active in the Ewe territory since 1847. The borders were fixed in treaties with France and Britain in the 1890s. German military expeditions into the hinterland met with little resistance, the administration was efficient but harsh in the treatment of forced native labour. Togo became the only economically viable German colony: from 1907 onwards it was able to balance its budget. Hence it was regarded as an ideal example of German *Kolonialpolitik*. In 1913, the 90,000 sq km territory was believed to have a population of 1,032,000. On 26 Aug 1914 the *Schutztruppe* had to surrender to the invading British and French colonial troops. In 1919 Togo was divided between the two occupying powers, who then administered it as a mandate.

Trade Unions. See *Gewerkschaften.*

Treitschke, Heinrich v (15 Sept 1834–28 Apr 1896); historian and politician. He heralded the foundation of the German Empire under Prussian leadership (*kleindeutsch*). A National Liberal deputy in the *Reichstag* from 1871, he opposed the *Kathedersozialisten* and preached *anti-Semitism*. In his lectures at the *Berlin University* he revered an 'ethically based power state'. His 'German History of the 19th Century' was intended for patriotic political education. It influenced the outlook of the German bourgeoisie in the Wilhelmine era, whereas abroad it won Treitschke the image of the theorist of *Weltpolitik.*

A Dorpalen: Heinrich v Treitschke (1957).

Treviranus, Gottfried (20 Mar 1891–7 June 1971); Conservative politician. In 1924 Treviranus entered the Reichstag for the *DNVP*, but he left the party in 1929 after differences with *Hugenberg* and founded the *Volkskonservative Vereinigung* (1930). Under *Brüning*, Treviranus became minister for the occupied territories and also commissioner for the *Osthilfe.* From Sept 1930 he was *Reichsminister* without portfolio; in Brüning's second cabinet he was minister of transport. In 1934 he emigrated to England, and lived later in the USA and Canada.

Trias. Idea of establishing a third, completely independent power in Germany beside Austria and Prussia. The precursor of the Trias was the Confederation of the *Rhine.* In the *Deutscher Bund* opposition by the medium size states was first led by Württemberg; after 1850 the concept of a triple division became the basis of the propositions for federal reform advanced by L v Pfordten and *Beust* on behalf of Bavaria and Saxony respectively. The suspicions felt by the middle states for each other prevented the Trias from coming to anything.

Triple Alliance. Secret defensive alliance between Germany, Austria-Hungary and Italy, which was concluded when the latter joined the *Dual Alliance* on 20 May 1882. The Triple Alliance, which had to be renewed every five years, stipulated that in the event of an attack by two or more great powers against one allied partner, the others were obliged to come to the victim's rescue (except against Britain). In 1883 Rumania was informally joined to the alliance by special treaties with Germany and Austria-Hungary. In 1887 supplements to the alliance provided adjustments between Austria and Italy for territorial changes in the Balkans, while Germany promised Italy assistance against France in the Mediterranean. These clauses illustrate that Italy was the weak point in the alliance. In 1902 she made a secret treaty with France, in 1914 Italy did not accept the 'casus foederis' by remaining neutral, and in 1915 entered the war against the *Central Powers*, thereby breaking the alliance. The Triple Alliance aimed at keeping Austria's back free from Italian aspirations in the event of a conflict with Russia, but it was used by Italy for colonial adventures and blackmail. It did not provide a solid diplomatic basis for Germany's *Mitteleuropa* plans; rather, it was a factor of uncertainty.

F Fellner: Der Dreibund (1960).

Trott zu Solz, Adam v (9 Sept 1909–26 Aug 1944); diplomat. He was German Rhodes scholar in Oxford, 1931–33, and as counsellor in the *Auswärtiges Amt* from 1940, used his contacts abroad to seek Allied understanding for the German resistance movement, but he found little response for the 'other Germany'. He was arrested in connection with the *July Plot* (1944) and executed.

C Sykes: Adam von Trott zu Solz (1968).

Tugendbund. Patriotic association founded in 1808 by young academics, officers in favour of reform, aristocrats and men of letters, belonging to the Königsberg Freemason's lodge. The association wished to revive morality, religiosity and public spirit. It wanted to strengthen patriotism in spite of Napoleonic domination. It quickly expanded and spread in the country. It entertained good relations with *Scharnhorst* and *Stein*. The Tugendbund was not a direct-membership organization but a network of sympathizers, whose number rose to 700 at its peak. On 31 Dec 1809 it was formally dissolved by royal decree, but it continued to function and was the starting-point for new patriotic associations (*Deutsche Gesellschaften*).

Turnen. Physical training with special emphasis on gymnastics. It was introduced in the early 19th century by F L *Jahn*, K F Friesen and others. The liberal and national ideas connected with the movement led to its prohibition in 1819. But it was illegally continued until the ban on it was lifted in 1842, when it was included in school curricula. In 1860 the 'Deutsche Turnerschaft' was founded as a national organization of all athletes practising Turnen in clubs. From 1891 Social Democratic Workers' Clubs sprang up. They were an important factor in the physical and political education of the working class until their dissolution in 1933. In National Socialist Germany Turnen and all other sports were exploited for military training and nationalist propaganda, reaching its climax with the staging of the Olympic Games of 1936 in Berlin.

U-Boat-Warfare. Submarine warfare opened on 4 Feb 1915 against the merchant shipping of the Allies as a reprisal against the tightening of the British blockade. All waters around the British Isles were declared a 'war zone' and a substantial tonnage was sunk with only 21 U-boats. After the sinking of the American vessel 'Lusitania' (in which 120 US citizens died) on 7 May 1915 this first phase of the warfare was restricted in Sept because of protests of neutral countries. On 29 Feb 1916 the escalation of blockade measures was answered by *Falkenhayn* with an intensified U-boat warfare, which quickly achieved a high rate of success, but the renewed loss of American lives (24 March 1916: 'Sussex') led to the cancellation of the tightened up rules of this transitional phase. In autumn 1916 the third *Oberste Heeresleitung* became the advocate of

160

an unrestricted U-boat warfare, which was supported by public opinion (*Zentrum* resolution). On 9 Jan 1917 *Bethmann Hollweg* consented and after the refusal of their ostensible peace offer of 12 Dec 1916 by the Entente, the Central Powers announced unrestricted submarine warfare on 1 Feb 1917. Then the U-boat warfare became a race between German sinkings and Allied ship construction. In Apr 1917, 430 ships (852,000 tons) were sunk; the peak of German strength was reached in Oct 1917 (140 boats). But the Allied convoy system and the US output overcame the German challenge. The U-boat warfare did not force Britain to surrender or sign a compromise peace and was instrumental in bringing the USA into the war against Germany (4 Apr 1917). By the armistice terms (*Compiègne*) Germany had to surrender all U-boats and the Treaty of *Versailles* forbade her to possess any. It was not until 1935 that the *London Naval Agreement* authorized Germany to build submarines up to the British strength, though the London protocol of 1936 expected her to observe the rules of international law. In 1939 Germany repeated the U-boat challenge with only 57 boats but with great success. In 1941, with bases along the Atlantic coast, German submarine groups ('wolf packs') operated across the Atlantic. In Mar 1943 they almost succeeded in cutting off American supplies to Britain, but after heavy losses inflicted by bombing, dared only to operate in remote waters until the snorkel allowed them to match radar. Still, in the remaining months of the war the U-boats suffered many losses and could not prevent the Allied invasion. In World War II Germany built 1,162 boats, 785 of which were destroyed; the remainder surrendered in 1945.

K E Birnbaum: Peace Moves and U-Boat Warfare (1958); S W Roskill: The War at Sea 1939–45.

Ullstein. Publishing house founded in 1877 by L Ullstein (1826–1899). Papers published by it included the *Vossische Zeitung*, 'Berliner Morgenpost', 'BZ', and various illustrated magazines. In 1933 Ullstein was expropriated because of his Jewish descent; the company was continued as 'Deutscher Verlag'. In 1952 the publishing company was restored to the Ullstein family.

Umsturzvorlage. Bill providing for tightening of the penal law for political subversion. It was presented to the *Reichstag* by *Hohenlohe* in Dec 1894. According to it, more severe penalties were threatened for inciting others to commit punishable offences, stirring up class-conflict, public offences relating to marriage, family and property, and insults to the state and its organs. Only the Conservatives supported it in full. The *Zentrum* made its approval dependent on the inclusion of penalties for offences against the Christian religion and the Church. When the government amended the bill, it was opposed by the *SPD*, the *Freisinnige* and the National Liberals whose protest was supported by many intellectuals who feared that such a law might serve to silence any academic criticism of religious and ecclesiastical issues. So the bill was rejected on 11 May 1895.

Unconditional Surrender. This was agreed upon by Churchill and Roosevelt at the Casablanca Conference (14–26 Jan 1943). This formula, which was criticized as un-Christian by Pope Pius XII, was grist to the mill of the German Ministry of Propaganda, for it seemed to support the thesis of a struggle for survival of the German people and also deprived the German resistance movement of the possibility of peace negotiations on a basis of equality. *Dönitz's* government was forced to accept unconditional surrender; on 7 May 1945 *Jodl* surrendered to the Western Allies in Reims; on 8 May 1945 *Keitel* capitulated to the Red Army.

Unemployment Insurance Act (Arbeitslosenversicherungsgesetz). An act passed by *Marx's* second cabinet on 16 July 1927. It determined the amount of unemployment benefit on the basis of the previous wage earned. The costs were evenly split between the employer and the employees, a fixed percentage of whose income was deducted. The act was an important landmark in the social legislation of the *Weimar Republic*, as it secured a minimum sustenance for the unemployed. When the dues under the act were raised to cover the costs of payments during the world economic crisis, the *SPD* withdrew from the last grand coalition (27 March 1930).

Union Plan (Unionsprojekt). Attempt to create a union of German states under Prussian leadership. This plan was devised by Gen J M v Radowitz (1797–1853), a Catholic Conservative who became foreign minister in autumn 1850. The plan had been introduced by the conclusion of the *Three Kings' Alliance* on 26 May 1849. It was intended to meet national and liberal demands in order to prevent new disorder. It envisaged a common customs, trade and foreign policy. The union parliament was to be elected according to the *three-class suffrage*: the executive power was to be vested in the Prussian King (*Friedrich Wilhelm IV*), who had the right of veto against parliamentary resolutions. In June 1849, at a conference in Gotha, the plan was approved by the *Erbkaiserliche*. A conference to discuss a new constitution for Germany on the basis of the plan met on 20 Mar 1850 (*Erfurt Parliament*). However, Austria began to oppose the plan at the *Dresden Conference* (Dec 1850–Mar 1851), whereupon Prussia's partners revised their positive attitude toward it. In Prussia, too, the nobility which had always been sceptical of the plan (*Camarilla*), regained influence. In autumn 1850 the plan was finally abandoned by Prussia in the *Olmütz Punktation*. The plan was the first, if abortive, attempt to found a united German empire 'from above', as it was later realized by *Bismarck* (*Kaiserproklamation*).

USPD (Unabhängige Sozialdemokratische Partei Deutschlands). Independent Social Democrats, founded in Apr 1917 by H Haase and K *Kautsky* as the party of a rigorous anti-war opposition. They disagreed with the majority of the *SPD* and had already opposed the war budget (*Burgfriede*) in 1914. During the *November Revolution* (1918) the USPD increased its strength. On 9 Nov 1918 the USPD and the SPD constituted the *Rat der Volksbeauftragten* as a provisional government, from which the USPD withdrew at the end of the year. In the elections for the *Weimar National Assembly* the USPD won only

7.6 per cent of the votes, but under the impact of the revolutionary ferment that gripped the broad masses it gained 18.8 per cent in the first *Reichstag* of the new republic in 1920, in which the USPD constituted the left wing opposition together with the *KPD*. At a party congress in Halle in Oct 1920, 300,000 out of 800,000 members broke away from it and joined the Communists. The remainder rejoined the SPD by 1922.

R E Wheeler: *USPD* und Internationale − sozialistischer Internationalismus in der Ziet der Revolution (1975).

D W Morgan: The Socialist Left and the German Revolution. A History of the German Independent Social Democratic Party, 1917−1922. (1975).

V1−V2 (Flying Bombs). Missiles developed at the end of World War II, with which the Nazis hoped to retaliate against Allied bombardment. They were bombs flying with rocket propulsion at 650 km/h (VI) and 5,000 km/h (V2) respectively and ranging 250 km. Several thousand V2 were used, especially against London, but did not produce a devastating effect. The Ministry of Propaganda exaggerated them as 'miracle weapons'.

D Irving: Die Wunderwaffen des Dritten Reiches (1975).

Vaterlandspartei. Patriotic party founded on 2 Sept 1917 by W *Kapp*. It was devised as a reservoir for all opponents of the *peace resolution* of the *Reichstag* majority. The party wanted to unite all patriotic forces disregarding their ideological background. It was supported by the *Fortschrittliche Volkspartei*, the National Liberals and the Conservatives and by influential industrialists. In July 1918 the party had 1.25 million members. It was to cease to exist after the conclusion of a victorious peace. Its war aims came close to those of the *Alldeutscher Verband*. It was dissolved on 10 Dec 1918.

Verdun, Battle of. German attempt to knock France out of World War I (Feb−July 1916). *Falkenhayn* hoped that an all-out offensive at so crucial a point as Verdun would 'bleed France to death' by annihilating her best troops. After it Britain would have lost 'her best sword'. The attack on Verdun was calculated on the basis of the strategy of localized attrition, ie methodical stages of hammer-strokes, each with a limited objective. German bombardment began on 21 Feb, advances were slight but cumulative in effect. Verdun was relieved by the Allied Somme offensive and the German attack ceased on 21 June, although the fighting continued until 11 July. The Germans crushed several French divisions but fell short of their final objective. However, the French army was so drained that in 1916 the British had to take the main burden.

Vereinigter Landtag. Prussian parliament first convened on 11 Apr 1847 on the basis of the patent of 3 Feb 1847. It consisted of all members of the *Provinzialstände*. Of its 613 members 307 belonged to the nobility, 306 to the bourgeoisie. It was to be summoned irregularly by the King. In practice this happened only twice (11 Apr 1847 and in Apr 1848). Parliamentary parties ranging from the Conservative to the Liberal wing were soon formed. The competence of the parliament extended to tax questions and public debts; it had an advisory function relating to legislative drafts of the government and petitions to the King. Its decisions were not binding except in financial questions. Thus the parliament lagged behind the representative bodies of the south and central German states (Baden, Hesse). The expectations of the Democrats and Liberals could not be fulfilled by it. Though not a representative of the Prussian population, it was at least the first parliament in the development of the Prussian state.

Versailles, Treaty of. Peace treaty signed on 28 June 1919 by Germany and 27 other nations. The peace conference had begun on 18 Jan 1919. Germany was not admitted to the negotiations and on 7 May 1919 the German delegation, headed by *Brockdorff-Rantzau*, was confronted with the terms dictated by the four great powers (Britain, France, Italy, USA) and forced to accept them. The treaty had 440 clauses in 15 parts. Part I contained the covenant of the League of Nations. Part II regulated cessions of territory on Germany's borders, totalling 70,000 sq km with 6.5 million inhabitants (*Alsace-Lorraine, Saar district, Plebiscite districts, Danzig, Memelland, Hultschin Territory*). Germany's rivers were internationalized and her sovereignty over the *Rhineland* was restricted. Part V determined disarmament and limitations of the new army (*Reichswehr*). Part VIII regulated the question of *reparations* on the basis of Germany's responsibility for the outbreak of World War I (§231). German war criminals, including *Wilhelm II*, were to be extradited. The treaty was only signed under protest by Germany. Its clauses were resented as a humiliation, in particular the *war-guilt clause*, the allegation that Germany was incapable of administering her colonies (*Schutzgebiete*) and to the denial of an *Anschluss* of Germany and Austria. The treaty was designed to initiate a period of permanent peace, but it became the cause of renewed international tension. It made Germany a second-rate power without punishing her so hard as to make her recovery impossible. The reparations clauses plunged her into economic chaos, which provided arguments for the propaganda of the extreme right. Thus the treaty was a permanent topic of debate in the politics of the *Weimar Republic* (*Revisionspolitik*, policy of *fulfilment*).

Vertreibung. Expulsion of the German population from their homes in the eastern provinces in accordance with the territorial reshaping of eastern Europe after World War II. According to art. 7 of the *Potsdam Agreement*, it was to have been carried out in an orderly and humanitarian way, but in reality it often assumed cruel forms. It was also extended to the *Volksdeutsche* in eastern and south eastern Europe and the entire number affected by it is estimated at 13.6 million.

A M de Zayas: Nemesis at Potsdam. The Anglo-Americans and the Expulsion of the Germans (1976).

Vienna, Congress of. International assembly of monarchs and diplomats in Vienna from 18 Sep 1814 to 9 June 1815 to re-establish the political order of

Europe after the *wars of liberation* against Napoleon. German agents were *Stein* (for Russia), *Hardenberg* (for Prussia) and F v Gentz (1764–1834), a Prussian in Austrian diplomatic service as advisor to Metternich, who acted as secretary-general of the congress. The Final Act of 9 June determined the territorial settlements. As far as the German lands were concerned, the results were as follows: Austria recovered her cessions to Bavaria; Prussia obtained the *Rhineland*, an enlarged *Westphalia*, almost half of the kingdom of Saxony, Swedish Pomerania, while ceding territory to Bavaria, Hanover (which was raised to a kingdom) and Russia. Britain retained *Heligoland*. The former Holy Roman Empire of the German Nation was replaced by a loose confederation of the German states. Non-territorial pronouncements included free navigation of the Rhine and the recommendation of the emancipation of *Jews* in Germany. The political principles of the congress were restoration, legitimism and solidarity against revolutionary movements, as later continued by the *Holy Alliance*.

Virchow, Rudolph (13 Oct 1821–5 Sept 1902); pathologist and politician. He was founder (1861) and leader (with E *Richter*) of the *Fortschrittspartei*. For his stern opposition during the *constitutional conflicts*, Virchow was challenged to a duel by *Bismarck* in 1865. From 1880 to 1893 he was a *Reichstag* deputy and participated in cultural and ecclesiastical affairs. He coined the word *Kulturkampf*.

E H Ackerknecht: Rudolph Virchow; Doctor, Statesman, Anthropologist (1953).

Vize-Kanzler. Office of a representative of the *Reichskanzler*, created by the law of 17 Mar 1878. This 'vice-chancellor' was authorized to represent the Reichskanzler in all affairs, including the signing of the imperial decrees. Such representation had become necessary, because *Bismarck* was frequently absent from Berlin. In respect of the federal states the law excluded those departments, in which the competence of the central government was confined to legislation and supervision, with the power of execution in federal hands. The Vize-Kanzler was also appointed to the chairmanship of the Prussian *Staats-ministerium* and became secretary of state of the 'Reichsamt des Innern'. The first holder of this office was Count Stolberg-Wernigerode.

Völkerschlacht. See *Leipzig, Battle of.*

Völkischer Beobachter. Central organ of the *NSDAP* acquired in Munich in 1920. The chief editor was *Rosenberg*. It reached its peak circulation in 1944 (c. 1.7 million copies). Its last issue appeared in Apr 1945.

Völkisch parties, movement. See *Anti-Semitism.*

Volksbegehren/Volksentscheid. Constitutional possibilities (§§ 73–77 of the Reich *constitution* of 1919) for legislation by plebiscite. One-tenth of the enfranchised population could move a bill in the *Reichstag* (Volksbegehren)

165

and if this was refused, the decision was taken in a Volksentscheid, needing a quorum of the majority of the enfranchised. A Volksentscheid could also be demanded by the *Reichspräsident*, if the *Reichsrat* disagreed with an act passed by the Reichstag, but this never occurred. In the history of the *Weimar Republic* there were seven Volksbegehren and two Volksentscheid, namely on the compensation for *princes* (1926) and the *Young Plan* (1929), both of which failed. A Volksbegehren was held on the 'Panzerkreuzerbau A' ('armoured cruiser A'). They were attempts to let the people participate directly in political decision-making, but these plebiscites were also apt to undermine the idea of representative democracy.

Volksdeutsche (ethnic Germans). Settlers of German origin living for centuries outside the frontiers of Germany (and Austria). They received German citizenship after resettling (*Umsiedlung*) in the *Grossdeutsches Reich* during the era of *National Socialism*, which propagated their return. The resettlement of the Volksdeutsche, together with the *Vertreibung*, extinguished the traditional German settlements in eastern and south-eastern Europe except for small groups.

Volksempfänger. Simple wireless set. The National Socialist leadership recognized the propaganda value of the radio as a medium and encouraged the purchase of inexpensive sets under the slogan 'the whole of Germany listens to the *Führer*'.

Volksgemeinschaft. Social concept of *National Socialism*, according to which neither descent nor class origin was important. All German citizens who served the nation by manual or intellectual labour were to be recognized as equals within the community of the nation. But after the *Nazi seizure of power* the position of the *Volksgenossen* remained virtually unchanged. The Volksgemeinschaft was only realized in propaganda enterprises like *Kraft durch Freude*, which were intended to conceal the continuing social disparities.
T W Mason: Arbeiterklasse und Volksgemeinschaft (1974).

Volksgenosse. Term of National Socialist propaganda, for the members of the *Volksgemeinschaft*, to which every German belonged by virtue of his nationality. The increasing application of the *Aryan racial doctrine* limited this criterion to racial purity.

Volksgerichtshof. National Socialist special court established on 24 Apr 1934. It had sole jurisdiction over high treason and political offences. Except for its presidents (Thierack, *Freisler*) it was composed of loyal lay-judges. It was an instrument for the suppression of political opposition and became notorious for its trial of the conspirators of the *Jul·· Plot* (1944).
W Wagner: Der Volksgerichtshof im nationalsozialistischen Staat (1974).

Volkskonservative Vereinigung. Conservative party formed in January 1930 by secessionists from the *DNVP* under the leadership of *Treviranus* and *Westarp*. They strove to reconcile monarchy and republicanism by a form of conservative Christian democracy. It had 10,000 members but, under the name of 'Konservative Volkspartei', won only 4 seats in the *Reichstag* elections of Sept 1930. Failing to realize a new basis for a Conservative mass party, it abstained from the elections in 1932–33.

E Jones: Die Volkskonservativen 1918–1933 (1965).

Volksmarinedivision. Marines coming to Berlin during the *November Revolution* of 1918 to protect the revolutionary government. By Dec 1918 their numbers had risen to 3,000 men and played a decisive role in the disturbances in Berlin. *Ebert* called the Old Guard to quell the uprising, whereupon the *USPD* members withdrew from the *Rat der Volksbeauftragten*.

Volksschulen. Elementary schools set up in Prussia to meet the demand for compulsory school attendance dating back to 1717. The legal basis for the establishment of the Volksschulen was the *Allgemeines Landrecht* of 1794, which ruled that the communities were responsible for the financing of the schools. By 1820 there existed 17,623 village schools and 2,462 urban schools. They were supervised by the state. By 1848 already 82 per cent of the children of school-age could read and write, although education in the countryside was still poor. The spread of the schools fostered a critical outlook on the part of the masses towards the old order. Therefore, in 1854 the Prussian state decreed a patriotic curriculum and under *Wilhelm II* several decrees demanded opposition to socialist ideas. Until 1914 more than 10 million attendants of the Volksschulen were annually influenced by such political education.

E N Anderson: 'The Prussian Volksschule in the 19th century', in Festschrift H Rosenberg (1970).

Volkssturm. Home guard formed at the end of World War II by *Hitler's* order of 18 Oct 1944. It called upon men between 16 and 60 to defend their fatherland. The Volkssturm, under the command of the *Gauleiter*, mainly comprised men not fit for active service, and later included women and girls. The Volkssturm lacked military training and equipment and was insufficient to prevent Germany's defeat.

Volksverein, Deutscher. Popular association of German Catholics. By 1914 it had 805,000 members, making it one of the biggest bourgeois mass organizations. It comprised c 40 per cent of the supporters of the *Zentrum*. The work of the Volksverein was largely responsible for the preservation of the social and moral characteristics of the Roman Catholics, who were thus isolated from the mainstream of Germany's social development.

Volksverein, Prussian. Popular union of the Prussian Conservatives founded in 1861. It was conceived as an anti-*Nationalverein* by its leading spirit H Wagener (1815-89), the chief editor of the *Kreuzzeitung*. Its members (50,000 in 1865) were mainly recruited from traditionally-minded artisans. It opposed all liberal constitutional reform. It supported the King in the *constitutional* *conflict* of 1862–3 and approved of German unification only under the proviso that the sovereignty of the princes was preserved. It declined after 1866 and was dissolved in 1872.

Volkswagen (VW). Small car type promoted by *Hitler* for propaganda. As the car industry delayed its production, the *DAF* erected the VW works at Wolfsburg, which developed into the biggest car company in Europe after World War II. During the National Socialist era only military vehicles were produced there instead of the family car promised to the public who saved 236 million marks, and whose VW accounts helped to finance rearmament.

Volkswirtschaftliche Vereinigung. Parliamentary group in the *Reichstag* formed in 1878. It consisted of 204 deputies (75 Conservatives, 87 *Zentrum*, 27 National Liberals). Its pronouncements in favour of a *protective tariff* on 17 Oct 1878 secured the parliamentary endorsement of tariff reform based on a coalition between the iron and steel industries and the Junkers (*Sammlungspolitik*), combined with the Zentrum, which was less interested in a protective tariff than in separating the National Liberals from *Bismarck's* supporters in the *Kulturkampf.*

Volkswirtschaftsrat. Extra-parliamentary body in Prussia, founded by *Bismarck* in 1881. Its members were partly elected by the *Handelskammer* and partly nominated by the government. They were largely industrialists and Junkers, although 15 represented craftsmen and workers. The members of the Volkswirtschaftsrat did not represent political parties but economic interests, with whom Bismarck expected to come to terms rather than with parliamentarians dominated by party spirit and political theories. The Volkswirtschaftsrat was to deliberate all economic and financial bills of the government, before they were moved in the *Abgeordnetenhaus*, because Bismarck hoped that, after obtaining the consent of the Volkswirtschaftsrat, he could compel the deputies to give consent as well. He envisaged the extension of the Volkswirtschaftsrat into a national 'collateral' parliament, but the *Reichstag* refused to grant the money for it, which was also cut by the Abgeordnetenhaus, when the Volkswirtschaftsrat declared itself against a tobacco monopoly, and so it had to suspend its activity.

Vollzugsrat. Supreme leadership of the German soviets (*Workers' and Soldiers' Councils*), founded on 10 Nov 1918 as a permanent organ of the Berlin councils to control the *Rat der Volksbeauftragten*. It consisted of 7 'revolutionary foremen', 7 *SPD* representatives and 14 soldiers. The respective competences of the Vollzugsrat and the people's delegates remained controversial after the latter were given executive power and the Vollzugsrat administrative power. The Vollzugsrat was superseded by the *Zentralrat.*

Vormärz. Period in German history prior to the (March) *Revolution of 1848.* The Vormärz in its widest sense comprised the years 1815 to 1848. In the first phase until 1830 the tone was set by the national movements for liberty and unity, supported by the bourgeois intelligentsia in the universities (*Burschenschaften*) and expressed in various assemblies and constitutions of south-west Germany (eg Baden). This trend was opposed by reactionary forces of the *Deutscher Bund* (*Carlsbad Decrees*, pursuit of *demagogues*). Inspired by the French July revolution of 1830, the *Hambach Festival* (1832) led to new reprisals (*Six Articles*), forcing the *Junges Deutschland* into emigration. This second phase was also marked by a rising influence of the liberal bourgeoisie, whose economic activities found expression in the foundation of the *Customs Union* (1834). The accession of *Wilhelm IV* ushered in the third phase, the Vormärz in its narrower sense. Early social unrest (*Silesian Weavers' uprising*) culminated in the severe economic crisis of 1846, which already shook the authorities of the states to their foundations and prepared the ground for revolution. At this stage the struggle between Liberals and radical Democrats intensified, as was shown at their respective congresses at *Heppenheim* and *Offenburg* in autumn 1847. On the eve of the Revolution of 1848 the principal source of discontent was the absence of personal freedom and the suppression of intellectual and political activities by police state methods. This oppressive nature of the German governments was responsible for the pre-revolutionary attitude that developed throughout the country in the final stage of the Vormärz.

W Conze (ed.): Staat und Gesellschaft im deutschen Vormärz 1815–1848 (2nd ed., 1970); H Rosenberg: Politische Denkströmungen im deutschen Vormärz (1972).

Vorwärts. Social Democratic weekly, published from 1876 to 1878 in Leipzig. It was forbidden by the *Sozialistengesetz*, but restarted in 1891 in Berlin as the central organ of the *SPD*. Again suppressed by the Nazis, it was revived in West Germany after 1945.

Vossische Zeitung. Traditional Liberal newspaper published in Berlin. Originally a weekly founded in 1704, it was owned by the Voss family (from 1751) appearing as 'Berlinische Privilegierte Zeitung' with Vossische Zeitung as its subtitle. From 1824 the Vossische Zeitung appeared daily. From 1913 it was taken over by *Ullstein*. It was discontinued in 1933.

Wagner, Richard (22 May 1813–13 Feb 1883); dramatic composer and theorist. In his youth he dreamed of a romantic-socialist society, became embroiled in the *Revolution of 1848*, took part in the uprising at Dresden in 1849 and had to flee Germany until 1861. He turned pessimist under the influence of Schopenhauer and his temporary friend *Nietzsche*. In 1864 he was invited to Munich by his admirer *Ludwig II*, who championed his ideas on social and artistic revolution. His new type of music drama sought to express national and human aspirations in symbolic form. His works (eg 'The Ring') are interwoven with leitmotifs such as German nationalism. His national and racial ideas (in 1850 he had been the first prominent artist to propagate extreme *anti-Semitism*) animated a Wagnerian cult under the Nazis, centred at Bayreuth, where a special theatre had been built to suit the performance of his works.

169

Waldersee, Count Alfred (8 Apr 1832–5 Mar 1904); Prussian field marshal (1900); in 1888 he succeeded *Moltke* as chief of the general staff. In summer 1892, accused by *Caprivi* of interfering too much in politics, Waldersee was dismissed, but continued to exert a strong influence on *Wilhelm II*. When the German minister in Peking was shot, the Kaiser insisted that Waldersee be appointed commander-in-chief of the European troops in China during the Boxer rising in 1900–01. Thus he was to command the first international force in history.

Walküre. Code word for planned emergency measures of the German army in World War II. It was used as an operational basis by the conspirators of the *July Plot* (1944).

Wandervogel. Youth movement to organize activities like hiking and folklore. It originated in 1897–1900. It mainly comprised grammar school-boys (*Gymnasium*) of Protestant bourgois families in provincial towns. It protested against school drill and cramming, devoting itself to nature and 'natural life' for an intellectual-cultural restoration. It was anti-liberal and anti-democratic, anti-urban and anti-industrial, even anti-Semitic. It took refuge in a national social neo-Romanticism, its irrationalism reaching a climax with the patriotism of 1914 (*Langemarck*). In 1929 the various Wandervogel organizations had 30,000 members. It was dissolved in 1933, but elements of it were revived by the *Hitler-Youth*.
W Z Laqueur: Die deutsche Jugendbewegung (1960).

Wannsee-Conference. Meeting in the Berlin suburb of Wannsee on 20 Jan 1942. Representatives of the security organs, the ministries, the administration of the occupied territories and the chancery of the *NSDAP* (including *Freisler, Eichmann*) conferred under *Heydrich's* chairmanship to co-ordinate measures for the *final solution* of the Jewish question. The meeting lasted only an hour and a half during which the systematic extermination of 11 million European Jews, although not explicitly formulated, was treated as a fact of bureaucratic routine.

War Food Office (Kriegsernährungsamt). War Food Office established on 22 May 1916 under Baron v Batocki. It had the authority to give directions to the state governments. Its control of food supplies averted an acute crisis in summer 1917.

War Guilt Clause (Kriegsschuldparagraph). War guilt clause of the Treaty of *Versailles* (§ 231), declaring Germany's general responsibility for the outbreak of World War I. It served as the legal basis for the *reparations* and was highly resented by German public opinion. From 1919 a special department of the *Auswärtiges Amt* organized a campaign against the 'war guilt lie' and tried to prove the innocence of German foreign policy by the publication of selected documents of the pre-war period (*Grosse Politik*). The official line was supported by German historiography and American 'revisionist' historians. The war guilt debate poisoned international relations in the inter-war years.

S T Possony: Zur Bewältigung der Kriegschuldfrage (1968).

War-in-sight crisis (Krieg-in-Sicht-Krise). Diplomatic crisis which was sparked off by an article in the Free-Conservative paper 'Die Post' entitled 'Is War in Sight?' on 8 Apr 1875, leading to a German press campaign directed against the French cadre law of Mar 1875, which was regarded as preparation for a war of revenge. *Bismarck* tried to restore calm in the *Norddeutsche Allgemeine Zeitung*, but *Moltke*'s soundings about a preventive war with the Belgian minister provoked France to approach Russia and Britain and to inspire an article in 'The Times' on 6 May ('The French Scare'). Bismarck assured Russia and Britain of Germany's desire for peace. The crisis was the first, if minor, defeat of Bismarckian diplomacy.

Wars of Liberation. Wars of 1813–1815 which liberated Germany from French domination. Russia's victory over the Grande Armée in spring 1813 inspired Germany's national resistance. The starting-point had been the convention of *Tauroggen* (1812). In the beginning many volunteers offered themselves; the *Lützow-Korps* was formed. Public opinion forced King *Friedrich Wilhelm III* to promulgate the *Landwehr* and to declare war on Napoleon (17 Mar 1813), after concluding an alliance with Russia at Kalisz (28 Feb). In East Prussia *Stein* and *Yorck von Wartenburg* organized the arming of the people. With 6 per cent of the population on active service Prussia bore the main burden of the wars. In the spring of 1813 the first battles were fought in Saxony (Lützen, 2 May; Bautzen 20–21 May), where the French succeeded in driving the enemy into Silesia. In May Swedish troops landed in Pomerania, in June Britain entered the Russo-Prussian coalition. A preliminary armistice (4 June–10 Aug 1813) and abortive peace negotiations in Prague were followed by the entry of Austria and Bavaria into the war on the side of the coalition. In their autumn campaign the allied troops encircled Napoleon near *Leipzig* (16–19 Oct 1813). The defeat forced Napoleon to retreat from German territory; the states in the Confederation of the *Rhine* deserted him, thereby ending the Napoleonic system on German soil. The liberation of Germany was completed, but Prussia's armies (led by *Blücher* and *Gneisenau*) continued in the fight of the coalition against Napoleon and had a decisive share in the victories of Laon (8–10 Mar 1814) and Waterloo (18 June 1815).

H Helmert and H J Usczeck: Der Befreiungskrieg 1813–14 (1963).

Wartburg Festival. Patriotic student festival held at Eisenach on 18 Oct 1817 on the tercentenary of the Lutheran Reformation and the fourth anniversary of the Battle of *Leipzig*. It was the first national congregation of the *Burschenschaften*, aiming at the revival of national ideas and the discussion of a national programme. For the first time the colours black-red-gold were shown to demonstrate the unity of the German nation. The burning of anti-national, reactionary books was suggested by *Jahn* and carried out by extremists. It must be regarded as a marginal incident of the festival, which was not conspiratorial.

171

Nevertheless, the Wartburg Festival helped to increase the mistrust of reactionary elements towards the national forces, which culminated in the *Carlsbad Decrees* (1819).

G Steiger: Aufbruch-Urburschenschaft und Wartburgfest (1967).

Weber, Max (21 Apr 1864–14 June 1920); economist and sociologist. He developed a synthesis of the theoretical and the historical method of the social sciences. He aimed at discovering the concrete relationship between the spiritual components of the historical/social process, for man could only master nature and society by rationalizing economic and social life ('Economy and Society', published in 1922). As a politician Weber, supported by F *Naumann*, fought for a 'national democracy' and helped to found the *DDP*.

W J Mommsen: Max Weber und die deutsche Politik, 1890–1920 (1959); G Abramowski: Das Geschichtsbild Max Webers (1966).

Week of the Long Knives. See *Röhm Putsch*.

Wehrmacht. Name for the armed forces, 1935–1945, which succeeded the *Reichswehr*. Its officers made an accommodation with the National Socialist leadership, with which it concurred in rejecting the Treaty of *Versailles* (*Revisionspolitik*), which was being broken by clandestine rearmament, introduction of conscription (*Wehrpflicht*), and the re-militarization of the *Rhineland*. In 1934 the *Röhm Putsch* put an end to plans for a people's army (militia), integrating the *SA* and the Wehrmacht. The Wehrmacht then appeared secure beside the *NSDAP*, but in 1938 *Hitler* pushed aside the Minister of War, *Blomberg*, and created the *OKW* as a means for controlling the Wehrmacht. The Wehrmacht was gradually turned into a willing instrument in the hands of *National Socialism*, which it assisted in the preparation and conduct of a war of aggression. Increasing resistance against an adventurous war policy within the Wehrmacht (*Beck*) was subdued by the successes of the *Blitzkriege*, only to be revived after *Stalingrad*. It culminated in the abortive *July Plot* (1944).

Wehrpflicht. (1) Conscription decreed by *Scharnhorst* in Feb 1813 within the framework of the Prussian army reforms. Its previous obstacles, created by the Peace of *Tilsit* and the *Paris Convention*, were removed by the outbreak of the *wars of liberation*. Wehrpflicht was finally fixed by *Boyen's* military law of 3 Sept 1814 which prescribed general conscription for all healthy men from the age of 20. Persons of all social ranks were equally obliged to serve, although there were difficulties in implementing the regulation. Conscription was an important part of the reconstruction of the army on the basis of a people's militia. It signified the end of the separation of the population from the army. Wehrpflicht was more than a mere organizational principle; it transformed an absolutist state army into a conscript army of a modern nation state. The democratization of the military constitution stood in contrast to the reactionary political conditions with no universal suffrage.

172

(2) From 1919 the size of the German armed forces (*Reichswehr*) was limited to 100,000 by the Treaty of *Versailles*, but *Hitler* ordered an increase of manpower of the *Wehrmacht* to 300,000 by 1 Oct 1934. This decree was accompanied by increased illegal rearmament: two battle-ships and submarines were being built, the *Luftwaffe* was rapidly strengthened. When these measures became known to the Western Allies, they were published in a British White Book and presented to the House of Commons. Thereupon the Nazis organized a press campaign which created an atmosphere enabling Hitler to announce the re-introduction of conscription on 16 Mar 1935. This unilateral German move was the climax of the *Revisionspolitik*. As an Allied reaction to it Italy, Britain and France held the conference at Stresa (11–14 Apr 1935), but this common front was soon to disperse (*Rome-Berlin Axis*).

Weimar Coalition. Term for the coalition of *SPD*, *DDP* and *Zentrum* in the *Weimar Republic*. The coalition provided the first (provisional) central government under *Scheidemann* after the elections to the National Assembly, which did not give a majority to the Socialist parties. The coalition was also the basis of the governments under *Bauer* (1919–20), *Müller* (1920) and *Wirth* (1921–22), the last one without parliamentary majority. The alternative to the Weimar Coalition was the bourgeois coalition of *DDP*, *DVP* and *Zentrum*.

Weimar National Assembly. Constitutional assembly of the *Weimar Republic*, elected on 19 Jan 1919 by proportional representation. All citizens from 20 years of age were enfranchised. The largest parliamentary party in the assembly was the *SPD* (165 seats), followed by Zentrum (91), *DDP* (75), *DNVP* (44), *USPD* (22) and *DVP* (19). The assembly passed the new constitution on 11 Aug 1919. On 30 Sept it was transferred from Weimar (Thuringia) to Berlin. It was dissolved on 25 May 1920, after the elections for its successor organ, the *Reichstag*, had been fixed for 6 June 1920.

Weimar Republic. Name given to the German Republic from 1919 to 1933 because of its inauguration in Weimar (Thuringia), where the National Assembly had retired from the *November Revolution* in Berlin to draft a constitution. Accordingly it was a democratic, federal state with a parliamentary form of government. From the start it suffered from instability, as is evident from its 21 cabinets and 8 general elections for the *Reichstag*. The initial phase until 1923 was marked by political disturbances from the Left and the Right (*Kapp Putsch*, *Hamburg Uprising*) and by separatist aspirations in Bavaria and the *Rhineland*. The political climate was poisoned by assassinations (*Rathenau*, *Erzberger*). The financial obligations from the Treaty of *Versailles* (*reparations*) and passive resistance during the *Ruhrkampf* led to inflation which was ended by a reform of the *Reichsmark*. This introduced a stable period until 1929. In foreign policy *Stresemann* succeeded in obtaining Germany's international recognition and reconciliation with the Western Allies, as expressed by the *Locarno Pact* (1925), the entry into the League of Nations (1926) and the premature evacuation of the Rhineland. Reparations were regulated by the *Dawes Plan* and the *Young Plan*. From 1929, due to the world economic crisis, the Weimar Republic experienced new crises, which were exploited by the united forces of the Right (*Harzburg Front*). After the fall of H *Müller*'s cabinet in 1930, its downfall set in. *Brüning* began a pattern of presidential cabinets, ruling by decrees which practically ended the parliamentary system. When unemployment reached 5.6 million at the end of 1931, the *NSDAP* gained 230 seats in the elections of July 1932. On 30 Jan 1933 *Hitler* was appointed *Reichskanzler*. His *Enabling Act* of 23 Mar 1933 suspended the Weimar Republic. The reasons for its failure must be seen in the lack of democratic spirit among all classes, in the burden of the peace settlement of 1919 and in the consequences of the world economic crisis.

A J Nicholls: Weimar and the Rise of Hitler (1968).

Welfenfonds. Royal fortune of the Welf dynasty, confiscated by *Bismarck* in 1868, when the deposed last Hanoverian King Georg V established a Welf legion. It then amounted to c 48 million marks. A part of the interest derived from it were used as a basis for the *Reptilienfonds*. The supporters of the Welfs gathered in the 'Deutschhannoversche Partei' (earlier 'Rechtspartei', later 'Landespartei'); they also gained influence in the *Zentrum*. It was not until 1913 that the Welfs became reconciled with the Hohenzollerns.

Wels, Otto (15 Sept 1873–16 Sept 1939); Social Democratic politician. Wels, who had been elected into the governing body of the *SPD* in 1913, voted for the war credits in 1914 (*Burgfriede*). During the *November Revolution* he was city commander of Berlin. In 1920 he organized the general strike against the *Kapp Putsch*. He was party president from 1919. On 23 Mar 1933, as leader of the parliamentary party, he spoke up against the *Enabling Act* and then emigrated to Czechoslovakia, where he presided over the SPD's governing body in exile. In 1938 he was forced to move to Paris. A moderate Socialist by conviction, he refused co-operation with the Communists, even against the Nazis.

H J L Adolph: Otto Wels und die Politik der deutschen Sozialdemokratie (1971).

Weltpolitik. Term for German version of imperialist policy, first used by *Wilhelm II* in a speech on 18 Jan 1896. The Wilhelmine generation, conscious of Germany's economic and military strength, strove for aims beyond the national borders. Looking at the British Empire with admiration and envy, many Germans wanted a similar position for their own Reich. Conservatives and Liberals alike were convinced that Germany had to catch up with the other great powers and that she had a natural claim to hegemony over Central Europe (*Geopolitik, Mitteleuropa*) and a fair share of the colonies (*Kolonialpolitik*). This claim to "world power" meant equality with other world powers, not world domination, although thoughts of domination were entertained by influential extremists (*Alldeutscher Verband*). Weltpolitik was morally founded on the view that the system of a European balance of power had to be adapted to the new circumstances in which Britain was to be compelled to share her dominant role with others. This theory was an organic development of *Ranke*'s ideas by his epigones (*Neo-Rankeans*). The pursuit of Weltpolitik deliberately included the risk of war, in the event of it being necessary to break British supremacy. Germany built up a navy (*Flottenpolitik*) intended to guarantee the 'freedom of the seas'. Besides the general aim of proving oneself by conquest, there was a certain missionary ambition to spread German Kultur (*Pan-Germanism*), but basically Weltpolitik served only one purpose: power. The consequence was a foreign policy of persistent intervention in international affairs with the sole aim of prestige for its own sake. Thus Weltpolitik was bound to appear in time to Germany's neighbours as a threat to their very existence and finally led to isolation (*Encirclement*) and conflict.

L Dehio: Germany and World Politics in the Twentieth Century (1959); F Fischer: Germany's Aims in the First World War (1967).

Werwolf. Partisan units whose formation, together with the *Volkssturm*, was suggested by National Socialist propaganda to achieve 'final victory' in World War II. Werwolf did not gain strategic importance.

C Whiting: Werewolf. The Story of the Nazi Resistance Movement, 1944–1945 (1972).

Weserübung. Code word for military operations against Denmark and Norway. After the Soviet attack on Finland in Nov 1939 the western powers thought of setting foot on Norway to support the Finns and to cut off Germany from iron ore supplies via Narvik. When Germany was informed of this by the Norwegian Fascist leader Quisling, Admiral *Raeder* pressed for German intervention and on 27 Jan 1940 Hitler ordered Weserübung. The operation started with the occupation of Denmark a few hours before the scheduled Allied actions on 9 Apr. The landing in Norway succeeded in spite of strong resistance. On 14 Apr British troops landed in several ports, but only the expeditionary corps in Narvik held out until 8 June. Norway surrendered on 10 June and was then administered as a *Reichskommissariat* under J Terboven.

W Hubatsch: Weserübung (2nd ed 1960); T K Derry: The Campaign in Norway (1952).

Wessellied. Song composed by the National Socialist student Horst Wessel, who died on 23 Feb 1930. In the *Third Reich* it was made the national anthem beside *Deutschland, Deutschland über alles*.

Westarp, Graf Kuno (12 Aug 1864–30 July 1945); Conservative politician. He became a member of the *Reichstag* for the *Deutschkonservative Partei* in 1908 and was leader of the parliamentary party, 1913–18, when he spoke against a compromise peace and internal reforms. From 1920 he was deputy of the *DNVP*, whose parliamentary party he led from 1925, becoming party president in 1926. Under him his party entered *Marx*'s government after recognizing the *Locarno* treaties. In autumn 1928 he laid down his party offices because he could not overcome *Hugenberg*'s opposition within the party. In summer 1930 he founded the *Konservative Volkspartei* to support *Brüning*. But in the elections this party only obtained 4 seats and remained uninfluential. After 1933 he withdrew from political life.

Westphalia, Kingdom of. Napoleonic vassal state formed in Aug 1807 out of electoral Hesse, Brunswick, the Prussian provinces west of the River Elbe, some smaller territories and, only to a small extent, of Westphalian districts. It was governed by Napoleon's brother Jérôme Bonaparte, who resided in Kassel, and administered it according to the pattern of the French Empire. Progressive legislation included the abolition of differences due to estates, the liberation of the peasants, the introduction of the Code Napoléon, and freedom of trade. Grievances were caused by the permanent tax pressure and the compulsory recruitment for the French army. During the advance of the Allied troops in the *wars of liberation*, Westphalia was dissolved in Nov 1813.

H Berding: Napoleonische Herrschafts- und Gesellschaftspolitik im Königreich Westphalen 1807–1813 (1973).

Westwall. Belt of fortifications on Germany's western front, whose construction was begun in June 1938. It was ready for defence at the outbreak of World War II. *Todt* was in charge of it. After 1945 the Allies demolished it.

Widerstand (Resistance). See *July Plot*.

Wilhelm I. (22 Mar 1797–9 Mar 1888); King of Prussia and *Deutscher Kaiser*. As second son of *Friedrich Wilhelm III* he was educated as a soldier and developed a conservative outlook. After the succession of his brother *Friedrich Wilhelm IV* he became heir presumptive in 1840 and took an active part in politics. He mistrusted his brother's constitutional plans of 1847 (*Vereinigter Landtag*). In 1848 he wanted to suppress the *revolution* by force (and hence was nicknamed 'Prince of Grapeshot'). He had to flee temporarily to England and his conservative prejudices were mitigated. His residence at Koblenz became the centre of the *Wochenblatt* party. When his brother was ill, he was appointed his deputy in Oct 1857, then regent in Oct 1858 and on 2 Jan 1861 he became King. As Prince Regent he had proclaimed the *New Era*. His first ministry included Conservatives and Liberals, but major concessions to Liberalism were blocked by the *Herrenhaus* or by Wilhelm's reluctance. The army reforms of his minister of war *Roon* led to a struggle with the liberal majority of the *Abgeordnetenhaus* and Wilhelm was even prepared to abdicate. *Bismarck*, whom he had summoned as minister-president, ended the *constitutional conflict* victoriously for Wilhelm. After the foreign political successes of 1864 (German-Danish War – See *Schleswig-Holstein*) and 1866 (*Seven Weeks' War*), German unity appeared feasible to Wilhelm only under Prussian leadership (*kleindeutsch*). This was achieved after the *Franco-Prussian War* of 1870–71 with the *Kaiserproklamation* on 18 Jan 1871. Bismarck remained Wilhelm's leading statesman. Veneration for the 'Old Emperor' was increased by two attempted assassinations in 1878, which were utilized by his Chancellor for repressive legislation (*Sozialistengesetz*). Wilhelm's devotion to duty had made possible German unity under the Prussian crown, but the conflict of the monarchy with the spirit of the times was due to his personality.

Wilhelm I (27 Sept 1781–25 June 1864); King of Württemberg. He succeeded his father *Friedrich I* in 1816. In 1819 he granted a constitution with a bicameral system. He was an unsuccessful exponent of the *Trias* concept, but he remained a lifelong opponent of Prussian hegemony. In the *revolution of 1848* he maintained a liberal ministry in office but refrained from identifying himself with the people's enthusiasms for a political re-organization of Germany. In June 1849 he dispersed the Rump Parliament at Stuttgart which consisted of the left-wing delegates of the *Frankfurt National Assembly*. The latter's Fundamental Laws of the German People (civil rights), previously adopted by Wilhelm, were discarded and the constitution of 1819 restored. In 1864 Wilhelm I was succeeded by his son *Karl I*.

Wilhelm II. (27 Jan 1859–4 June 1941); *Deutscher Kaiser* and King of Prussia. The eldest son of *Friedrich III*, he ascended the throne on 15 June 1888. He became the representative of a new generation of Prussian society, combining traditional military virtues (ideal of his grandfather *Wilhelm I)* with a belief in modern technology. He tried to embody two images, that of the Prussian Junker and that of the English gentleman, feeling committed to the latter by his ancestry (being a nephew of Queen Victoria). Since his admiration for England was not reciprocated by the British, it developed into a 'love-hate' feeling for the Anglo-Saxons. His character was unsteady and he was easily influenced because of his impulsiveness. Intuitive in his judgments (as revealed in the marginal notes in *Die Grosse Politik*) and uncritical towards his advisers (*Camarilla*), he was unable to pursue a clear and continuous policy, though his strong constitutional position demanded of him or his *Reichskanzler* firm leadership. Wilhelm II failed in his attempt at 'personal rule', ie to act without even consulting his ministers. At first, in *Sozialpolitik*, he aimed at a reconciliation with the working class but ended by denouncing the Social Democrats as 'unpatriotic companions'. His short-lived reform plans brought him into opposition to *Bismarck*, whose resignation he enforced in 1890. Then followed the *Neuer Kurs* with an approach to Britain (*Heligoland-Zanzibar-Treaty*). But colonial collisions led him to foster the idea of a *Continental League*. Anglo-German relations deteriorated after the *Krüger Telegram* of 1896, which established Wilhelm as an exponent of *Weltpolitik*, in particular of *Flottenpolitik*. From 1908 he acted strictly constitutionally, because his self-confidence was shaken by the *Daily Telegraph Affair*. By then public opinion was highly critical of him. At home *Harden* revealed his connections with P *Eulenburg*; abroad Wilhelm's enjoyment of military splendour and the tactlessness of many of his speeches (*Huns speech*) suggested despotic inclinations and bellicose intentions. In spite of such 'sabre-rattling', Wilhelm cannot be blamed for diplomatic failures. In most decisions of foreign policy he followed ministerial advice, sometimes even unwillingly (*Tangier, Panther's Spring*). His reaction to the crisis in 1914 was undiplomatic, but 'Kaiser Bill' did not plot the outbreak of World War I, as Allied propaganda insinuated. During the war his restraint left a vacuum that was filled by the *Oberste Heeresleitung*, which forced Wilhelm to appoint and dismiss chancellors at their will. When his promise for parliamentarization ('Easter message' of 1917) could not ease interior tensions, Wilhelm sought refuge in the general headquarters. At the beginning of the *November Revolution, Max von Baden* could only recommend abdication. On 10 Nov 1918 Wilhelm went into exile in the Netherlands, and he abdicated on 28 Nov. In spite of his intellectual abilities and intentions, to make his country prosperous, to establish good relations with Britain and to defend the position of Europe against the 'yellow danger', Wilhelm achieved the opposite and discredited the monarchy in Germany.

M Balfour: The Kaiser and his Times (1964); V Cowles: The Kaiser (1963).

Wilhelmstrasse. Street in Berlin. As seat of the *Reichskanzler* (*Reichskanzlei*), of the *Auswärtiges Amt* and other ministries, it was the symbol for German foreign policy, 1871–1945.

P Seabury: The Wilhelmstrasse (1954).

Windthorst, Ludwig (17 Jan 1812–14 Mar 1891); parliamentary leader. He was Hanoverian minister of justice, 1851–53 and 1862–65. From 1867 deputy in the *Abgeordnetenhaus* and the *Reichstag*, he soon became the uncontested leader of the *Zentrum*. He was the champion of a federal-constitutional union, representing the particularists and Catholics of north-West Germany. During the *Kulturkampf* Windthorst was the vociferous opponent of *Bismarck*, whom he then supported on *protective tariff* and *Sozialpolitik*, though Windthorst's interview with *Wilhelm II* on Mar 1890 is said to have played a part in the chancellor's dismissal. The 'little excellency' was the most prominent opposition leader in the Bismarckian era, distinguished for his tactical and rhetoric abilities.

W Spael: Ludwig Windthorst (1962).

Wirth, Joseph (6 Sept 1879–3 Jan 1956); statesman. He became a *Zentrum* deputy of the Baden *Landtag* in 1913, and member of the *Reichstag* in 1914. In 1921 he succeeded Erzberger as *Reichsminister* of finance. From May 1921 to Dec 1922 he presided over two cabinets as *Reichskanzler*, pursuing a strict policy of *fulfilment*. His government accepted the *London Ultimatum* and passed the *Republikschutzgesetz*. He initiated a rapprochement with the Soviet Union (*Rapallo*, 1922) as a basis for a *Revisionspolitik* in the East. In H *Müller*'s second cabinet (1929) he was minister for the occupied territories. In 1933 he emigrated to Switzerland.

Wirtschaftspartei. Party representing the interests of the self-supporting middle classes after World War I. At times it attracted large sections of the urban middle class. Its membership was 50,000 in 1921, and increased to more than

80,000 in 1928. The party was then represented in the *Reichstag* by 23 deputies.

M Schumacher: Mittelstandspartei und Republik. Die Wirtschaftspartei – Reichspartei des deutschen Mittelstands 1919–1933 (1972).

Wissel, Rudolf (8 Mar 1869–13 Dec 1962); trade unionist and Social Democratic politician. Wissel, who was secretary of the *ADGB*, entered the *Reichstag* for the *SPD* in 1918. In Dec 1918 he became a member of the *Rat der Volksbeauftragten*. From Feb to July 1919 he was the first *Reichsminister* of economics. He represented the idea of a planned communal economy controlled by society. From 1920 to 1930 again in the Reichstag, he was minister of labour in H *Müller*'s second cabinet (1928–30). He was detained on 2 May 1933 but released in June.

Wochenblattpartei. Conservative group founded in Prussia in 1851, deriving its name from the *Wochenblatt* journal in which it discussed current political issues. Its members were higher civil servants and diplomats (Bunsen, Mathis, Goltz) and its stronghold was in the Rhineland. It stood in opposition to the *Camarilla*. It wanted to preserve the constitution of 11 Mar 1850 and demanded a foreign policy independent of Austria.

M Behnen: Das preussische Wochenblatt 1851–1861 (1971).

Wolff-Metternich zur Gracht, Graf Paul (1853–1934); diplomat. From 1890 he was first secretary of the German embassy in London and became ambassador in 1901. He strove for Anglo-German understanding and enjoyed a position of respect in London's diplomatic circles. He came into conflict with *Tirpitz* and was replaced by his counsellor *Kühlmann* in 1912.

Wolfsschanze ('Wolf's Lair'). Headquarters of the *Führer* in East Prussia, renowned as the place of the assault on *Hitler* by the conspirators of the *July Plot* (1944).

Women's Associations (Frauenvereine). Associations of the German women's movement. Politically inspired by the *revolutions of 1848*, they aimed at achieving better educational and professional opportunities for women, who had been excluded from political activities until 1908. The first of the women's associations was founded in 1865 in Leipzig. From 1894 all organized women were united in the league of German Women's Associations led by Helene Lange (1848–1930). The bourgeois associations had a marked nationalist attitude, while the Progressives developed radical feminist programmes and were engaged in practical self-help activities (1896: first day-nursery and canteen for working women). In 1902 the suffragettes founded the German Association for Women's Suffrage. The right to vote was granted to women by article 22 of the Weimar Constitution.

R J Evans: The Feminist Movement in Germany, 1894–1933 (1975).

Workers' and Soldiers' Councils (Arbeiter- und Soldatenräte). These were councils which emerged spontaneously from local or shop elections. The first German soviet was formed on 16 Apr 1917 in Leipzig; the best organized was the 'Council of Revolutionary Foremen' in Berlin, where a national conference of workers' and soldiers' councils met from 16 to 18 Dec 1918. They determined elections of the *Nationalversammlung* and the *Zentralrat*, thus favouring a transition from the soviet to a parliamentary system. The councils failed to overcome the differences between the socialist parties during the *November Revolution*. They were without a theoretical concept and concentrated on practical duties (eg food supplies, demobilization). They lacked a programme to solve the problems of a modern industrial society.

E Kolb: Die Arbeiter- und Soldatenräte in der deutschen Innenpolitik 1918–1919 (1962).

Works Council Act (Betriebsrätegesetz). Shop committees law of 1920, which prescribed the election of a works council in every shop with more than 20 employees or of a trustee in shops with at least 5 employees. The law provided for the representation of workers' interests in co-operation with the management. Its intentions were only partly realized in practice.

Wrangel, Friedrich Graf v (13 Apr 1784–1 Nov 1877); Prussian general. On 18 Apr 1848 he received the supreme command over the troops exercising federal authority against Denmark (*Schleswig-Holstein*). After the armistice of 26 Aug 1848 he commanded the troops stationed around Berlin. On 10 Nov they marched into the capital and restored royal authority over the people and the *Berlin National Assembly*. During the German-Danish war of 1864 he had supreme command over the Austro-Prussian troops. In spite of his reverence for the *Camarilla*, he enjoyed wide popularity as 'Papa Wrangel'.

Yangtse Agreement. Anglo-German agreement of 10 Oct 1900 on the principle of the 'open door' (ie unrestricted trade) for all nations on the rivers and along the coast of China. Both signatories to the agreement wanted to guarantee free trade in those parts of China where they could exert influence, and they relinquished further territorial advantages. In the event of other powers seeking to make territorial acquisitions as a result of the Boxer rising, Germany and Britain were to consult each other on counter-measures. The agreement was a compromise between *Weltpolitik* and a diplomacy that was against antagonizing either Britain or Russia over the Chinese question.

Yorck von Wartenburg, Graf Ludwig (26 Sept 1759–4 Oct 1830); Prussian general. Representative of the Prussian traditionalists, he opposed the reforms of *Stein*. In the war against Napoleon he, without authorization from the King, concluded the convention of *Tauroggen* (1812), which in *Friedrich Wilhelm III*'s eyes was the act of an insubordinate soldier. Later as governor of Königsberg he endorsed the plan for an East Prussian *Landwehr*. In the *wars of liberation* he led a corps which forced the way over the River Elbe near Wartenburg. This success, for which Yorck was rewarded by being elevated to an earldom and by the addition of the battleplace to his name, was a decisive precondition for the Battle of *Leipzig*.

Young Plan. Financial scheme for the regulation of German *reparations*. It was worked out by a commission which met in Paris in 1929 under the chairmanship of the American Owen D Young. The plan, which was enforced in 1930, succeeded the *Dawes Plan* and reduced the cost to about a quarter of the sum originally demanded in 1921. Payments were to be stretched over 62 years. In practice the plan was only in force up to 1931. Its acceptance on 11 Mar 1930 was preceded by a referendum (*Volksbegehren, Volksentscheid*). The debate over the Young Plan strengthened the Nazi movement and led to the fall of the last parliamentary government (H *Müller*). The impracticability of the plan during the world economic crisis was acknowledged by the Allies, who annulled it in July 1932.

M Vogt (ed): Die Entstehung des Young-Plans (1970).

Z-Plan. Naval programme of Nazi Germany for World War II, providing for the production of a powerful fleet of 13 battleships, 33 cruisers, 4 aircraft carriers, and 250 U-boats. The Z-Plan, according to which Germany was to be equipped for victory at sea against the world powers until 1944–46, went ahead on this schedule, because *Hitler* had promised *Raeder* that war would not break out before 1944–5.

Zabern (Saverne). Town in *Alsace-Lorraine* where, after a local protest demonstration in 1913, 28 indigenous civilians were detained by the commander whose regiment was stationed at Zoberne. This was against the constitution, but the resulting court-martial acquitted the commander on the ground that a cabinet order of 1820 justified the unauthorized detention of civilians by the military, if the civil administration could no longer maintain public order, which had not been the case at Zabern. *Bethmann Hollweg* and the *Reichstag* protested in vain against the judgment, which underlined the military's claim to power.

Zentralrat. Council established by the national conference of the soviets (*Workers' and Soldiers' Councils*) on 16–18 Dec 1918 for a transition period until the election of the National Assembly. The Zentralrat was to replace the *Vollzugsrat* as a sovereign representation for the control of the *Rat der Volksbeauftragten*. It was elected without participation of the *USPD* and other radical left-wing groups and was thus an organ of the majority Socialists (*SPD*).

Zentrum (Centre party). Party of German Catholicism, whose first parliamentary party was formed in the *Frankfurt National Assembly* (1848): a Roman Catholic party existed in the Prussian *Landtag* during the *New Era* up to 1862. The Zentrum was founded as a national party in 1870 by *Windthorst* and the brothers Reichensberger. It derived its name from the sitting order in parliament. Though inter-confessional by its programme, its voters came primarily from Roman Catholic regions. In the *Kulturkampf* the party opposed *Bismarck* and also disapproved of his *kleindeutsch* solution. In the first *Reichstag* the Zentrum obtained 58 seats; from 1878 to 1914 it had between 90 and 100 seats, being the strongest parliamentary party in 1878. After Bismarck turned to protection (1879), the Zentrum supported his economic and social policy. From 1890 the Zentrum was one of the ruling parties. It was not until 1911–14 that a firm party structure was established. In World War I the Zentrum formed a coalition with the *SPD* and the *Fortschrittspartei*, standing for parliamentarization (*Interfraktioneller Ausschuss*) and a negotiated peace. After the *November Revolution* (1918) the Zentrum was loyal to the *Weimar Republic*. From 1919 it had 60–70 seats in the *Reichstag* and was the main ruling party, providing four chancellors (*Fehrenbach, Wirth, Marx, Brüning*). The Zentrum defended the policy of *fulfilment* and was linked with the Social Democrats. It tried in vain to defend the constitutional stage against the extremists from the left and the right, even though it voted for the *Enabling Act*. It was dissolved on 5 July 1933.

M Morsey: Die deutsche Zentrumspartei 1917–1923 (1955); J K Zeender: The German Center Party 1890–1906 (1976).

Zeppelin. Type of rigid airship named after its inventor Count Ferdinand v Zeppelin (1838–1917). The first Zeppelin was lifted above Lake Constance on 2 July 1900 and in 1908 the first 12-hour flight over Switzerland aroused national interest. A public donation of 6 million marks enabled Count Zeppelin to found an air-travel company, providing five Zeppelins for commercial and pleasure flights. In World War I, 88 Zeppelins were used for naval reconnaissance (eg Battle of *Jutland*) and bombing raids on London 1916–17. In 1918 the remainder was dismantled or delivered to the Allies. The first post-war Zeppelin was built as *reparations* payment to the USA in Oct 1924. From 1928 to 1937 Zeppelins maintained the first transatlantic air service, which came to an abrupt end after the crash of the Zeppelin 'Hindenburg' on its arrival in New York on 6 May 1937. In 1939 Zeppelin construction was discontinued and in July 1944 Allied bombing destroyed the hangers at Friedrichshafen.

J G Vaeth: Graf Zeppelin (1958).

Zetkin, Clara (5 July 1857–20 June 1933); Communist politician. From the 1870s she belonged to the left wing of the *SPD* and became a leading member of the women's movement. It was not until 1 May 1919 that she changed over from *USDP* to *KPD*. She was frequently elected to the Central Committee. From 1920 to 1933 she was a member of the *Reichstag*, but from 1924 she (being married to a Russian) lived in Moscow, directing the women's secretariat of the Third International. In spite of her many decorations she became isolated because of her opposition to Stalin. In 1932, one year before her mysterious death, she opened the Reichstag as its senior president.

Zimmerman Telegram. Telegram of 19 Jan 1917 from the secretary of state of the

Auswartiges Amt, Arthur Zimmermann (1864–1940), to the German minister in Mexico. It authorized the latter to propose an alliance with Germany to the President of Mexico and to encourage the reconquest of Texas, New Mexico and Arizona, in the hope that Mexico would begin hostilities on the American frontier if the USA entered war against Germany which was expected as a reprisal for the resumption of unrestricted *U-Boat-Warfare* on 1 Feb 1917. The coded message (sent via Washington) was intercepted and deciphered by British intelligence, which forwarded it to President Wilson, who had it published on 1 Mar 1917. The telegram helped to persuade the Americans of the necessity of an imminent US declaration of war (it was declared on 6 Apr 1917).

B W Tuchmann: The Zimmermann Telegram (1958).

Zivilkabinett (Civil Cabinet). Office directly subordinated to the Prussian monarch for his personal affairs. Officially it was only for technical administration (preparation of expeditions, correspondence with ministries), but in practice the chief of the extra-constitutional Zivilkabinett often had more influence than the Staatsministerium, and the reign of *Wilhelm II* provided an opportunity for his 'personal rule' as well as for the rise of a new *Camarilla.*

H Potthoff (ed): Friedrich v Berg als Chef des Geheimen Zivilkabinetts 1918 (1972).

Zollunion. Customs union projected between Austria and Germany during the negotiations on 23 Mar 1931. It had economic reasons but it also revived aspirations for *Anschluss.* It was therefore opposed by France and the Little Entente. On 5 Apr the Hague Court declared (by 8 votes to 7 votes) that the Zollunion was incompatible with existing treaties. The failure of the Zollunion gave new arguments to the champions of *Revisionspolitik.* Economically it led to a withdrawal of foreign capital.

S Suval: The Anschluss Question in the Weimar Republic 1918–1932 (1974).

Zollverein. See *Customs Union.*

Zuchthausvorlage (Hard Labour Bill). Bill proposing prison sentences for picketing and threatening blacklegs. It was presented to parliament by *Posadowsky* on 26 May 1899, but it was rejected by all parties except the Conservatives. By demanding a special penal law for workers, the bill contradicted the principle of legal equality. Its failure put an end to the government's active repressive policy towards the *SPD.*

Zwanzigster Juli. See *July Plot.*

CHRONOLOGICAL TABLE

1806	Dissolution of the Holy Roman Empire
	Foundation of the Confederation of the Rhine
	Battle of Jena and Auerstädt
1807	Peace of Tilsit
	Prussian Reforms initiated by Stein
1810	Hardenberg appointed Staatskanzler
	Humboldt Minister of Education
1812–14	Emancipation of the Jews in Prussia
	Prussian Army Reforms (Landwehr, Conscription)
	by Scharnhorst, Gneisenau, Clausewitz
1813–15	Wars of Liberation:
Mar 1813	Appeal 'To my people' by Friedrich Wilhelm III (1797–1840)
Oct 1813	Battle of Leipzig
1814–15	Congress of Vienna
1815–66	Deutscher Bund (German Confederation)
Sept 1815	Holy Alliance
	Foundation of the Deutsche Burschenschaft in Jena
1817	Wartburg Festival
1818	Congress of Aachen
1819	Murder of Kotzebue by Sand
	Carlsbad Decrees
1820	Congress of Troppau
1822	Provincial Estates
1832	Hambach Festival
	Six Articles
1834	*Zollverein* (customs union)
1835	First German Railway from Nuremberg to Fürth
1836–40	Cologne disorders
1837	Protest and dismissal of the Göttingen Seven
1840–61	Reign of Friedrich Wilhelm IV of Prussia

1844	Silesian Weavers' Revolt
1847	Vereinigter Landtag
1848	German Revolution:
	Barricade Uprising in Berlin (18 Mar)
	Revolt in Baden (April)
	Inauguration of a Constituent National Assembly in Frankfurt's Paulskirche (18 May) and a Prussian National Assembly in Berlin
1848–49	Deliberations of the Frankfurt National Assembly
	Rejection of the Kaiser deputation by Friedrich Wilhelm IV (April 1849)
	Uprisings in South West Germany and Saxony (May–July)
	Abdication of the *Reichsverweser* (Dec 1849)
1849	Three Kings' Alliance
1850	Erfurt Parliament
	Treaty of Olmütz
1850–51	Dresden Conference
1859–62	New Era in Prussia
1861–88	Wilhelm I, King of Prussia
1862–66	Constitutional conflict in Prussia
1862	Bismarck appointed Prussian Prime Minister (22 Sept)
1863	Alvensleben Military Convention
	Frankfurt Congress of the German Princes
1864	German-Danish War (Schleswig-Holstein)
1865	Treaty of Gastein
1866	Austro-Prussian War (Seven Weeks' War):
	Battles of Langensalza (29 June) and Königgrätz (3 July)
	Peace of Nikolsburg (26 July), Peace of Prague (23 Aug)
	Indemnity Bill accepted (Sept)
1866–67	Formation of the North German Confederation
1870–71	Franco-Prussian War:
	Battle of Sedan (1 Sept 1870)
	Peace of Frankfurt (10 May 1871)
1871	Foundation of the (Second) German Empire:
	Proclamation of Wilhelm I as German Emperor in Versailles on 18 Jan 1871
1872–78	Kulturkampf:
	Pulpit clause (1871), School Supervision (1872)
	May Laws (1873–74), Civil Marriage (1874–75)
1872	Three Emperors' League
1875	War-in-Sight Crisis
	Gotha Programme of the SPD
1878	Congress of Berlin
	Introduction of a protective tariff
	Sozialistengesetz (Law against the Social Democrats)
1879	Dual Alliance

1882	Triple Alliance
1883–89	Social legislation:
	Sickness Insurance Act (1883), Industrial Accident
	Insurance Act (1884), Old-Age Pension Insurance Act (1889)
1884–85	Berlin Congo-Conference
	South-West Africa first German colony (*Schutzgebiet*)
1887	Re-insurance Treaty with Russia
1888–1918	Kaiser Wilhelm II
1890	Suspension of the *Sozialisten-Gesetz*
	Re-insurance Treaty not renewed
	Heligoland-Zanzibar Treaty
	Dismissal of Bismarck (d. 1898)
1890–91	Legislation for protection of labour
1890–94	Caprivi Reichskanzler
1890–1904	*Neuer Kurs* (New Course)
1894–1900	Chlodwig Prince of Hohenlohe-Schillingsfürst Reichskanzler
1898	Launching of the naval programme (*Flottenpolitik*)
1898–1901	Anglo-German Alliance negotiations
1899	Baghdad Railway concession
1900	Introduction of the Civil Code (*Bürgerliches Gesetzbuch*)
1900–09	Bülow Reichskanzler
1905	Tangier Landing: First Moroccan Crisis
1908	Daily Telegraph Interview
	Bosnian Crisis (*Nibelungentreue*)
1909–17	Bethmann Hollweg Reichskanzler
1911	Autonomy for Alsace-Lorraine
	Panther's Spring to Agadir (Second Moroccan Crisis)
	Reichsversicherungsordnung
1912	Social Democrats (SPD) strongest parliamentary party in the Reichstag
	Anglo-German naval negotiations in Berlin
1914	Outbreak of World War I:
	Burgfrieden for the parties
	Blank cheque for Austria (6 July)
	Invasion of Belgium (3–4 Aug) followed by British declaration of war
	September-Programme of German war aims
	Battle of the Marne (Schlieffen Plan)
	Battle of Tannenberg in East Prussia
1916	Battle of Verdun
	Battle of Jutland
	Hindenburg and Ludendorff in Supreme Command (OHL)
	Central Powers' peace offer (12 Dec)
1917	Retreat to the Siegfried Line (Feb–March)
	Unrestricted U-boat warfare (from 1 Feb)

	Foundation of the Independent Social Democrats (USPD)
	Peace Resolution of the Reichstag
1918	Peace of Brest-Litovsk (3 Mar)

Foundation of the Independent Social Democrats (USPD)
Peace Resolution of the Reichstag
1918 Peace of Brest-Litovsk (3 Mar)
   Failure of Last Offensive (Operation Michael)
   Black Day of the German Army (8 Aug)
   Prince Max of Baden Reichskanzler
   Naval Mutinies at Kiel (29 Oct)
   November Revolution in Munich and Berlin (9 Nov)
   Abdication of the Kaiser, proclamation of the Republic
   Armistice on the basis of the 'Fourteen Points' (11 Nov)
1919 Spartacus Rising in Berlin (Jan)
   Inauguration of the National Assembly at Weimar (Feb)
   Treaty of Versailles signed (28 June)
1919–25 Friedrich Ebert Reichspräsident
1920 Kapp Putsch
   Foundation of NSDAP
1922 Rapallo-Treaty
1923 Climax of the inflation
   Occupation of the Ruhr by French troops
   Communist revolt in Hamburg
   Munich Putsch by Hitler and Ludendorff
   Stresemann Reichskanzler (Aug–Nov)
1924 Dawes Plan
1925–34 Hindenburg Reichspräsident
1925 Locarno Treaties
1926 Germany enters the League of Nations
1930 Evacuation of the Rhineland
   Young Plan
   Death of Stresemann
1930–32 Presidential Cabinets (Brüning, Papen, Schleicher)
1931 Crash of the DANAT Bank (13 July)
1931–32 End of reparations
1933 Hitler appointed Reichskanzler (30 Jan)
   Nazi seizure of power (*Machtergreifung*)
   Reichstag Fire (27 Feb)
   Enabling Act (Ermächtigungsgesetz) (23 Mar)
1933–34 Gleichschaltung
   Reichskonkordat
1934 Röhm Putsch (30 June)
   Non-Aggression Pact with Poland
   Death of Hindenburg (2 Aug): Hitler becomes 'Führer'
1935 Re-introduction of conscription
   Nuremberg Laws
   Return of the Saar district
   Anglo-German Naval Agreement
1936 Occupation of the Rhineland (Mar)

	Four-Year Plan
	Olympic Games in Berlin
	Rome-Berlin Axis
	Anti-Comintern Pact
1937	Hitler reveals his war aims (Hossbach Minutes)
1938	Dismissal of Blomberg and Fritsch
	Anschluss of Austria (13 Mar)
	Munich Agreement (29 Sept)
	Reichskristallnacht (9–10 Nov)
1939	Establishment of the protectorate over Bohemia-Moravia
	Nazi-Soviet Pact (23 Aug)
	Beginning of the German attack on Poland (1 Sept)
1940	Blitzkriege in the West, occupation of Denmark and Norway
	Armistice with France (22 June)
	Three Powers' Pact
1940–41	Battle of Britain
1941	Formation of the Afrika Korps
	War against Yugoslavia and Greece
	Beginning of the war against Russia (Operation Barbarossa)
	Declaration of war on the USA
1942	Climax of the Battle of the Atlantic
	Assassination of Heydrich (26 May)
	Wannsee Conference (20 Jan)
1943	Surrender at Stalingrad
	Goebbels declares total war (Sportpalast Speech)
	German surrender in Africa
1944	Conspiracy against Hitler (July Plot) fails
	Mobilization of the Volkssturm
1945	Hitler commits suicide (30 April), succeeded by Dönitz
	Unconditional surrender (7–8 May) of the Wehrmacht
	Potsdam Agreement
	Nuremberg Trials